ZOMBIES ASSEMBLE 2

Writer/Artist
YUSAKU KOMIYAMA

Script
JIM ZUB

Letters
VC's TRAVIS LANHAM

Cover
KIICHI MIZUSHIMA

SPECIAL THANKS TO
Rumi Okayama, Salena Mahina, Lisa Montalbano & Aki Yanagi

ADAPTATION EDITOR: **Jeff Youngquist** EXECUTIVE EDITORS: **C.B. Cebulski & Tom Brevoort** ASSISTANT EDITOR: **Caitlin O'Connell**
ASSOCIATE MANAGER, DIGITAL ASSETS: **Joe Hochstein** SENIOR EDITOR, SPECIAL PROJECTS: **Jennifer Grünwald**
ASSOCIATE MANAGING EDITOR: **Kateri Woody** EDITOR, SPECIAL PROJECTS: **Mark D. Beazley** SVP PRINT, SALES & MARKETING: **David Gabriel**
PRODUCTION: **Ryan Devall & Joe Frontirre** DESIGNER: **Jay Bowen**

EDITOR IN CHIEF: **C.B. Cebulski** CHIEF CREATIVE OFFICER: **Joe Quesada** PRESIDENT: **Dan Buckley** EXECUTIVE PRODUCER: **Alan Fine**

ZOMBIES ASSEMBLE VOL. 2. Contains material originally published in magazine form as ZOMBIES ASSEMBLE 2 #1-4. First printing 2018. ISBN 978-0-7851-9461-3. Published by MARVEL WORLDWIDE, INC., a subsidiary of MARVEL ENTERTAINMENT, LLC. OFFICE OF PUBLICATION: 135 West 50th Street, New York, NY 10020. Copyright © 2018 MARVEL. No similarity between any of the names, characters, persons, and/or institutions in this magazine with those of any living or dead person or institution is intended, and any such similarity which may exist is purely coincidental. **Printed in the U.S.A.** DAN BUCKLEY, President, Marvel Entertainment; JOE QUESADA, Chief Creative Officer; TOM BREVOORT, SVP of Publishing; DAVID BOGART, SVP of Business Affairs & Operations, Publishing & Partnership; DAVID GABRIEL, SVP of Sales & Marketing, Publishing; JEFF YOUNGQUIST, VP of Production & Special Projects; DAN CARR, Executive Director of Publishing Technology; ALEX MORALES, Director of Publishing Operations; SUSAN CRESPI, Production Manager; STAN LEE, Chairman Emeritus. For information regarding advertising in Marvel Comics or on Marvel.com, please contact Jonathan Parkhideh, VP of Digital Media & Marketing Solutions, at jparkhideh@marvel.com. For Marvel subscription inquiries, please call 888-511-5480. **Manufactured between 12/8/2017 and 1/9/2018 by SHERIDAN, CHELSEA, MI, USA.**

10 9 8 7 6 5 4 3 2 1

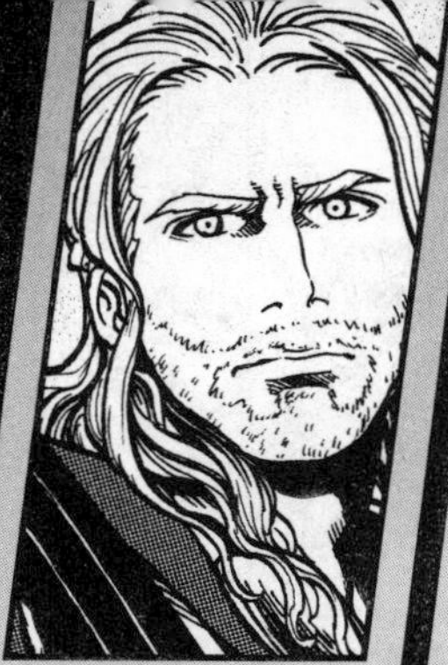

THOR

REAL NAME:
Thor Odinson

Thor is the Asgardian God of Thunder and an Avenger. Wielding Mjolnir, a mystical Uru hammer of immense power, the son of Odin fights to protect Earth and all the Nine Realms.

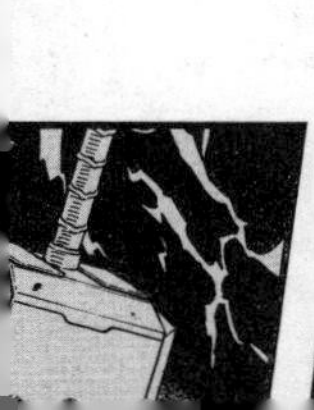

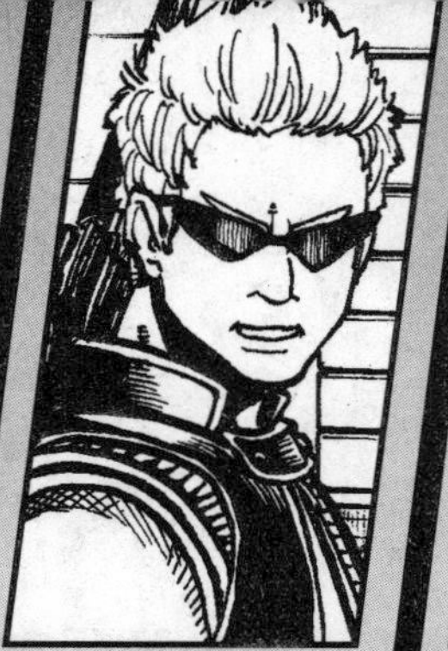

HAWKEYE

REAL NAME:
Clint Barton

Former criminal Clint Barton used his circus training to become the greatest sharpshooter the world has ever seen. He reformed and joined the Avengers, quickly becoming one of the team's most stalwart members.

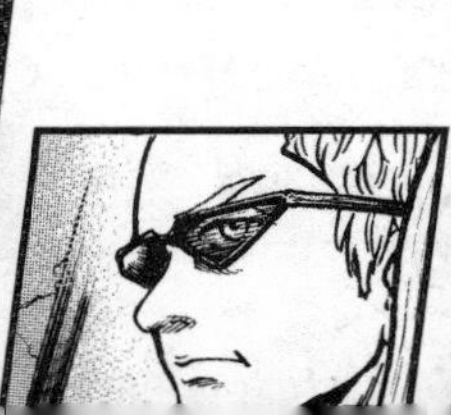

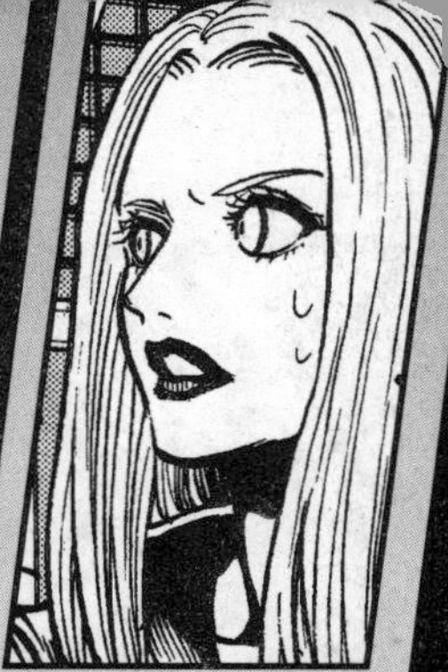

BLACK WIDOW

REAL NAME:
Natasha Romanoff

Natasha Romanoff is a deadly operative equipped with state-of-the-art weaponry and extensive hand-to-hand combat training. Before joining S.H.I.E.L.D. and the Avengers, she was an enemy spy; now, she uses her unique skills to atone for her past.

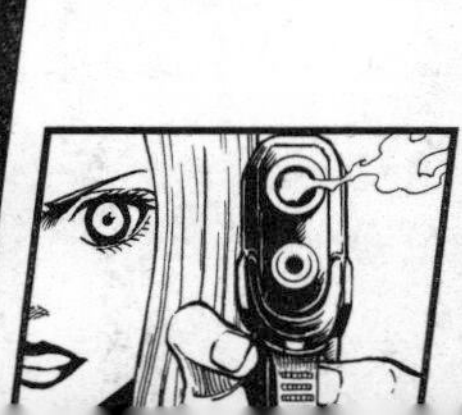

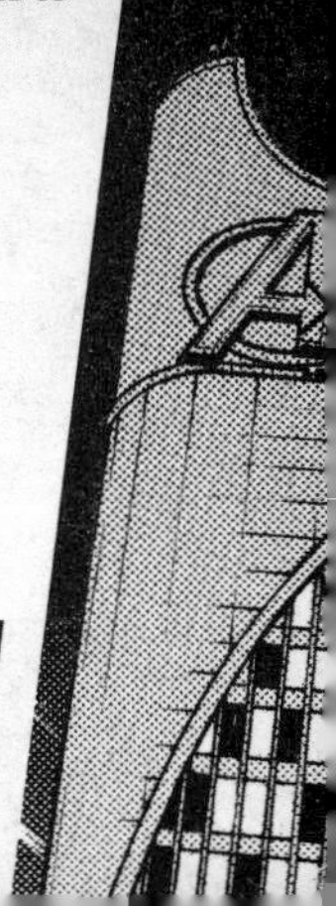

IRON MAN

CAPTAIN AMERICA

HULK

REAL NAME:
Anthony Edward Stark

Billionaire playboy and genius industrialist Tony Stark was kidnapped during a routine weapons test. His captors attempted to force him to build a weapon of mass destruction. Instead, he created a powerful suit of armor that saved his life. From that day on, he has used the suit to protect the world as the invincible Avenger Iron Man.

REAL NAME:
Steven Rogers

During World War II, a secret military experiment turned scrawny Steve Rogers into America's first Super-Soldier, Captain America. Near the end of the war, Rogers was presumed dead in an explosion over the English Channel. Decades later, Cap was found frozen in ice and was revived. Steve Rogers awakened to a world he never imagined—a man out of time. He again took up the mantle of Captain America, defending the United States and the world from threats of all kinds.

REAL NAME:
Bruce Banner

Bruce Banner was a brilliant scientist working for the Army when he was caught in the explosion of a gamma bomb of his own creation and transformed into the nearly indestructible Hulk. Now, Dr. Banner struggles to control his anger and anxiety to keep the Hulk in check while he fights alongside the Avengers.

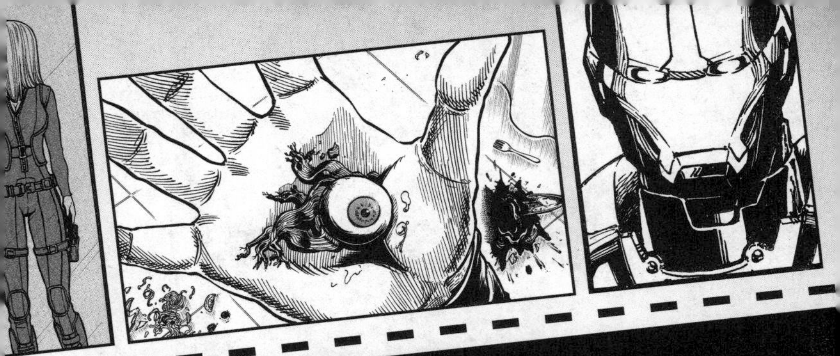

WHAT STARTED AS A SURPRISE BIRTHDAY party for Tony Stark has quickly spiraled into an alien infestation in New York City! Dr. Toshiko Amano thought she was helping mankind, but instead unleashed the virus responsible for transforming ordinary citizens and super heroes alike into Chitauri hybrids with zombie-like appetites. Two attempts at creating an antivirus have failed, and the situation looks bleak for the Avengers — Thor, Black Widow and Dr. Amano have all been infected. Bruce Banner has little time to test a new antidote before his teammates explode! Further complicating matters is the disappearance of Tony's best friend, James "Rhodey" Rhodes, and the emergence of the mysterious "Jasper." Is he the true mastermind behind the outbreak? And what is his connection to Tony?

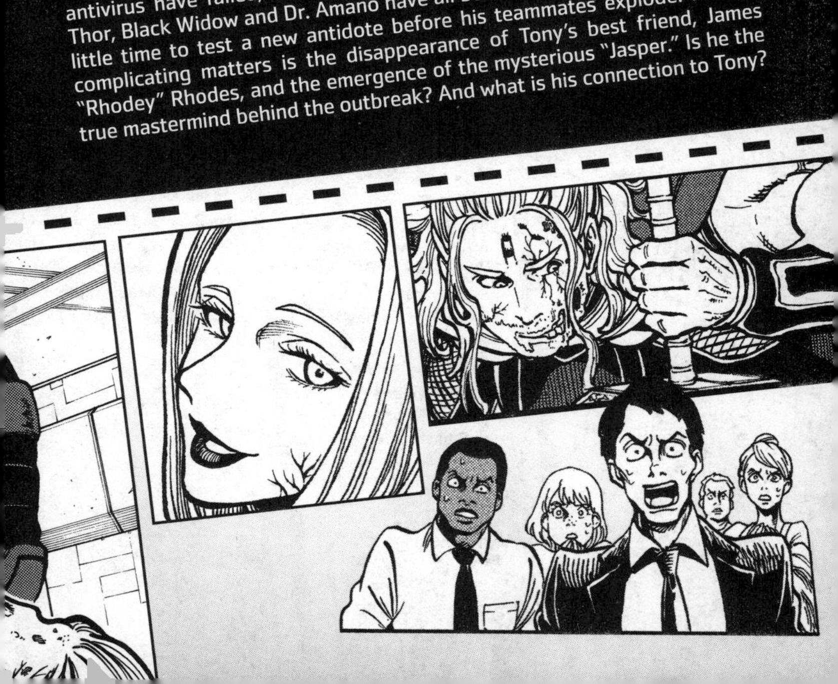

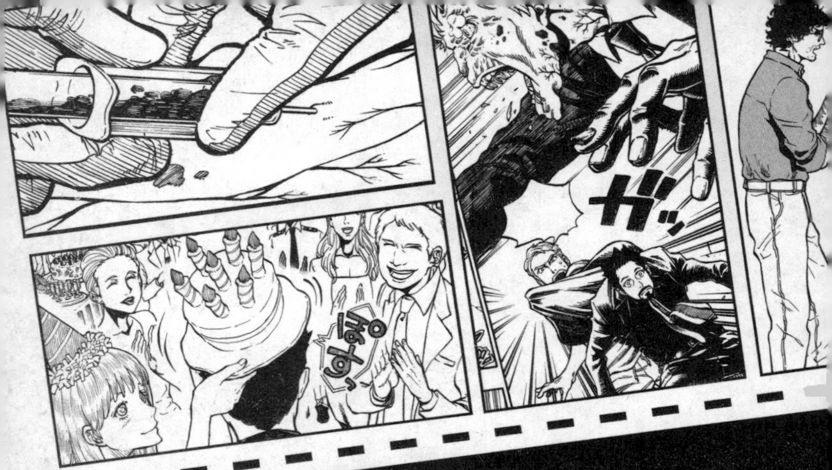

PREVIOUSLY IN...

ZOMBIES ASSEMBLE

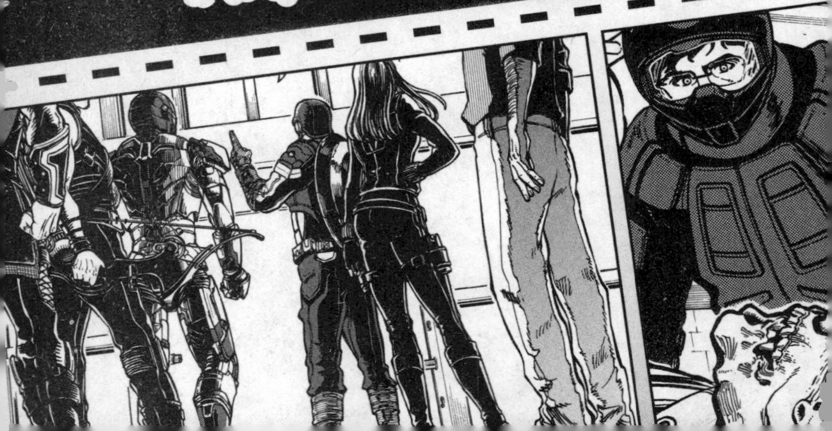

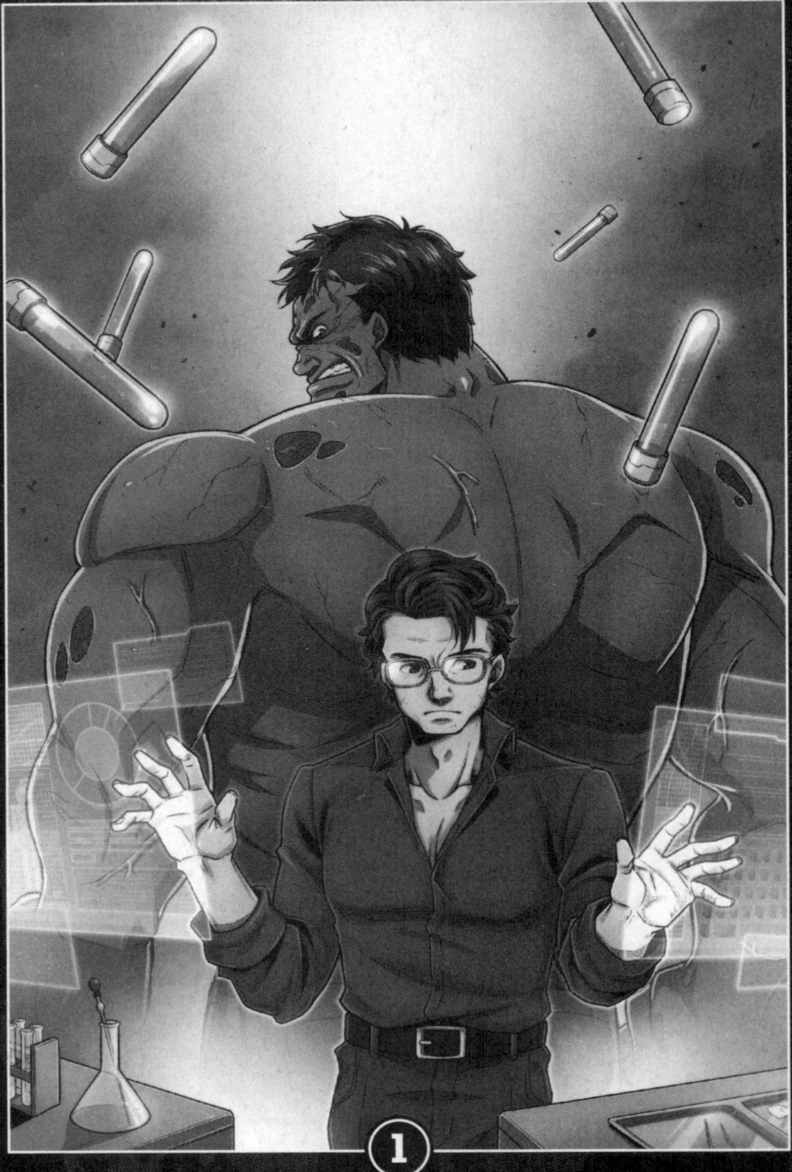

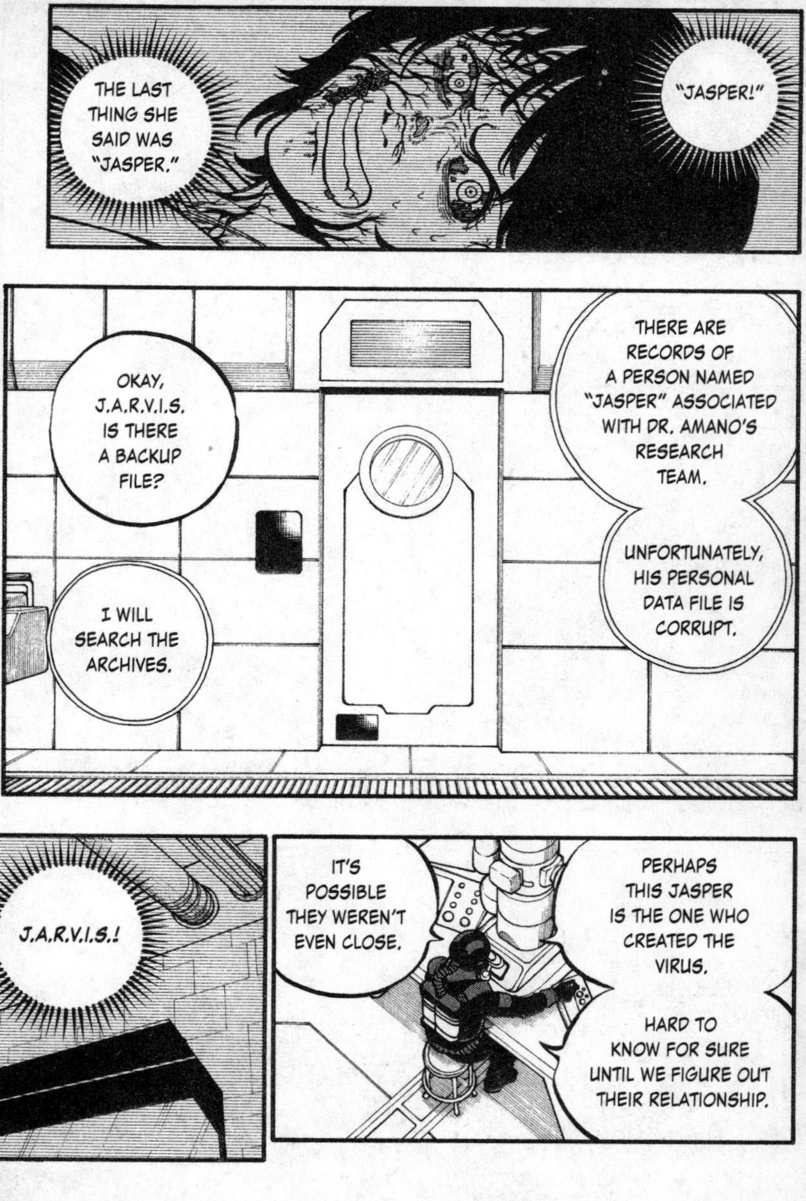
"JASPER!"
THE LAST THING SHE SAID WAS "JASPER."
THERE ARE RECORDS OF A PERSON NAMED "JASPER" ASSOCIATED WITH DR. AMANO'S RESEARCH TEAM.
UNFORTUNATELY, HIS PERSONAL DATA FILE IS CORRUPT.
OKAY, J.A.R.V.I.S. IS THERE A BACKUP FILE?
I WILL SEARCH THE ARCHIVES.
PERHAPS THIS JASPER IS THE ONE WHO CREATED THE VIRUS.
HARD TO KNOW FOR SURE UNTIL WE FIGURE OUT THEIR RELATIONSHIP.
IT'S POSSIBLE THEY WEREN'T EVEN CLOSE.
J.A.R.V.I.S.!

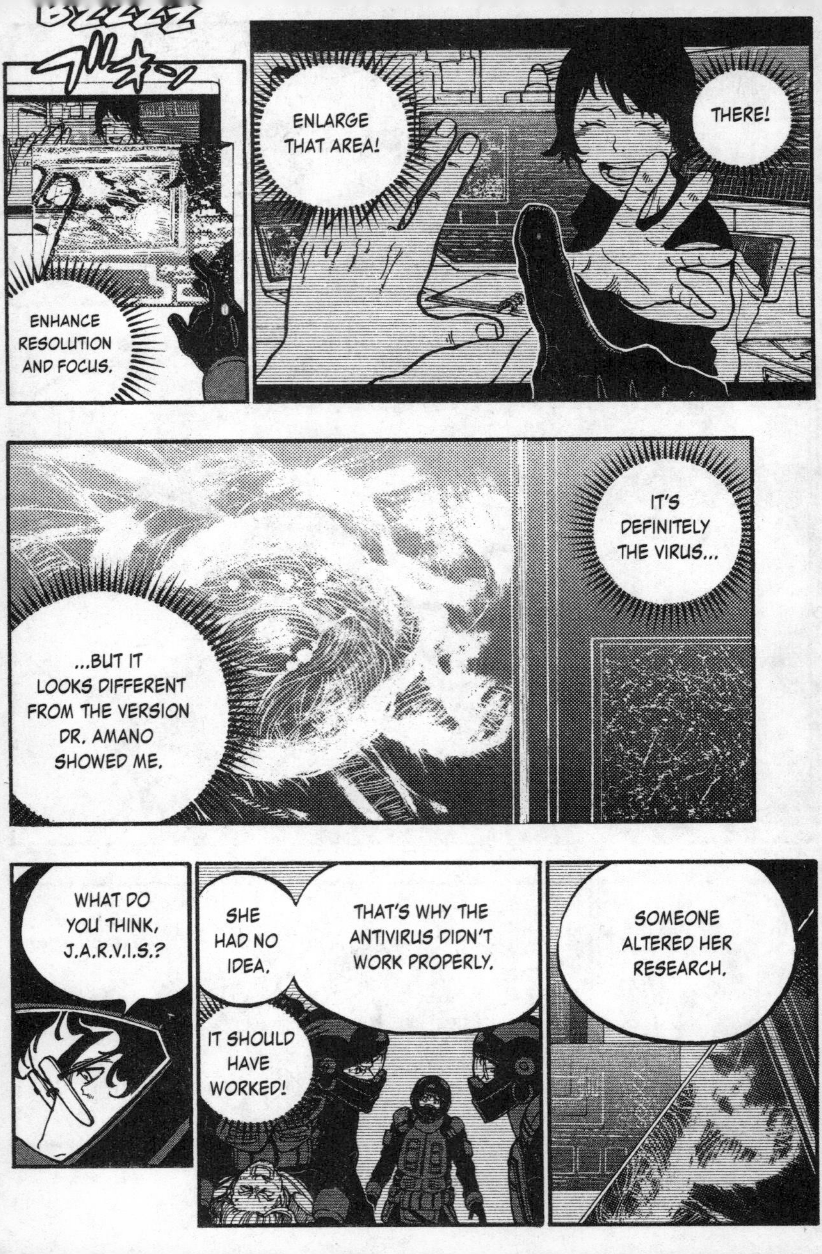
THERE!
ENLARGE THAT AREA!
ENHANCE RESOLUTION AND FOCUS.
IT'S DEFINITELY THE VIRUS...
...BUT IT LOOKS DIFFERENT FROM THE VERSION DR. AMANO SHOWED ME.
SOMEONE ALTERED HER RESEARCH.
THAT'S WHY THE ANTIVIRUS DIDN'T WORK PROPERLY.
SHE HAD NO IDEA.
IT SHOULD HAVE WORKED!
WHAT DO YOU THINK, J.A.R.V.I.S.?

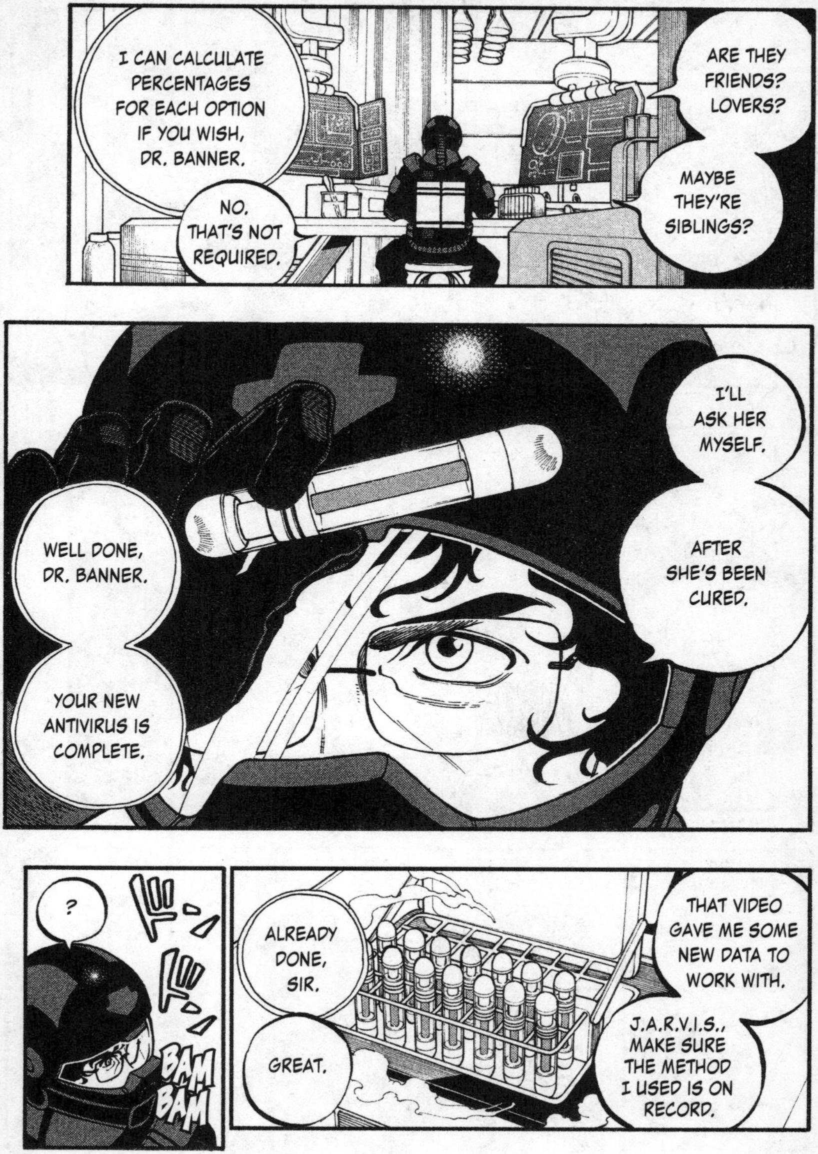
ARE THEY FRIENDS? LOVERS?
MAYBE THEY'RE SIBLINGS?
I CAN CALCULATE PERCENTAGES FOR EACH OPTION IF YOU WISH, DR. BANNER.
NO. THAT'S NOT REQUIRED.
I'LL ASK HER MYSELF.
AFTER SHE'S BEEN CURED.
WELL DONE, DR. BANNER.
YOUR NEW ANTIVIRUS IS COMPLETE.
THAT VIDEO GAVE ME SOME NEW DATA TO WORK WITH.
J.A.R.V.I.S., MAKE SURE THE METHOD I USED IS ON RECORD.
ALREADY DONE, SIR.
GREAT.
?
BAM BAM

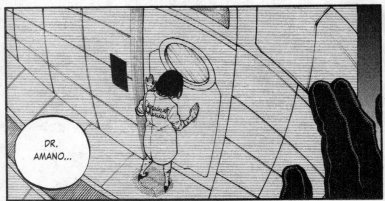

DR. AMANO...

...I'LL OPEN THE DOOR.

JUST A MOMENT...

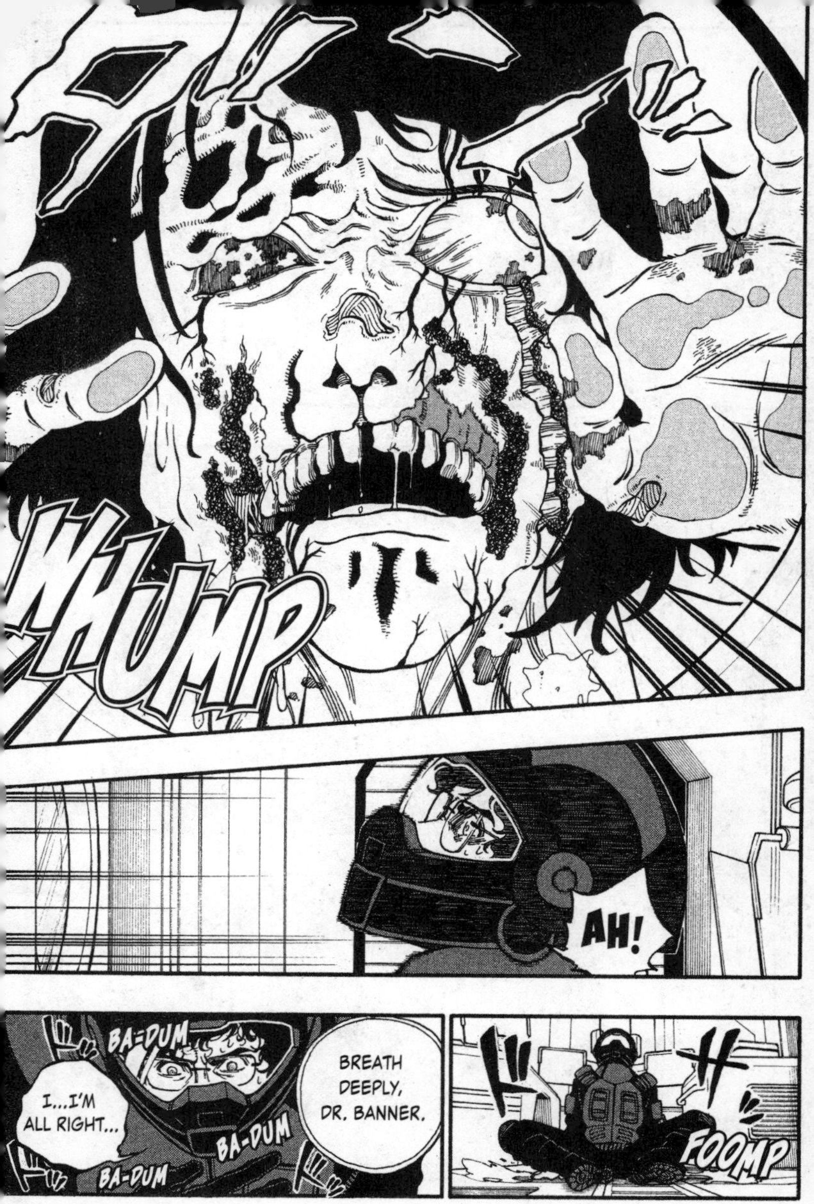
WHUMP
AH!
FOOMP
BREATH DEEPLY, DR. BANNER.
BA-DUM
I...I'M ALL RIGHT...
BA-DUM
BA-DUM

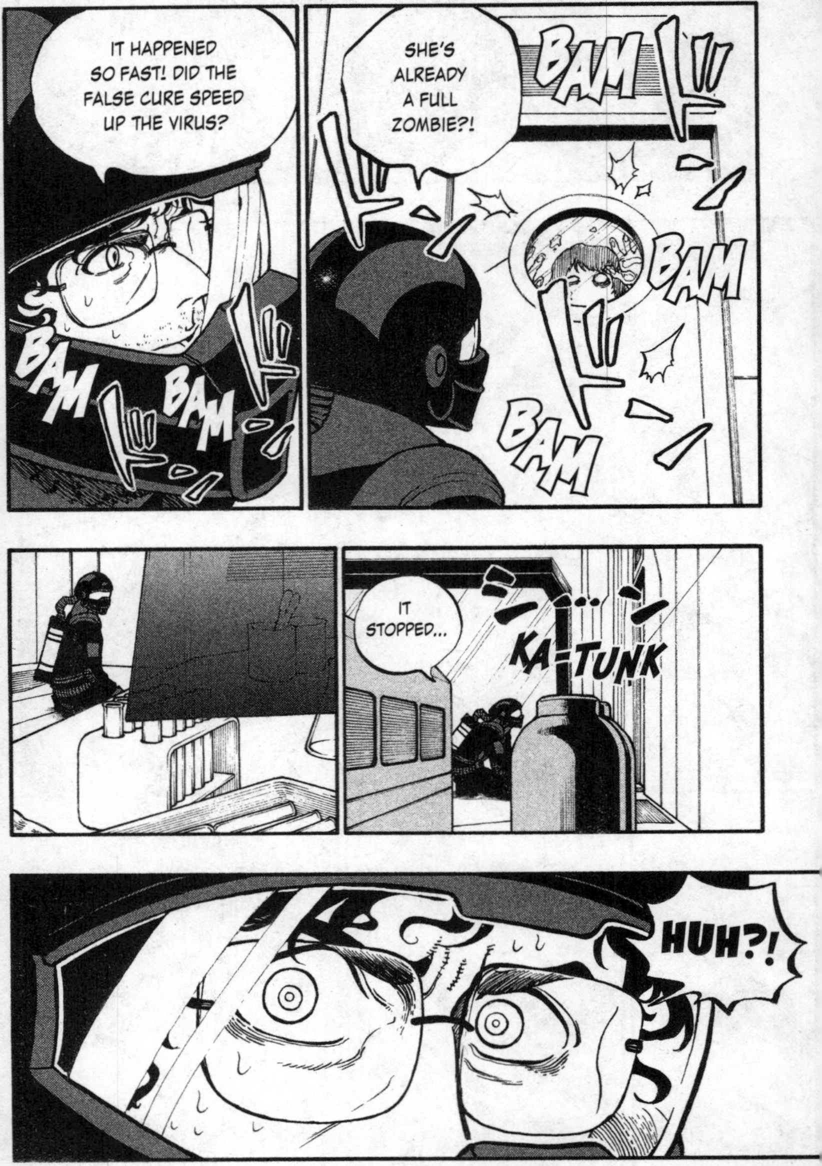
SHE'S ALREADY A FULL ZOMBIE?!
BAM
BAM
BAM
IT HAPPENED SO FAST! DID THE FALSE CURE SPEED UP THE VIRUS?
BAM
BAM
IT STOPPED...
KA-TUNK
HUH?!

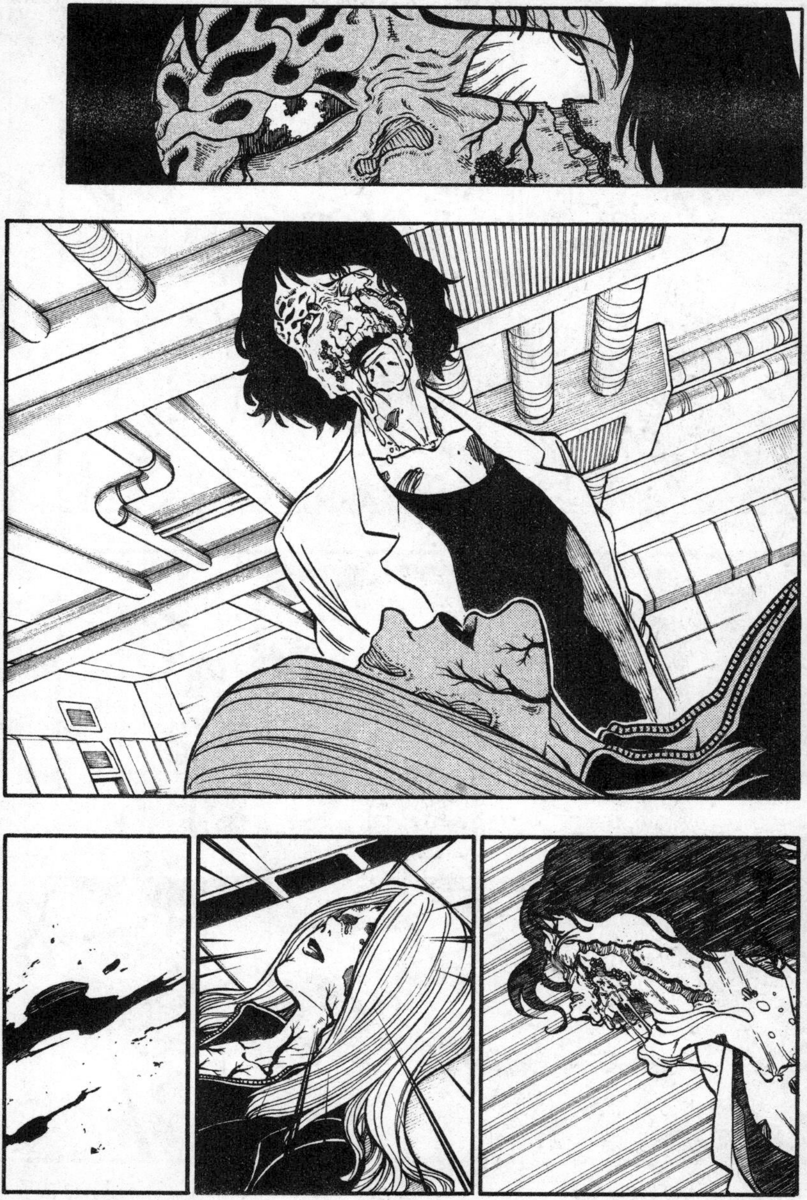

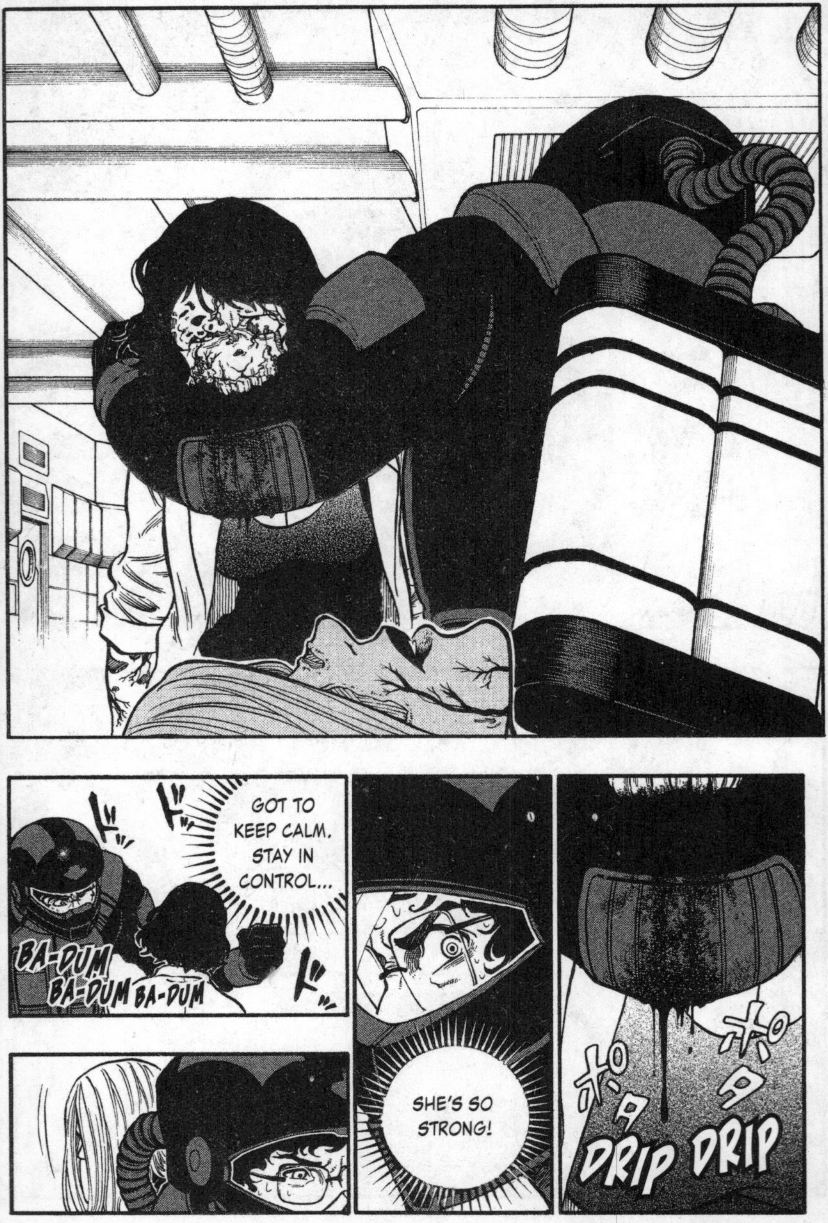
ポタ ポタ
DRIP DRIP
SHE'S SO STRONG!
ド ド
GOT TO KEEP CALM. STAY IN CONTROL...
ド
BA-DUM BA-DUM BA-DUM

N-NATASHA...!

BA-DUUUUM!

BA-DUM BA-DUM BA-DUM BA-DUM

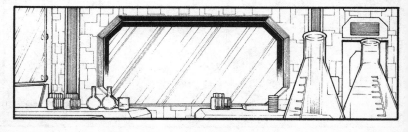

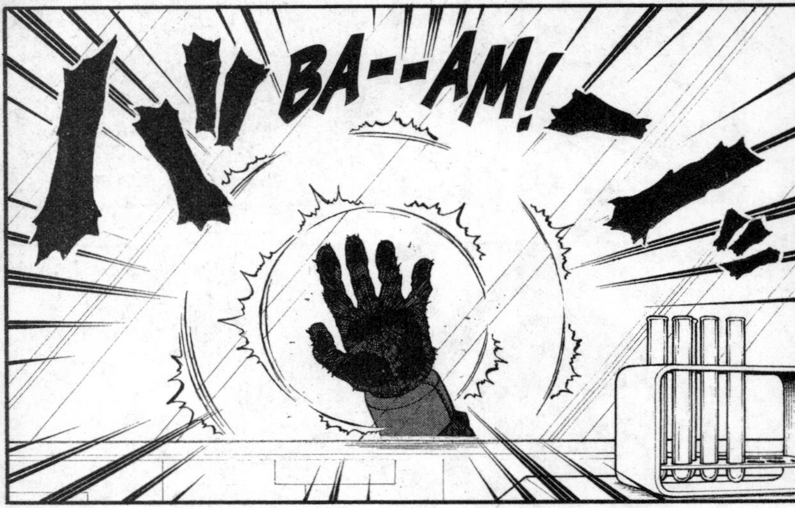
BA--AM!
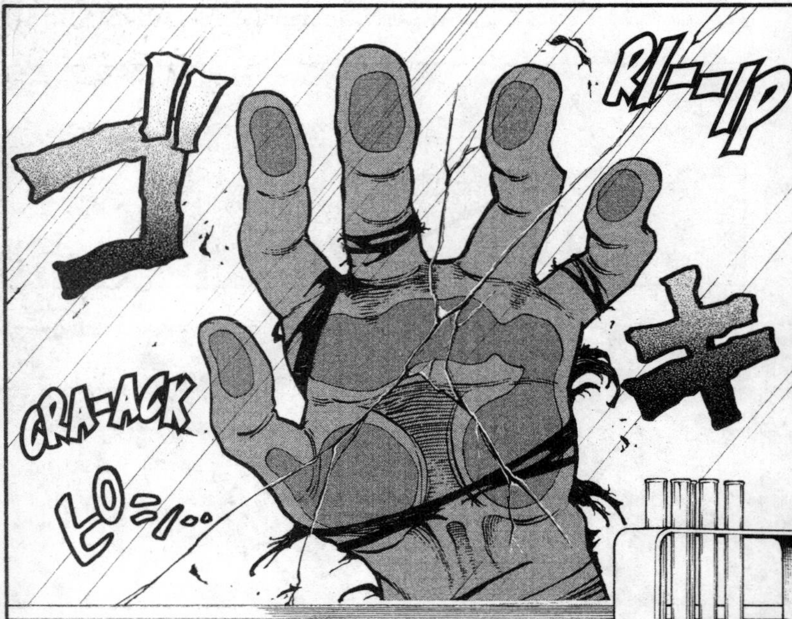
RI--IP
CRA-ACK

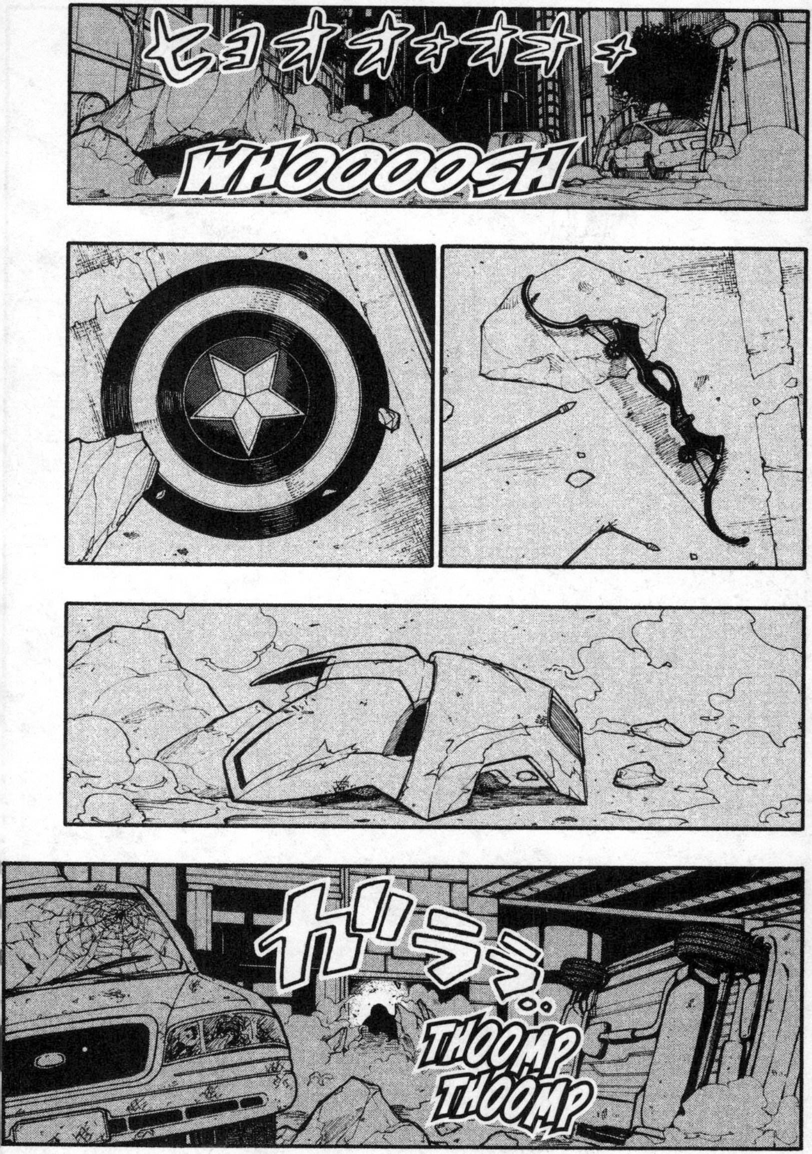
ヒョオオォオオォ
WHOOOOSH
ガララ..
THOOMP
THOOMP

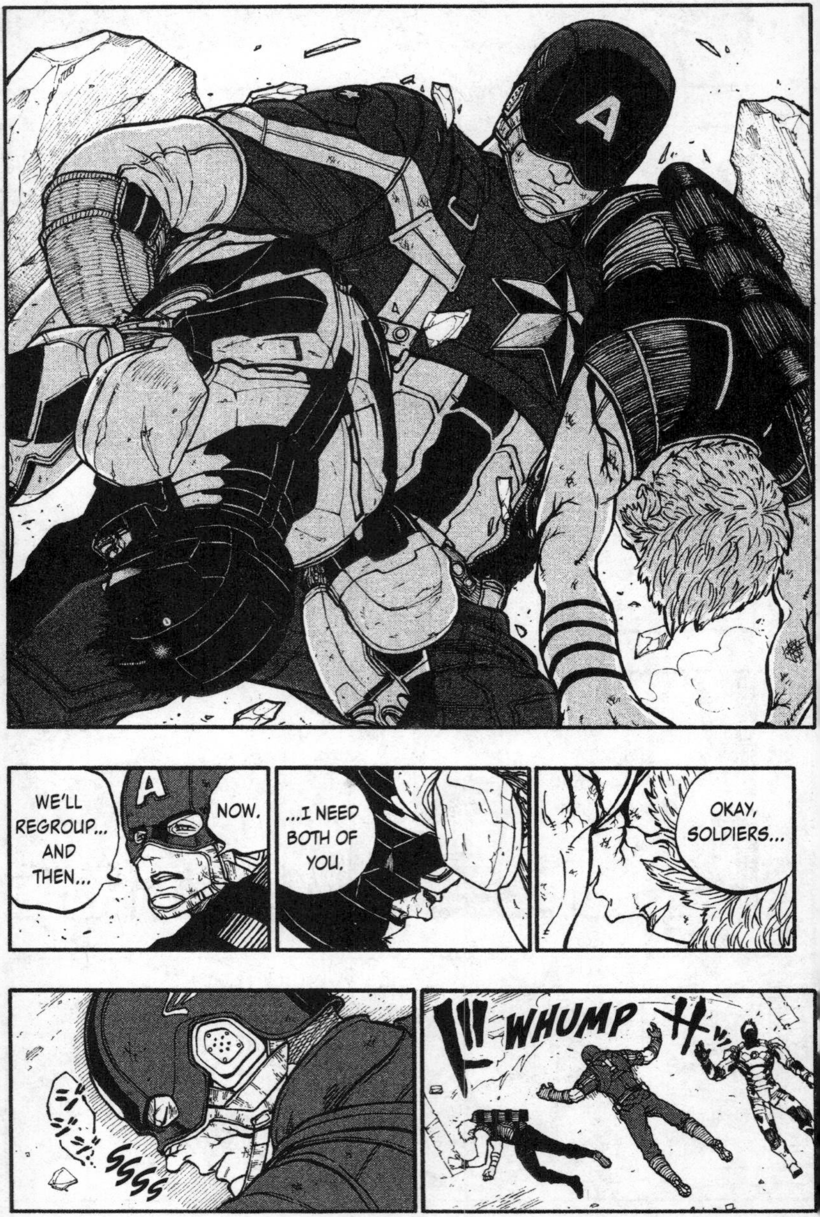
OKAY, SOLDIERS...
...I NEED BOTH OF YOU.
NOW.
WE'LL REGROUP... AND THEN...
WHUMP
SSSS

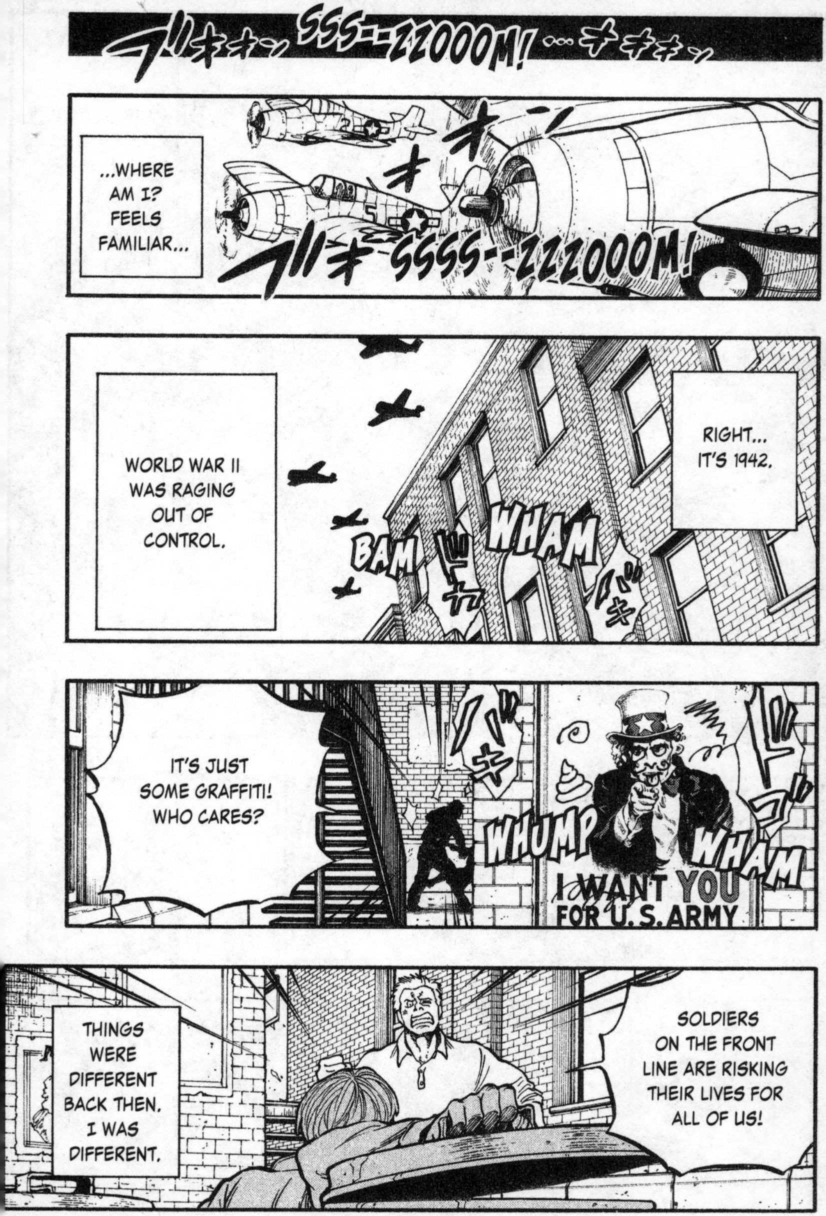
SSS--ZZOOOM! ...
SSSS--ZZZOOOM!
...WHERE AM I? FEELS FAMILIAR...
RIGHT... IT'S 1942.
WHAM
BAM
WORLD WAR II WAS RAGING OUT OF CONTROL.
WHAM
I WANT YOU FOR U.S. ARMY
WHUMP
IT'S JUST SOME GRAFFITI! WHO CARES?
SOLDIERS ON THE FRONT LINE ARE RISKING THEIR LIVES FOR ALL OF US!
THINGS WERE DIFFERENT BACK THEN. I WAS DIFFERENT.

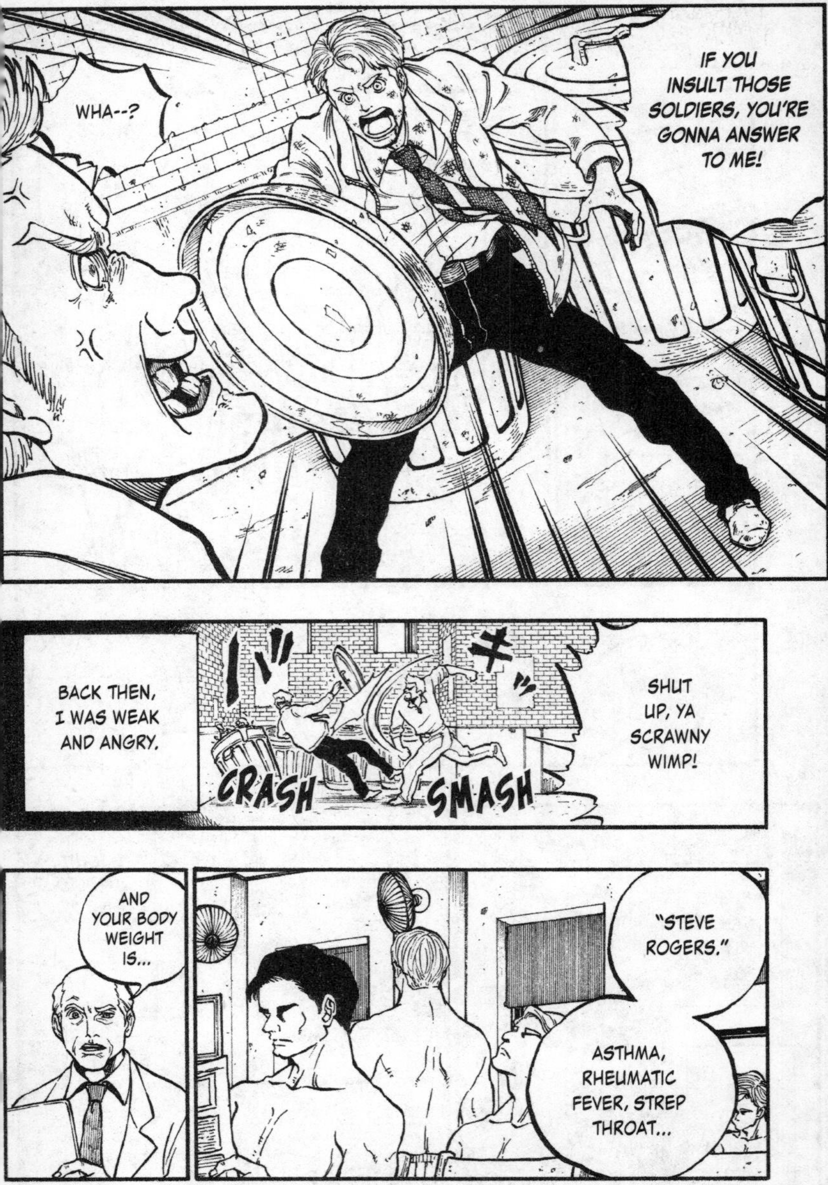
IF YOU INSULT THOSE SOLDIERS, YOU'RE GONNA ANSWER TO ME!
WHA--?
SHUT UP, YA SCRAWNY WIMP!
SMASH
CRASH
BACK THEN, I WAS WEAK AND ANGRY.
"STEVE ROGERS."
ASTHMA, RHEUMATIC FEVER, STREP THROAT...
AND YOUR BODY WEIGHT IS...

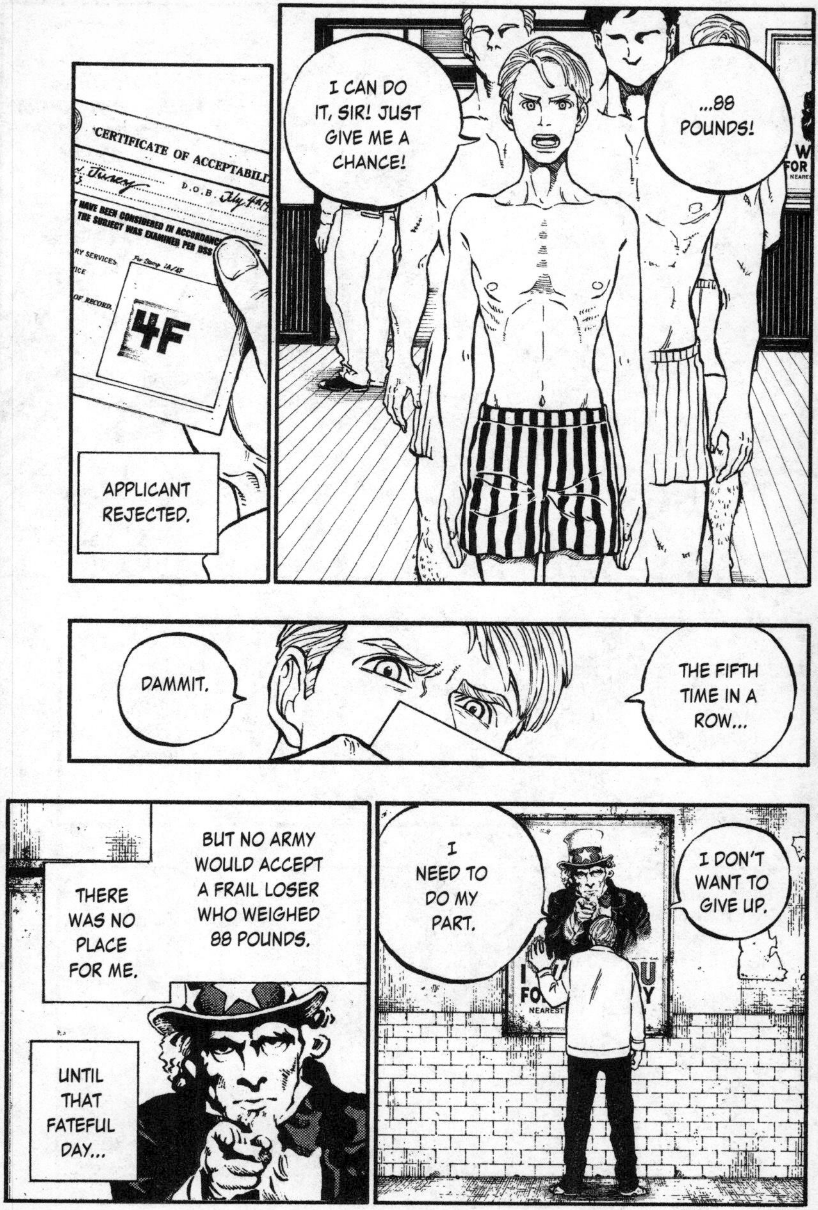
...88 POUNDS!
I CAN DO IT, SIR! JUST GIVE ME A CHANCE!
4F
APPLICANT REJECTED.
THE FIFTH TIME IN A ROW...
DAMMIT.
I DON'T WANT TO GIVE UP.
I NEED TO DO MY PART.
BUT NO ARMY WOULD ACCEPT A FRAIL LOSER WHO WEIGHED 88 POUNDS.
THERE WAS NO PLACE FOR ME.
UNTIL THAT FATEFUL DAY...

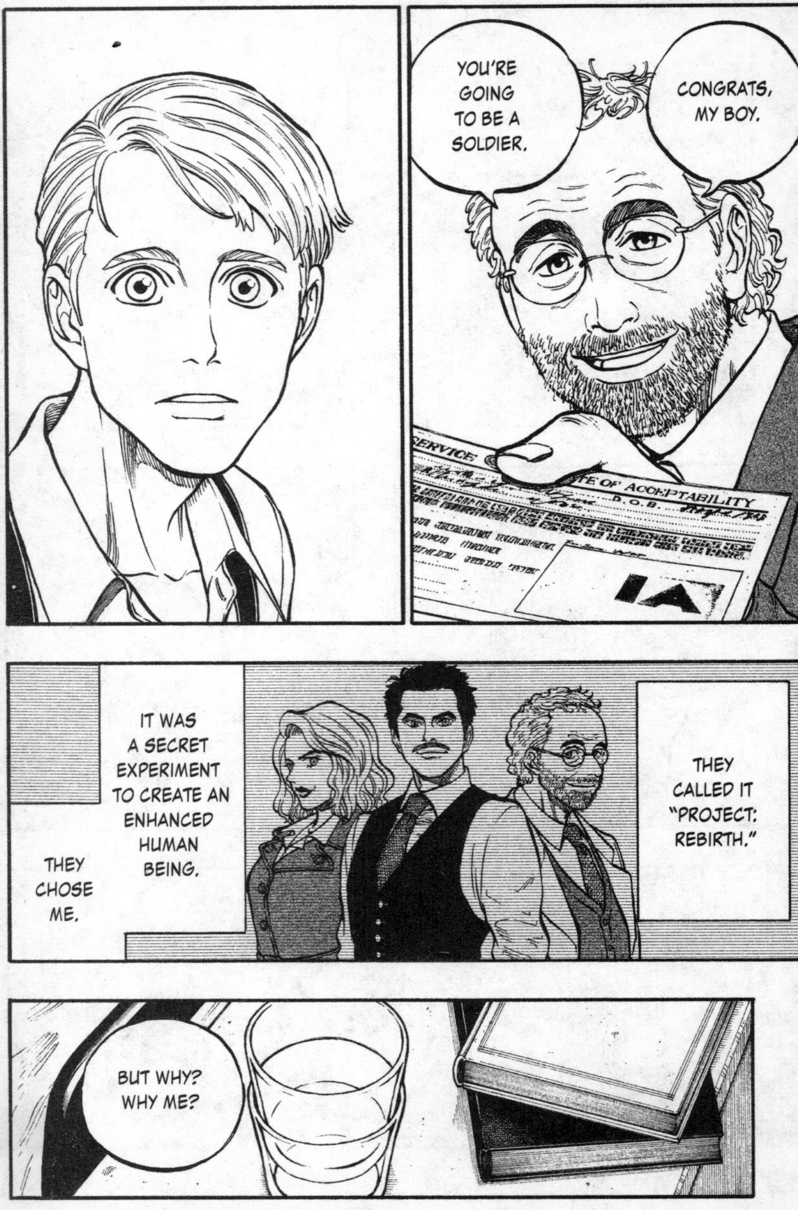
CONGRATS, MY BOY.
YOU'RE GOING TO BE A SOLDIER.
SERVICE
D.O.B.
THEY CALLED IT "PROJECT: REBIRTH."
IT WAS A SECRET EXPERIMENT TO CREATE AN ENHANCED HUMAN BEING.
THEY CHOSE ME.
BUT WHY? WHY ME?

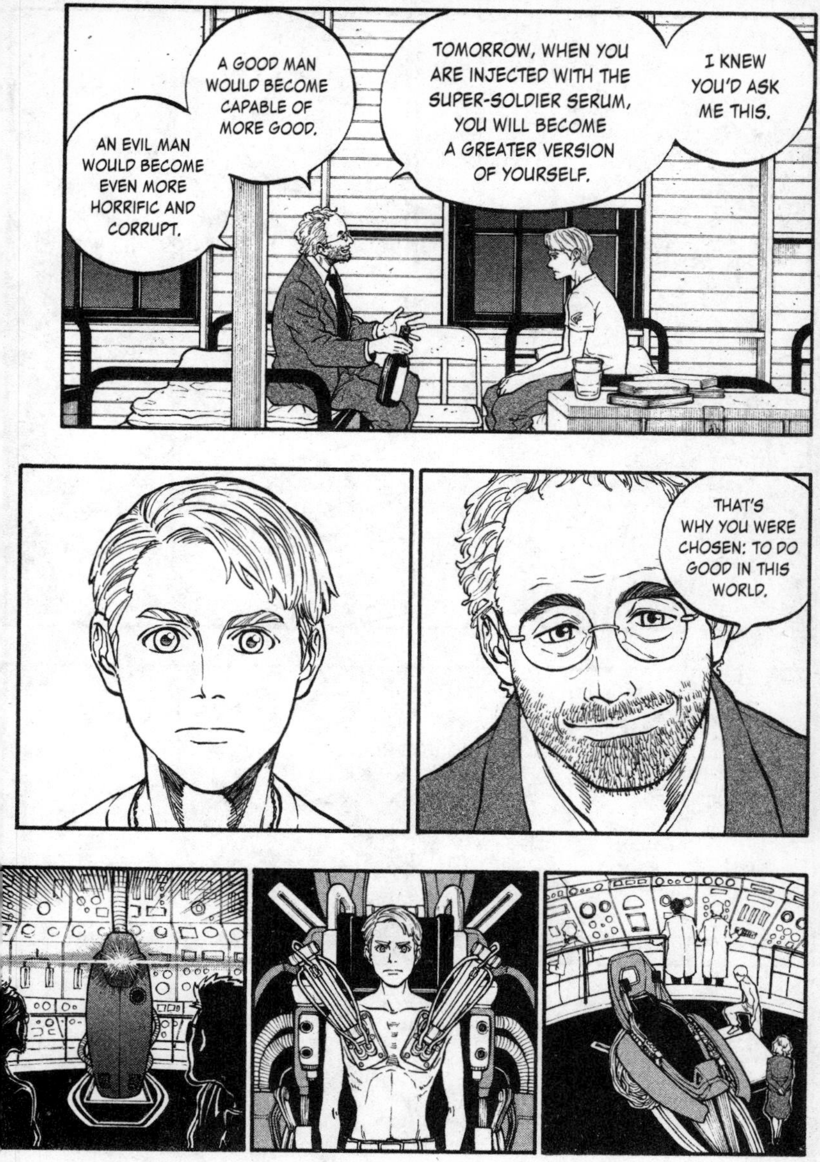
I KNEW YOU'D ASK ME THIS.
TOMORROW, WHEN YOU ARE INJECTED WITH THE SUPER-SOLDIER SERUM, YOU WILL BECOME A GREATER VERSION OF YOURSELF.
A GOOD MAN WOULD BECOME CAPABLE OF MORE GOOD.
AN EVIL MAN WOULD BECOME EVEN MORE HORRIFIC AND CORRUPT.
THAT'S WHY YOU WERE CHOSEN: TO DO GOOD IN THIS WORLD.

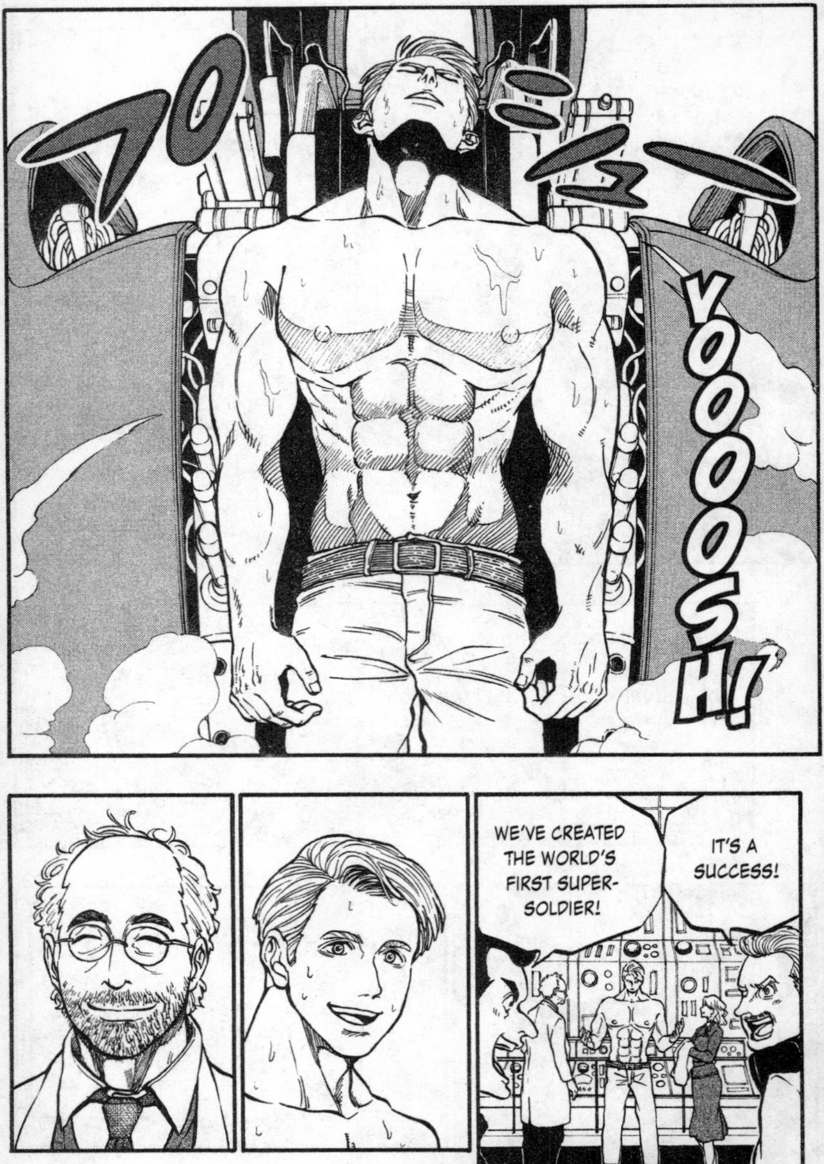
VOOOOOSH!
IT'S A SUCCESS!
WE'VE CREATED THE WORLD'S FIRST SUPER-SOLDIER!

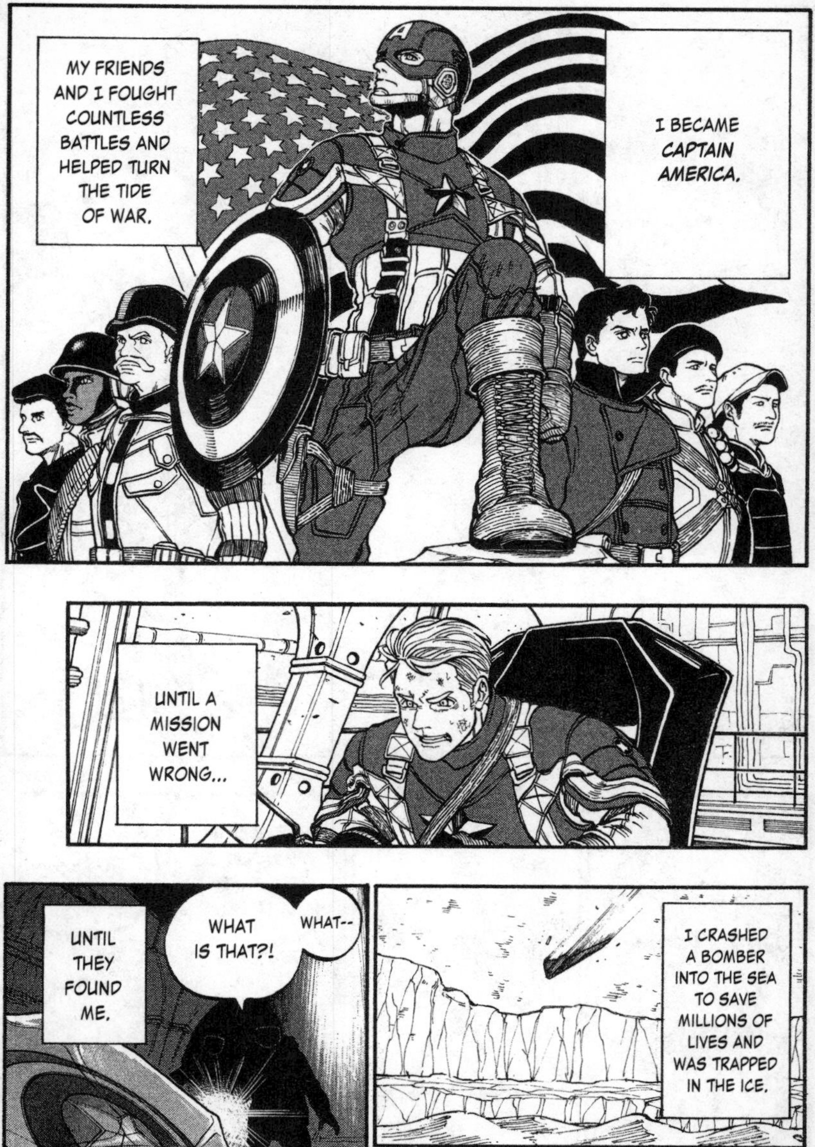
I BECAME CAPTAIN AMERICA.
MY FRIENDS AND I FOUGHT COUNTLESS BATTLES AND HELPED TURN THE TIDE OF WAR.
UNTIL A MISSION WENT WRONG...
I CRASHED A BOMBER INTO THE SEA TO SAVE MILLIONS OF LIVES AND WAS TRAPPED IN THE ICE.
WHAT--
WHAT IS THAT?!
UNTIL THEY FOUND ME.

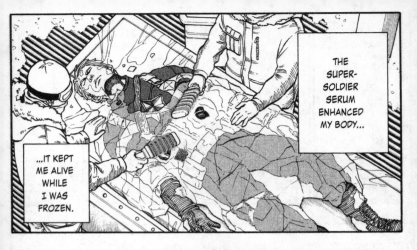

THE SUPER-SOLDIER SERUM ENHANCED MY BODY...

...IT KEPT ME ALIVE WHILE I WAS FROZEN.

I WOKE UP.

SEVENTY YEARS HAD PASSED. THE WORLD HAD CHANGED.

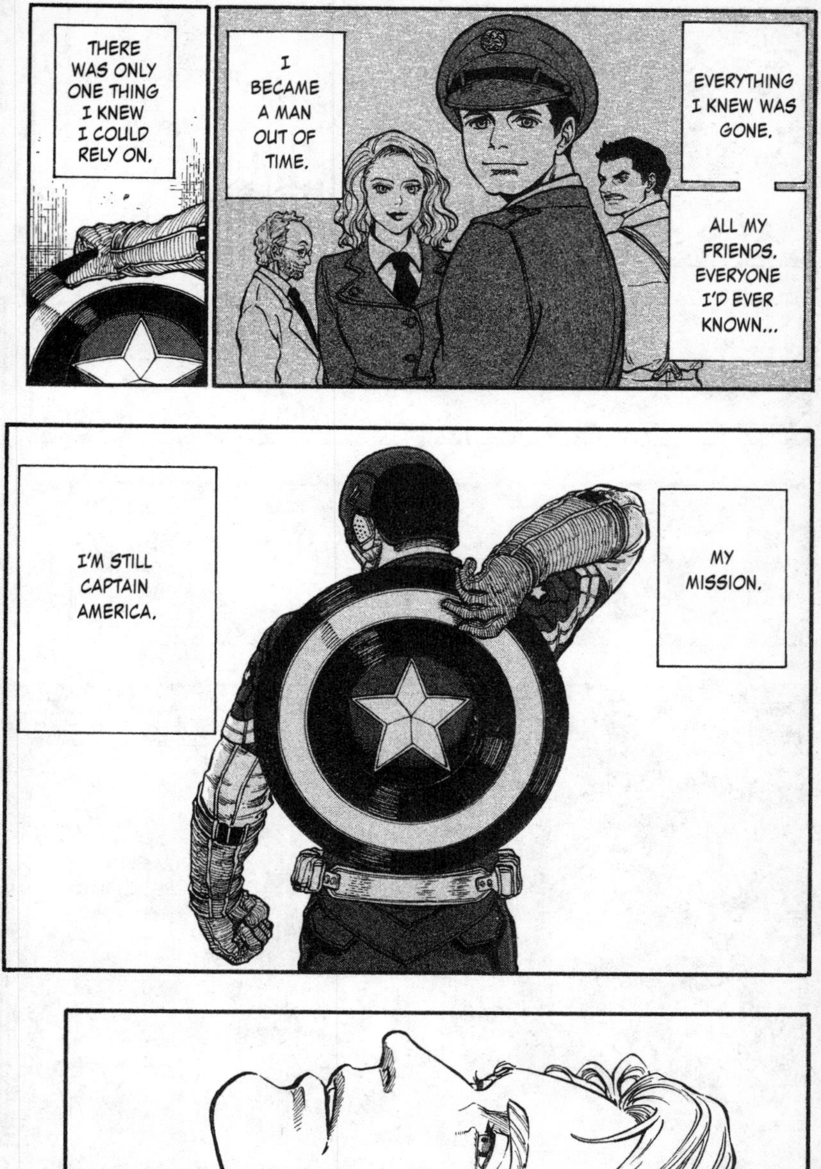
EVERYTHING I KNEW WAS GONE.
ALL MY FRIENDS. EVERYONE I'D EVER KNOWN...
I BECAME A MAN OUT OF TIME.
THERE WAS ONLY ONE THING I KNEW I COULD RELY ON.
MY MISSION.
I'M STILL CAPTAIN AMERICA.

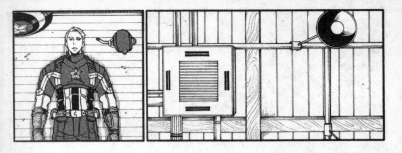

TONY! CLINT!

AHHH!

I'M NOT A ZOMBIE?

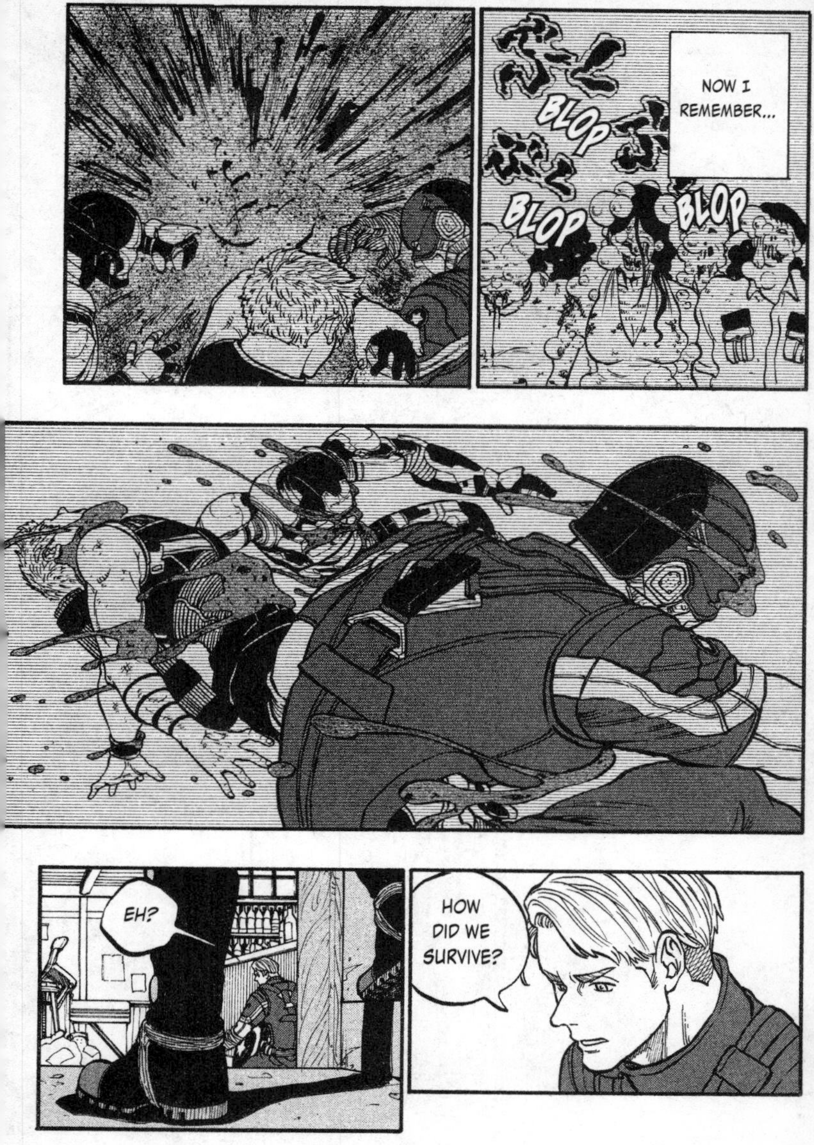
NOW I REMEMBER...
BLOP
BLOP
BLOP
HOW DID WE SURVIVE?
EH?

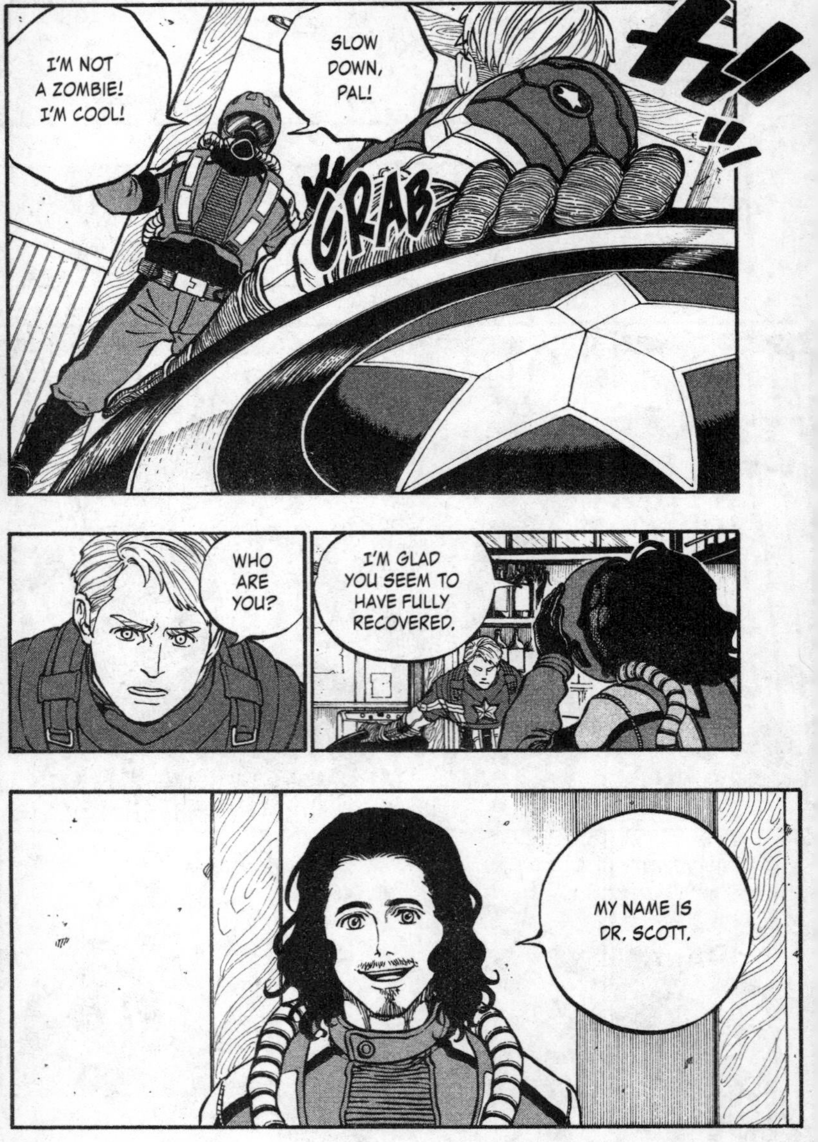
SLOW DOWN, PAL!
I'M NOT A ZOMBIE! I'M COOL!
GRAB
I'M GLAD YOU SEEM TO HAVE FULLY RECOVERED.
WHO ARE YOU?
MY NAME IS DR. SCOTT.

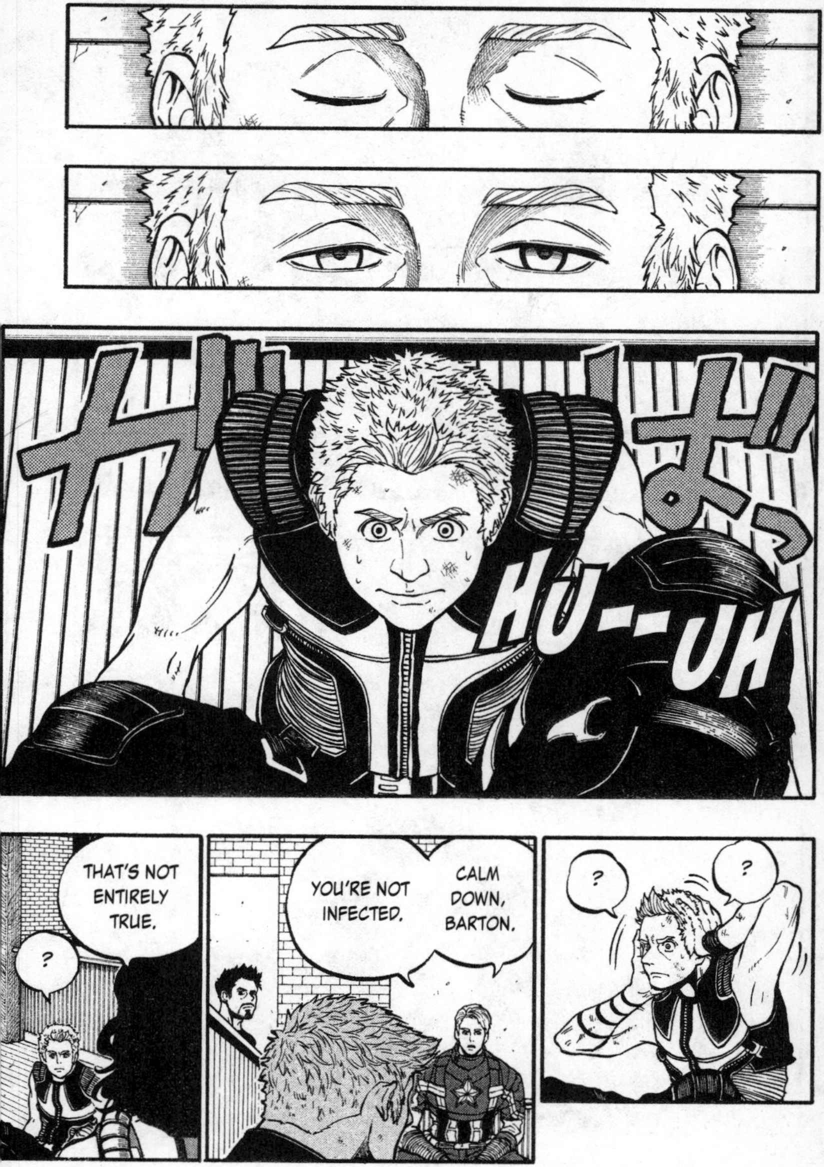
HU--UH
?
?
CALM DOWN, BARTON.
YOU'RE NOT INFECTED.
THAT'S NOT ENTIRELY TRUE.
?

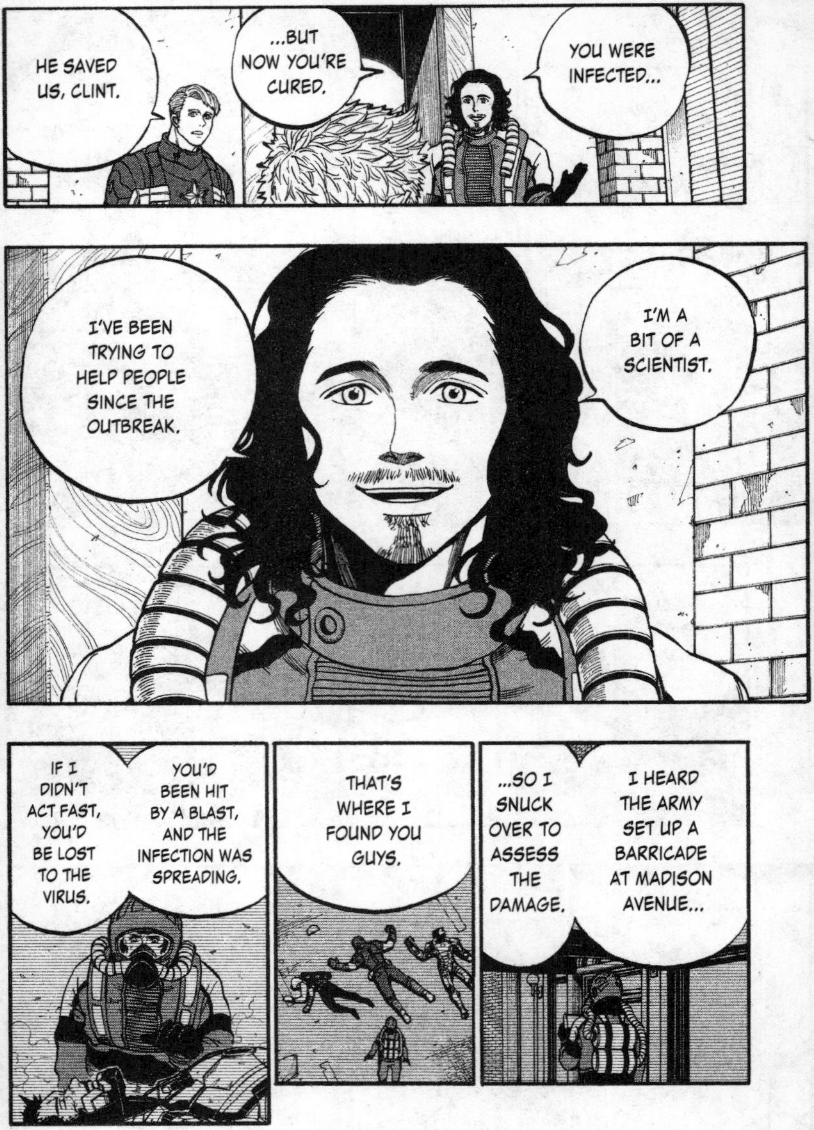
YOU WERE INFECTED...
...BUT NOW YOU'RE CURED.
HE SAVED US, CLINT.
I'M A BIT OF A SCIENTIST.
I'VE BEEN TRYING TO HELP PEOPLE SINCE THE OUTBREAK.
I HEARD THE ARMY SET UP A BARRICADE AT MADISON AVENUE...
...SO I SNUCK OVER TO ASSESS THE DAMAGE.
THAT'S WHERE I FOUND YOU GUYS.
YOU'D BEEN HIT BY A BLAST, AND THE INFECTION WAS SPREADING.
IF I DIDN'T ACT FAST, YOU'D BE LOST TO THE VIRUS.

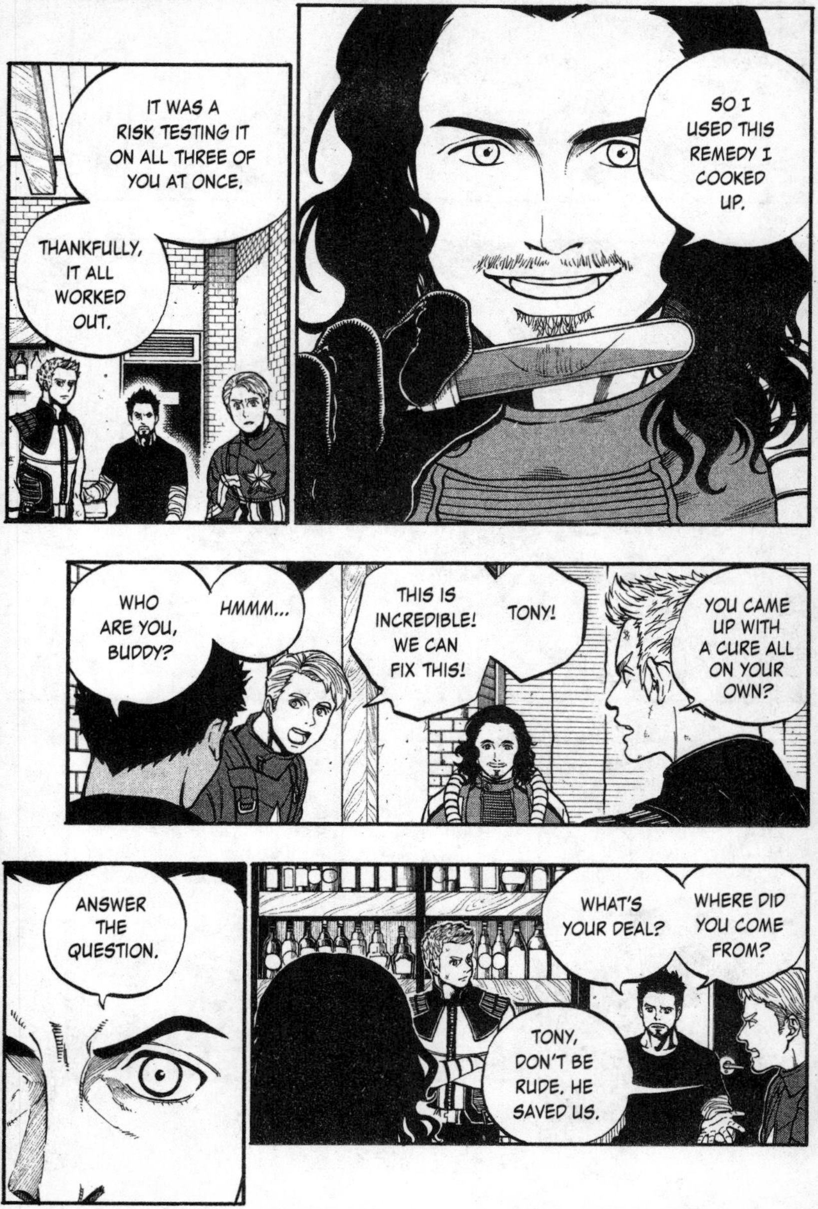
SO I USED THIS REMEDY I COOKED UP.
IT WAS A RISK TESTING IT ON ALL THREE OF YOU AT ONCE.
THANKFULLY, IT ALL WORKED OUT.
YOU CAME UP WITH A CURE ALL ON YOUR OWN?
TONY!
THIS IS INCREDIBLE! WE CAN FIX THIS!
HMMM...
WHO ARE YOU, BUDDY?
WHERE DID YOU COME FROM?
WHAT'S YOUR DEAL?
TONY, DON'T BE RUDE. HE SAVED US.
ANSWER THE QUESTION.

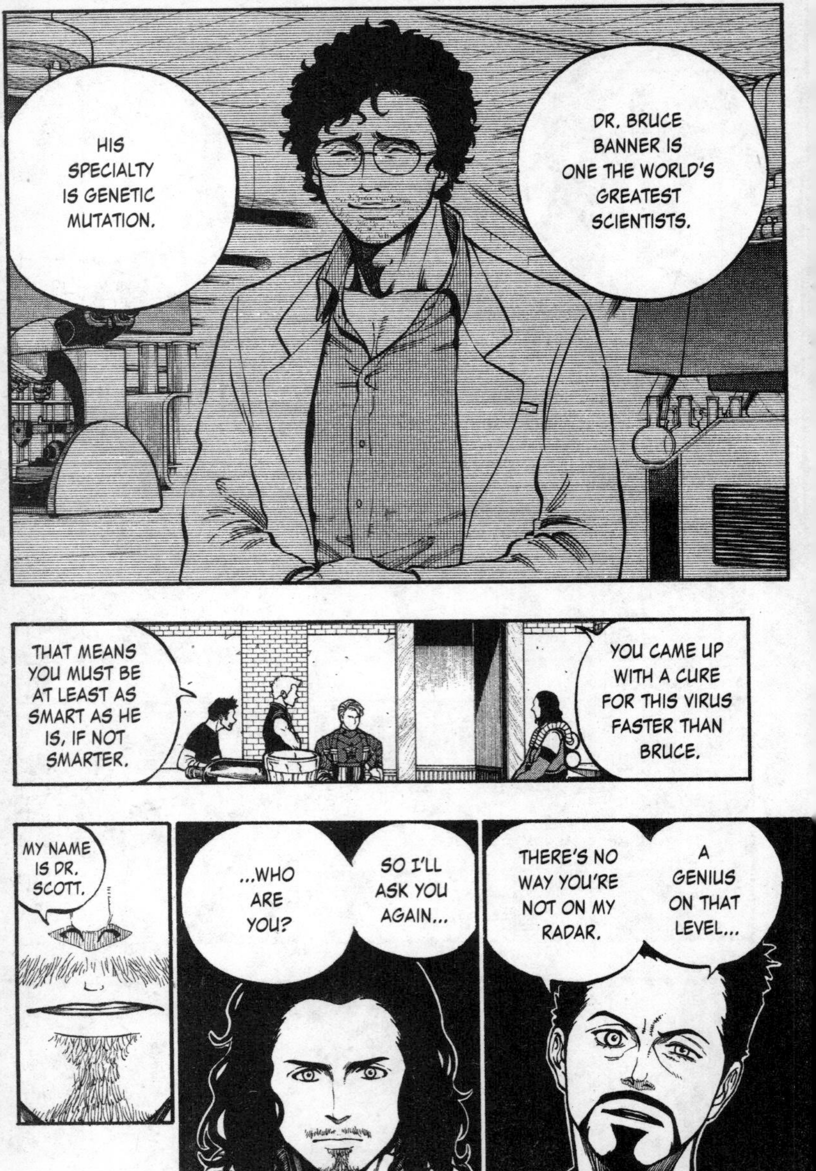
DR. BRUCE BANNER IS ONE THE WORLD'S GREATEST SCIENTISTS.
HIS SPECIALTY IS GENETIC MUTATION.
YOU CAME UP WITH A CURE FOR THIS VIRUS FASTER THAN BRUCE.
THAT MEANS YOU MUST BE AT LEAST AS SMART AS HE IS, IF NOT SMARTER.
A GENIUS ON THAT LEVEL...
THERE'S NO WAY YOU'RE NOT ON MY RADAR.
SO I'LL ASK YOU AGAIN...
...WHO ARE YOU?
MY NAME IS DR. SCOTT.

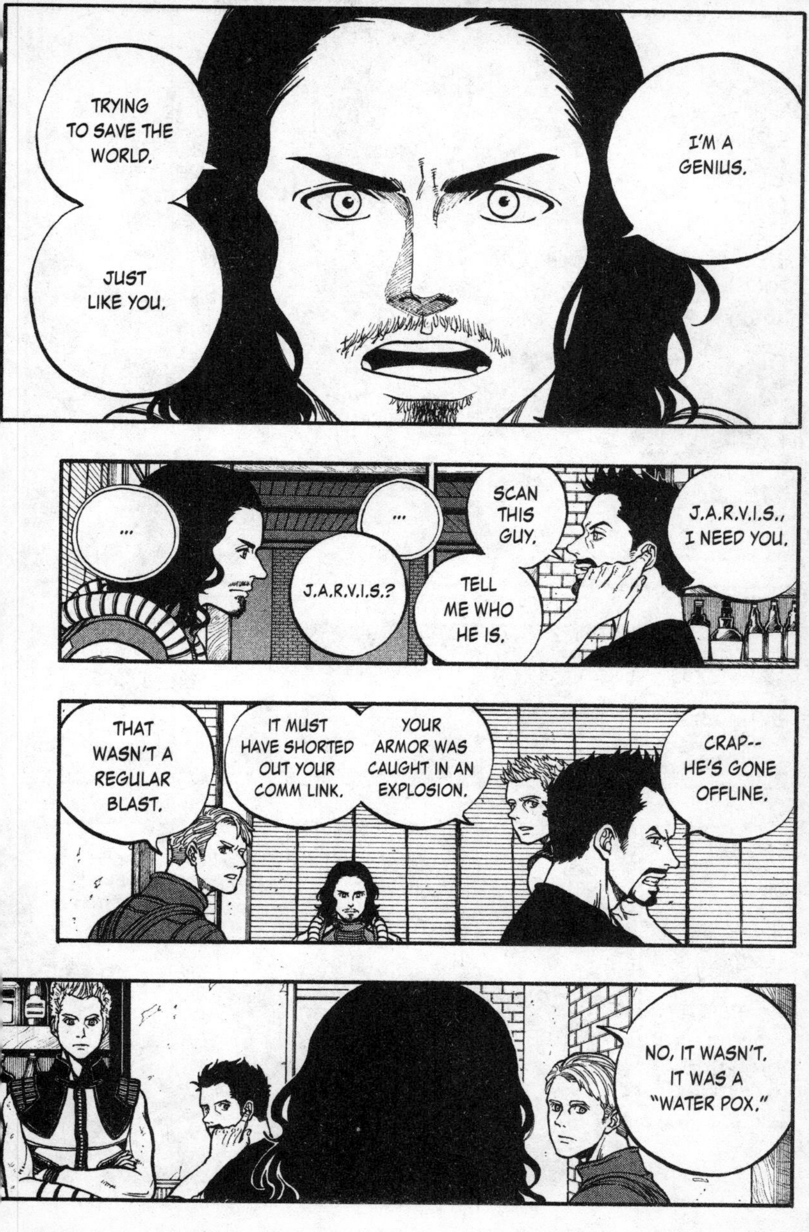
I'M A GENIUS.
TRYING TO SAVE THE WORLD.
JUST LIKE YOU.
J.A.R.V.I.S., I NEED YOU.
SCAN THIS GUY.
TELL ME WHO HE IS.
...
J.A.R.V.I.S.?
...
CRAP-- HE'S GONE OFFLINE.
YOUR ARMOR WAS CAUGHT IN AN EXPLOSION.
IT MUST HAVE SHORTED OUT YOUR COMM LINK.
THAT WASN'T A REGULAR BLAST.
NO, IT WASN'T. IT WAS A "WATER POX."

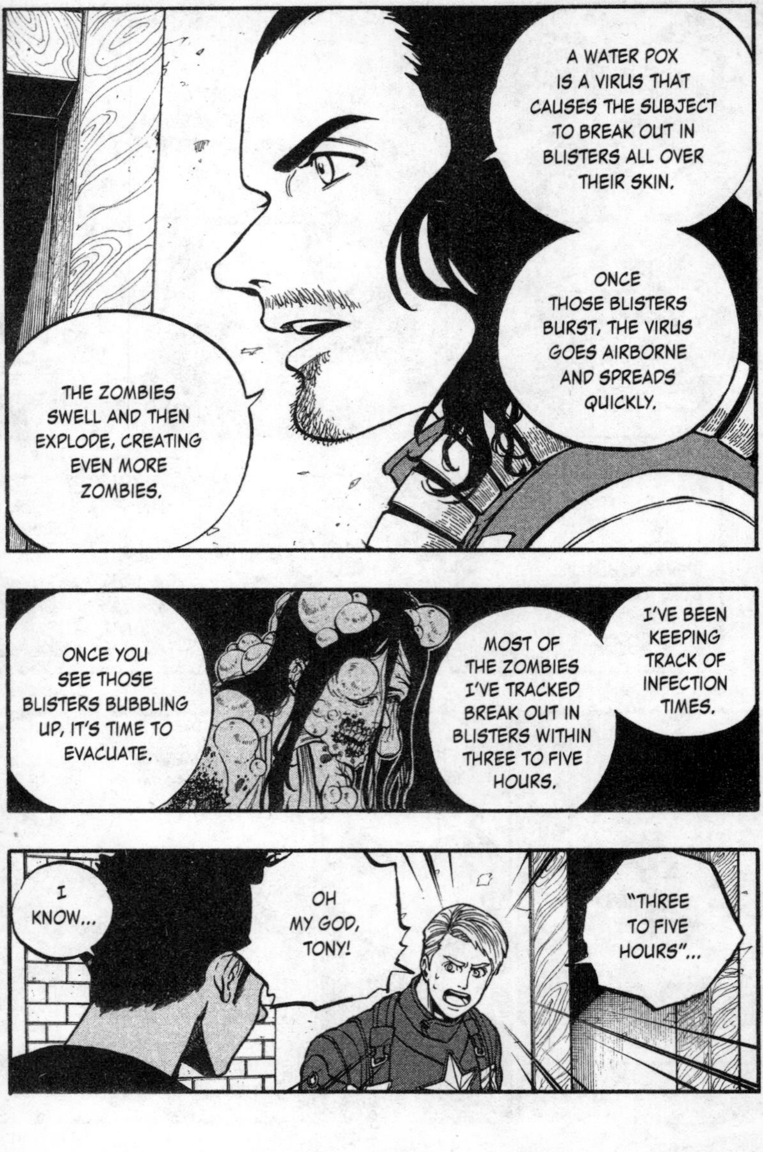
A WATER POX IS A VIRUS THAT CAUSES THE SUBJECT TO BREAK OUT IN BLISTERS ALL OVER THEIR SKIN.
ONCE THOSE BLISTERS BURST, THE VIRUS GOES AIRBORNE AND SPREADS QUICKLY.
THE ZOMBIES SWELL AND THEN EXPLODE, CREATING EVEN MORE ZOMBIES.
I'VE BEEN KEEPING TRACK OF INFECTION TIMES.
MOST OF THE ZOMBIES I'VE TRACKED BREAK OUT IN BLISTERS WITHIN THREE TO FIVE HOURS.
ONCE YOU SEE THOSE BLISTERS BUBBLING UP, IT'S TIME TO EVACUATE.
"THREE TO FIVE HOURS"...
OH MY GOD, TONY!
I KNOW...

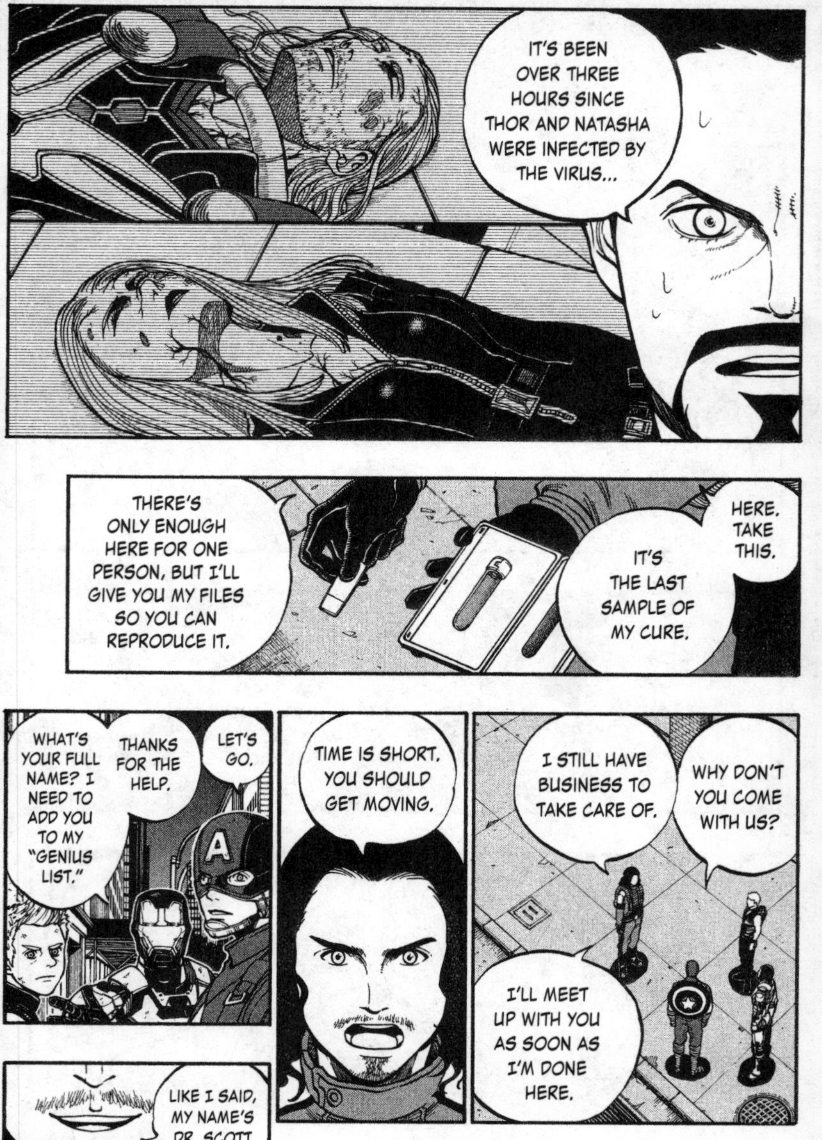
IT'S BEEN OVER THREE HOURS SINCE THOR AND NATASHA WERE INFECTED BY THE VIRUS...
HERE. TAKE THIS.
IT'S THE LAST SAMPLE OF MY CURE.
THERE'S ONLY ENOUGH HERE FOR ONE PERSON, BUT I'LL GIVE YOU MY FILES SO YOU CAN REPRODUCE IT.
WHY DON'T YOU COME WITH US?
I STILL HAVE BUSINESS TO TAKE CARE OF.
I'LL MEET UP WITH YOU AS SOON AS I'M DONE HERE.
TIME IS SHORT. YOU SHOULD GET MOVING.
LET'S GO.
THANKS FOR THE HELP.
WHAT'S YOUR FULL NAME? I NEED TO ADD YOU TO MY "GENIUS LIST."
LIKE I SAID, MY NAME'S DR. SCOTT.

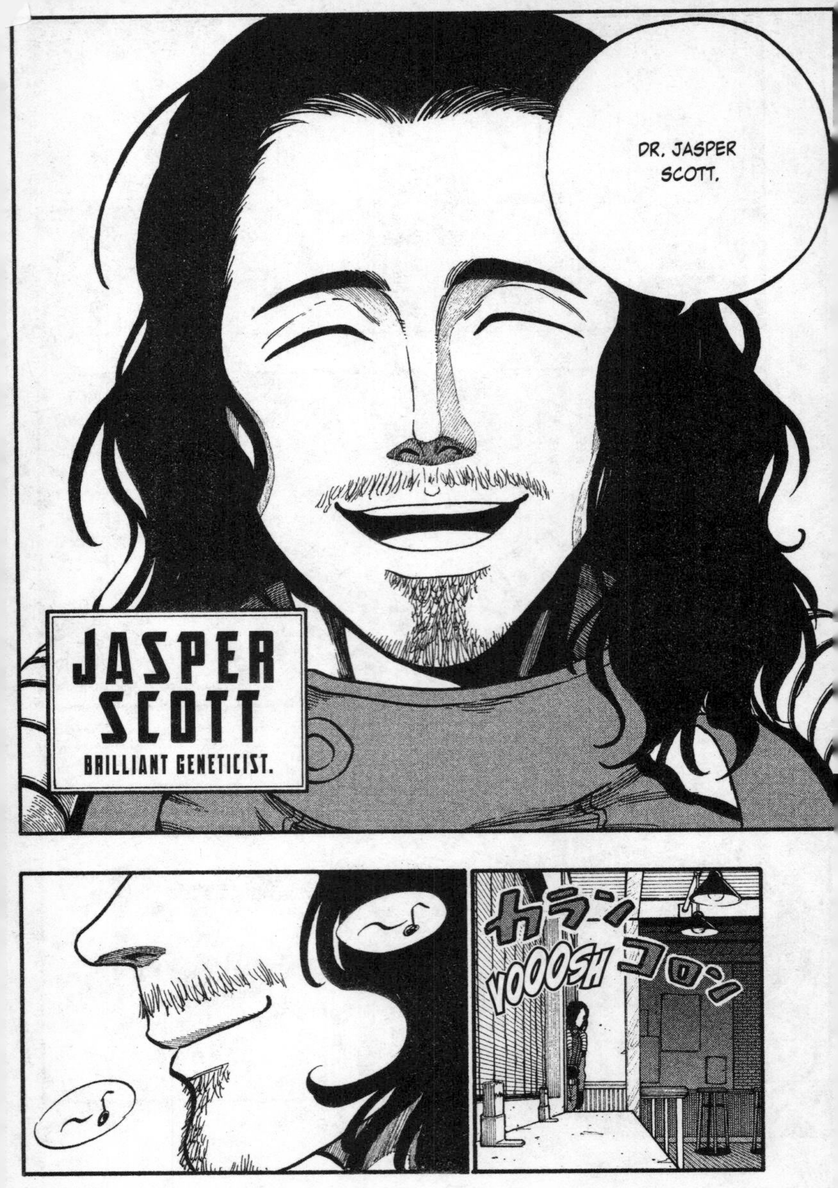
DR. JASPER SCOTT.
JASPER SCOTT
BRILLIANT GENETICIST.
カラーン
VOOOSH
コローン

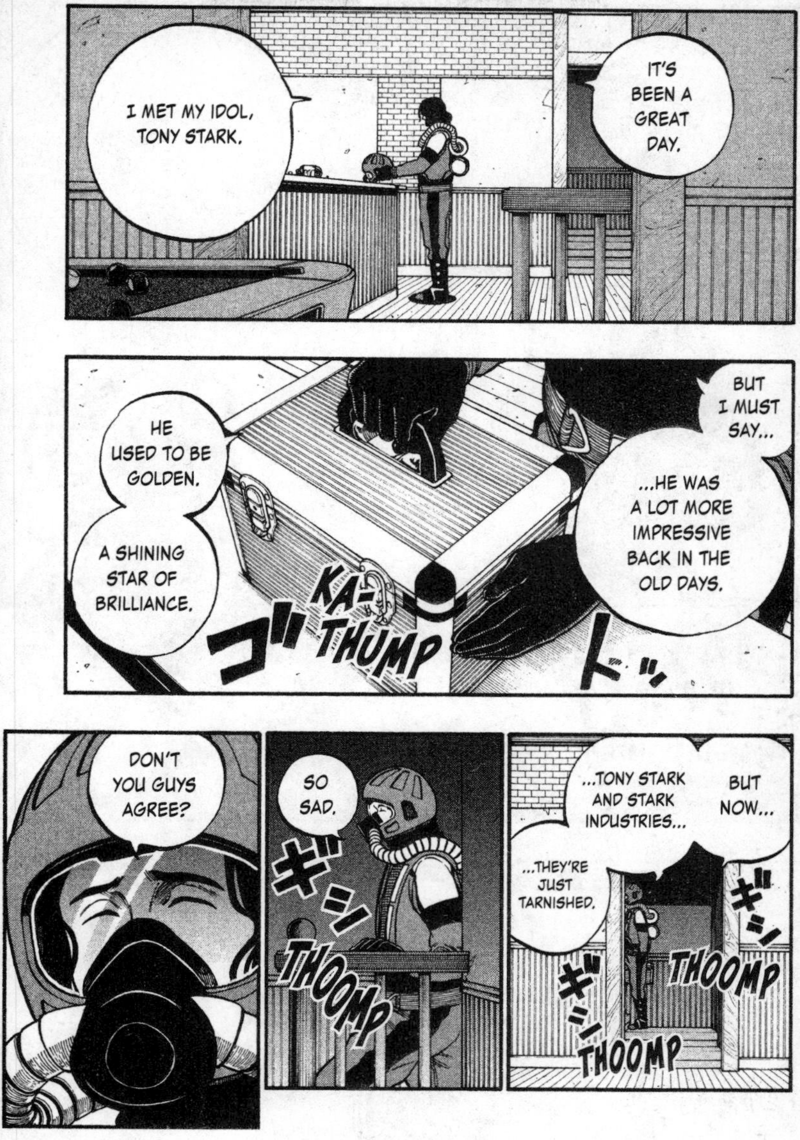
IT'S BEEN A GREAT DAY.
I MET MY IDOL, TONY STARK.
BUT I MUST SAY...
...HE WAS A LOT MORE IMPRESSIVE BACK IN THE OLD DAYS.
ドッ
HE USED TO BE GOLDEN.
A SHINING STAR OF BRILLIANCE.
KA-THUMP
ゴッ
BUT NOW...
...TONY STARK AND STARK INDUSTRIES...
...THEY'RE JUST TARNISHED.
ギッ
THOOMP
ギッ
THOOMP
SO SAD.
ギッ
THOOMP
DON'T YOU GUYS AGREE?

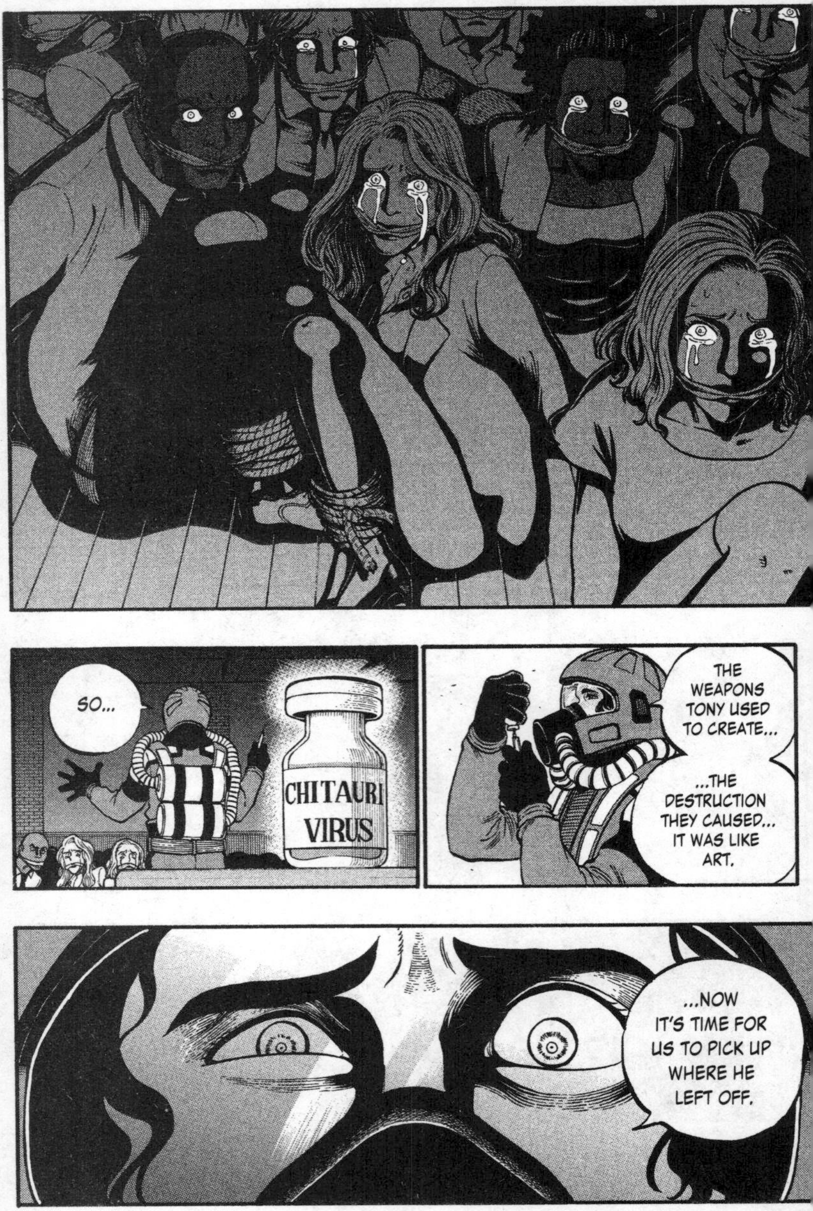
THE WEAPONS TONY USED TO CREATE...
...THE DESTRUCTION THEY CAUSED... IT WAS LIKE ART.
SO...
CHITAURI VIRUS
...NOW IT'S TIME FOR US TO PICK UP WHERE HE LEFT OFF.

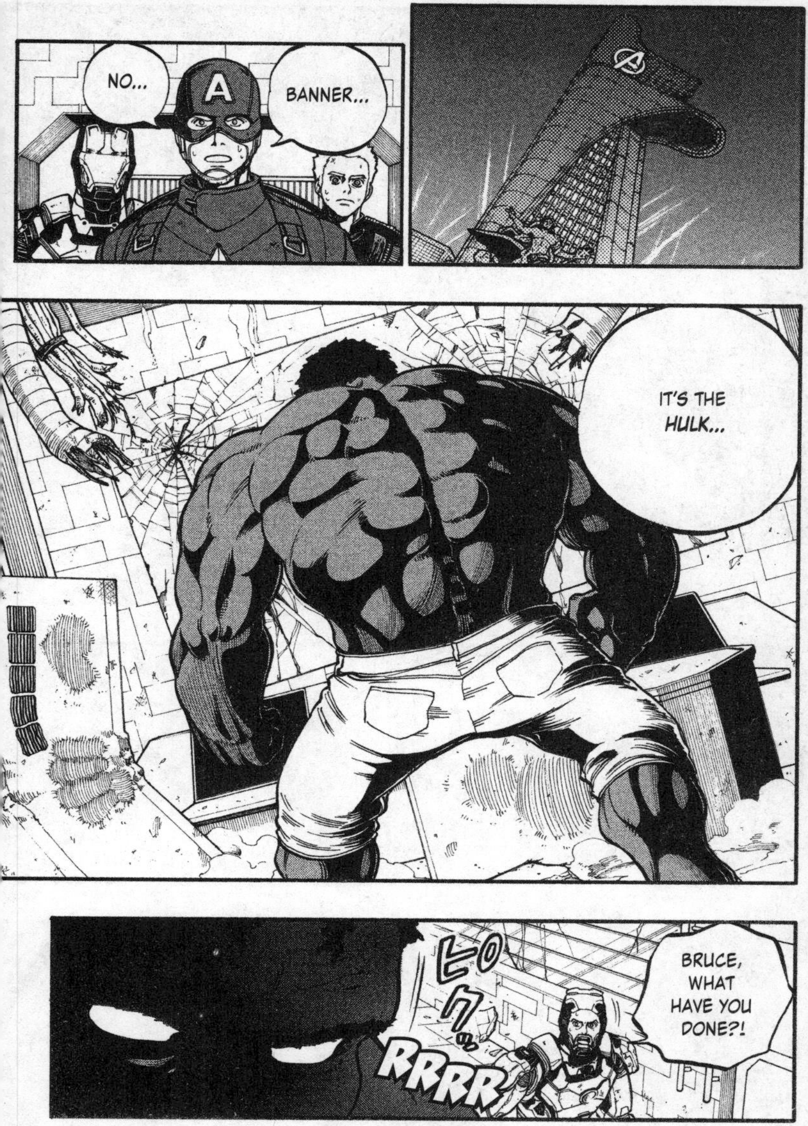
BANNER...
NO...
IT'S THE HULK...
BRUCE, WHAT HAVE YOU DONE?!
ピクッ
RRRR

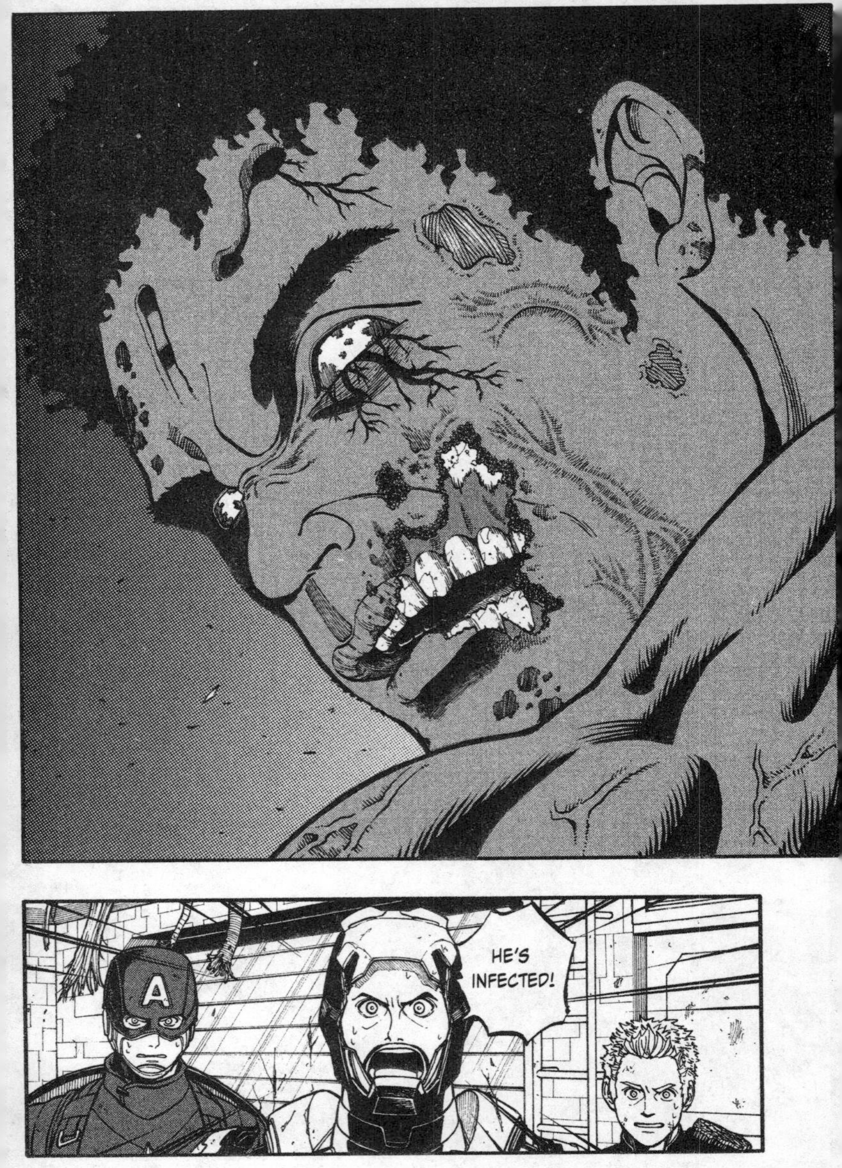
HE'S INFECTED!

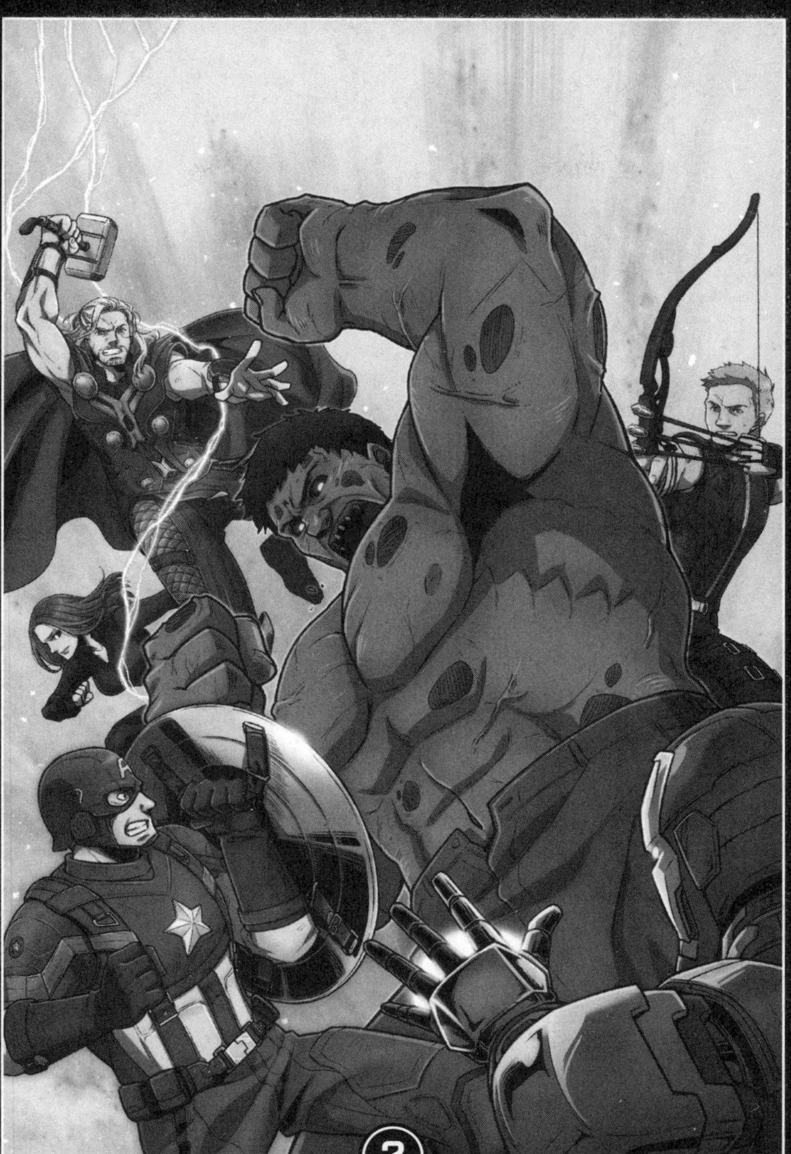

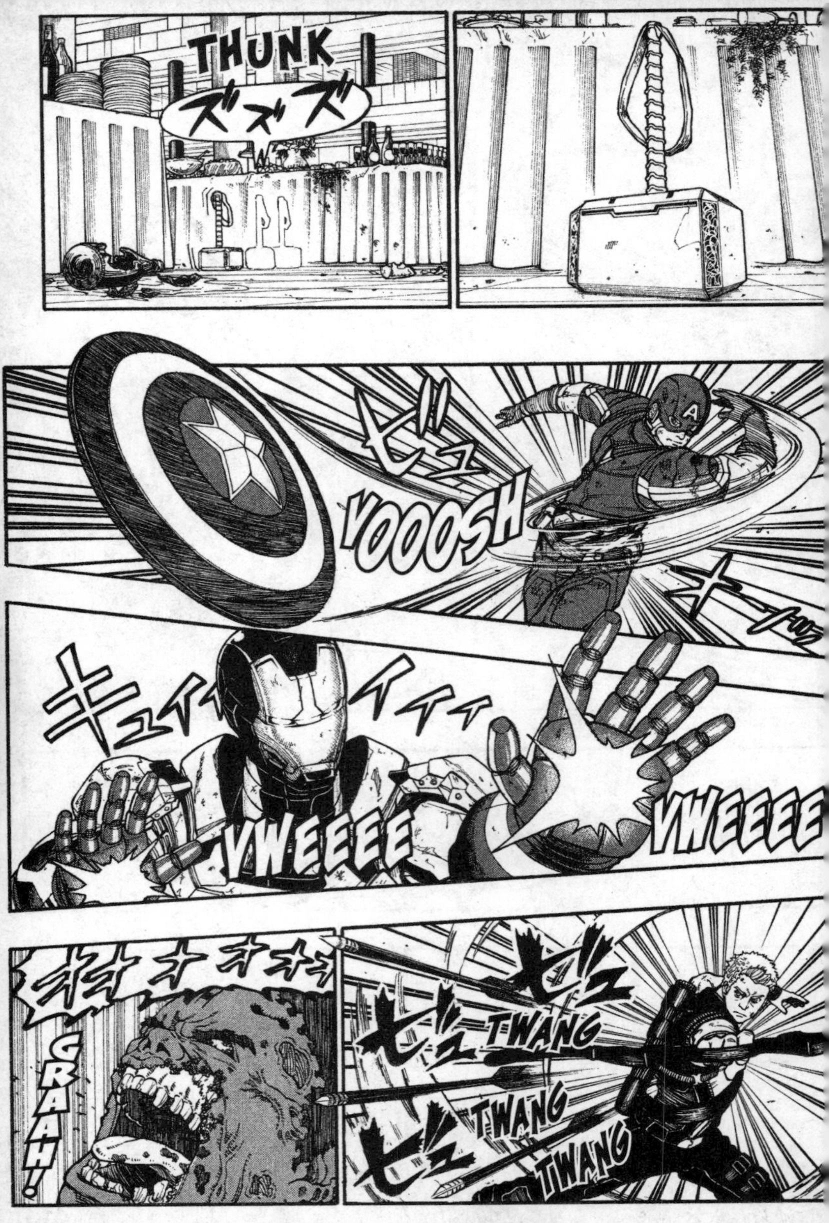
THUNK
ズズズ
ビュ
VOOOSH
VWEEEE
キュイイイイイ
VWEEEE
ビュ
TWANG
ビュ
TWANG
ビュ
TWANG
オオオオオオッ
GRAAAH!

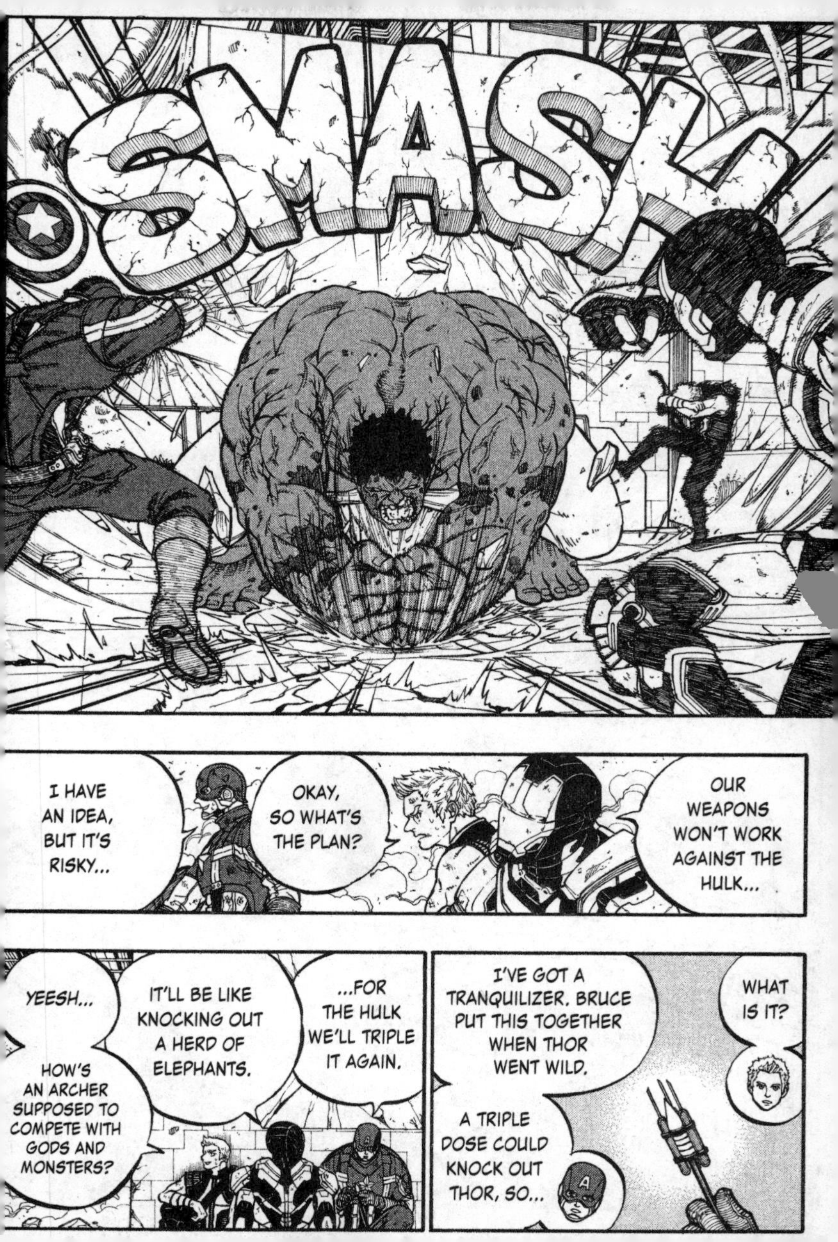
SMASH
OUR WEAPONS WON'T WORK AGAINST THE HULK...
OKAY, SO WHAT'S THE PLAN?
I HAVE AN IDEA, BUT IT'S RISKY...
WHAT IS IT?
I'VE GOT A TRANQUILIZER. BRUCE PUT THIS TOGETHER WHEN THOR WENT WILD.
A TRIPLE DOSE COULD KNOCK OUT THOR, SO...
...FOR THE HULK WE'LL TRIPLE IT AGAIN.
IT'LL BE LIKE KNOCKING OUT A HERD OF ELEPHANTS.
YEESH...
HOW'S AN ARCHER SUPPOSED TO COMPETE WITH GODS AND MONSTERS?

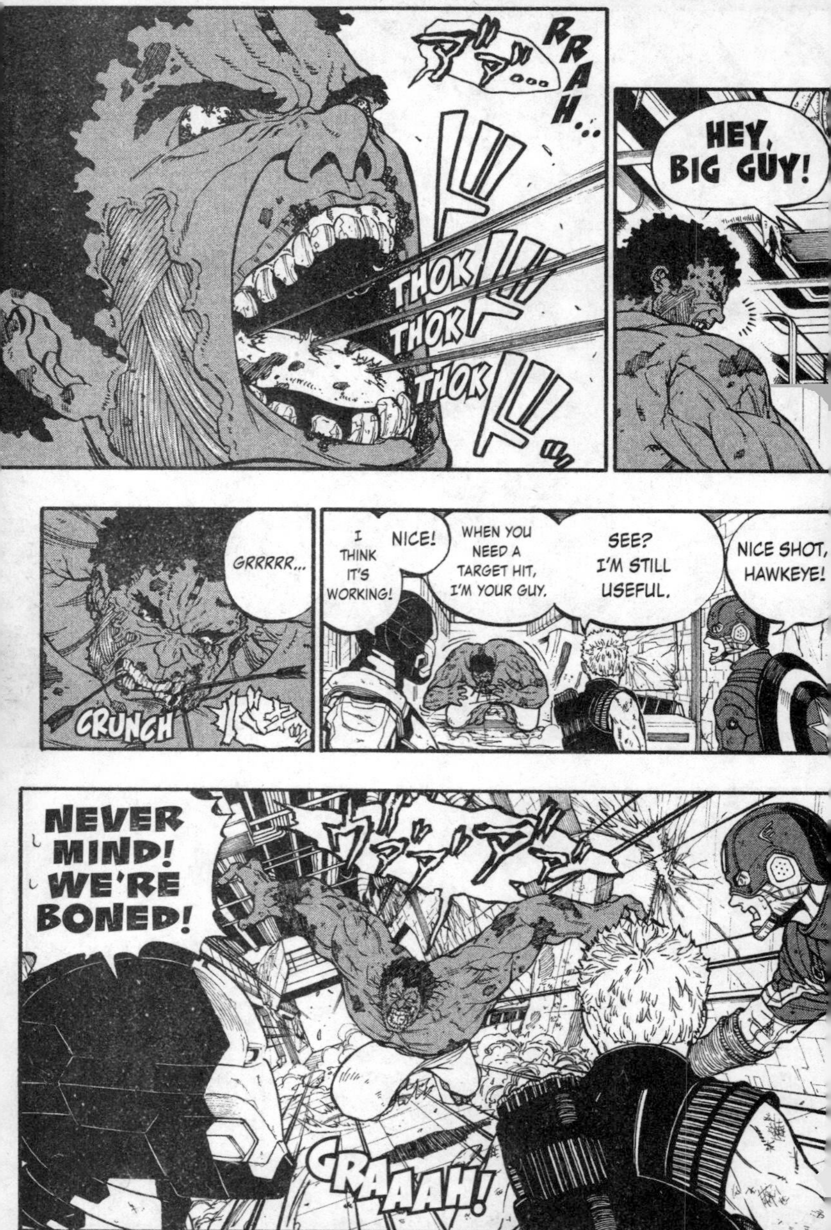
HEY, BIG GUY!
RRAH...
THOK
THOK
THOK
NICE SHOT, HAWKEYE!
SEE? I'M STILL USEFUL.
WHEN YOU NEED A TARGET HIT, I'M YOUR GUY.
NICE!
I THINK IT'S WORKING!
GRRRRR...
CRUNCH
NEVER MIND! WE'RE BONED!
GRAAAH!

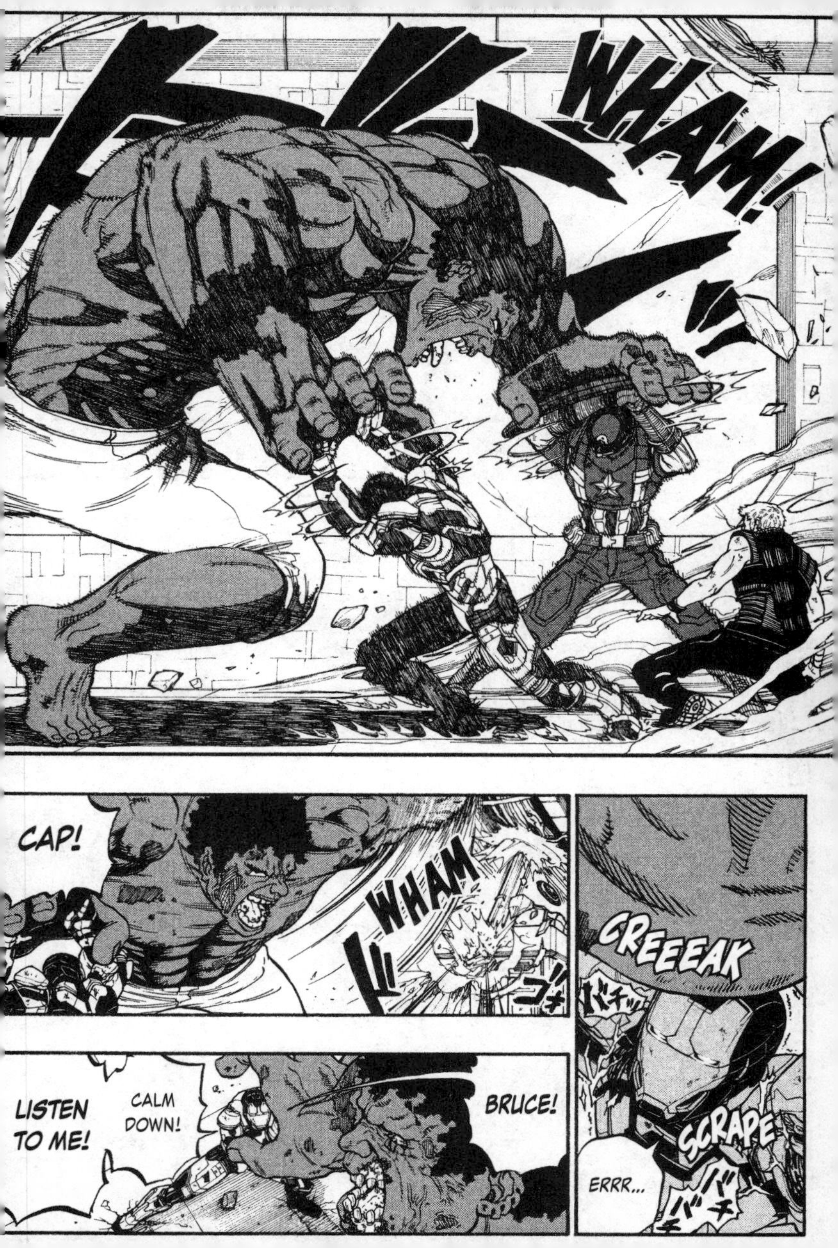
WHAM!!
CREEEAK
バチッ
SCRAPE
ERRR...
バチバチ
CAP!
WHAM
BRUCE!
CALM DOWN!
LISTEN TO ME!

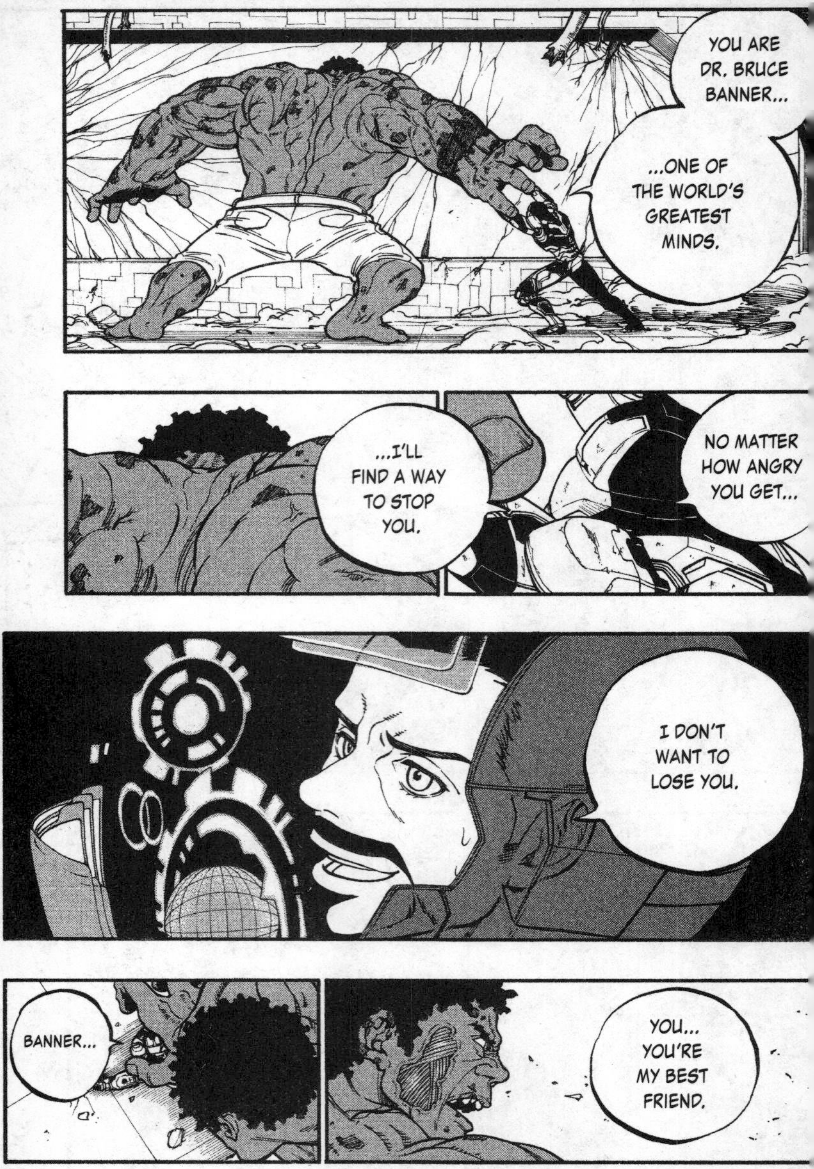
YOU ARE DR. BRUCE BANNER...
...ONE OF THE WORLD'S GREATEST MINDS.
NO MATTER HOW ANGRY YOU GET...
...I'LL FIND A WAY TO STOP YOU.
I DON'T WANT TO LOSE YOU.
YOU... YOU'RE MY BEST FRIEND.
BANNER...

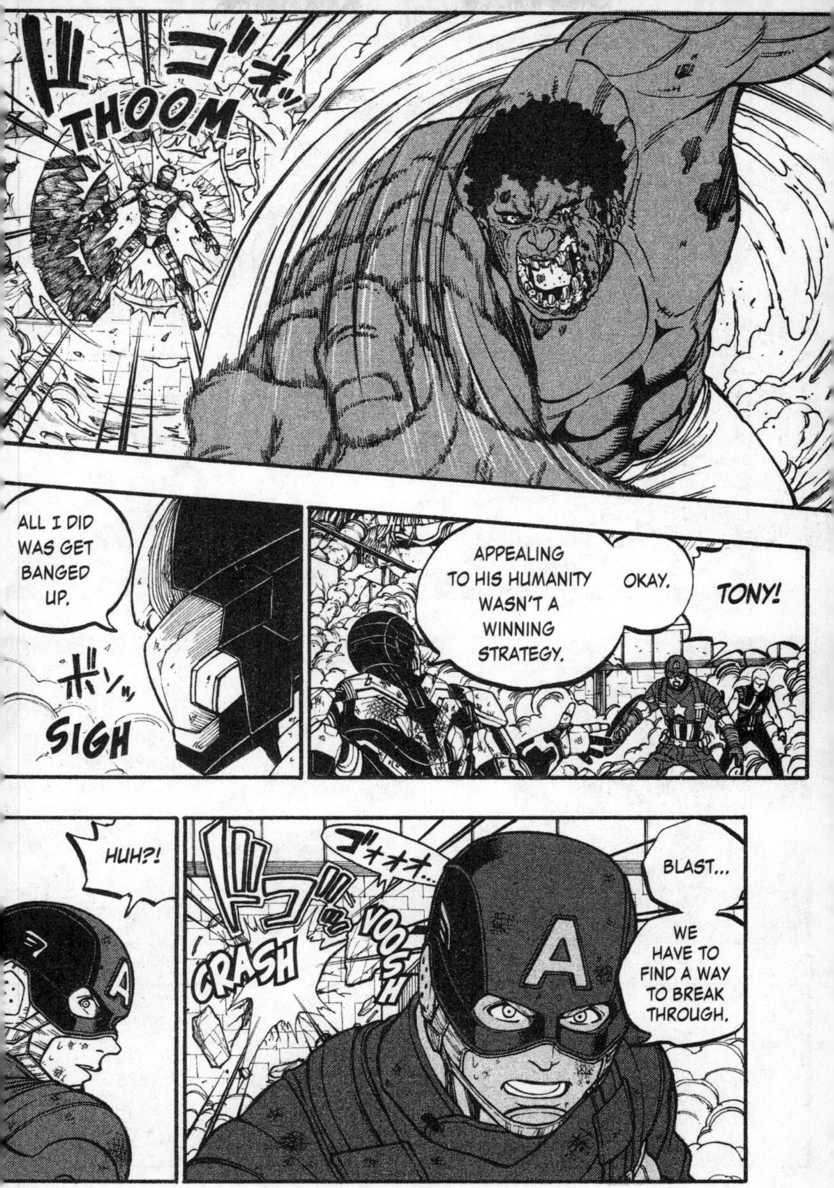
THOOM
TONY!
OKAY.
APPEALING TO HIS HUMANITY WASN'T A WINNING STRATEGY.
ALL I DID WAS GET BANGED UP.
SIGH
BLAST...
WE HAVE TO FIND A WAY TO BREAK THROUGH.
VOOSH
CRASH
HUH?!

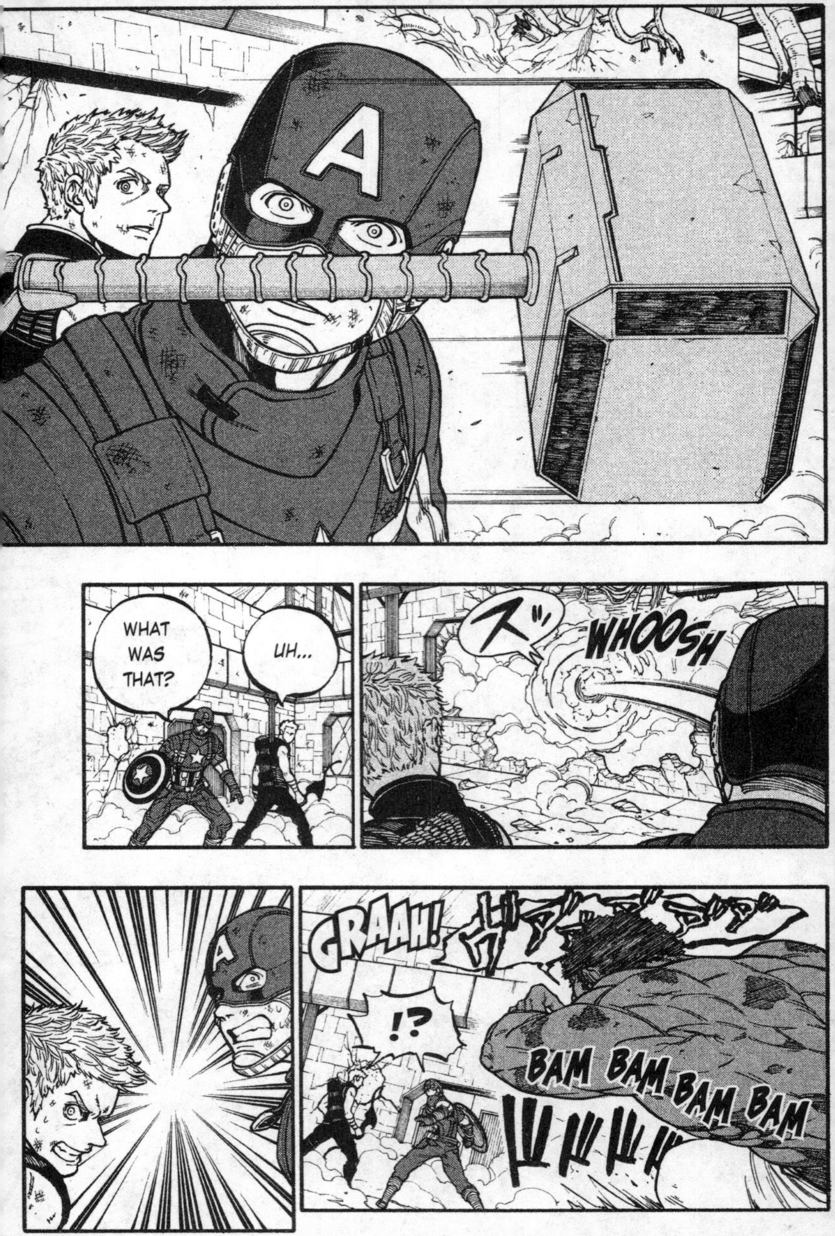
ズッ
WHOOSH
UH...
WHAT WAS THAT?
GRAAH!
!?
BAM BAM BAM BAM BAM

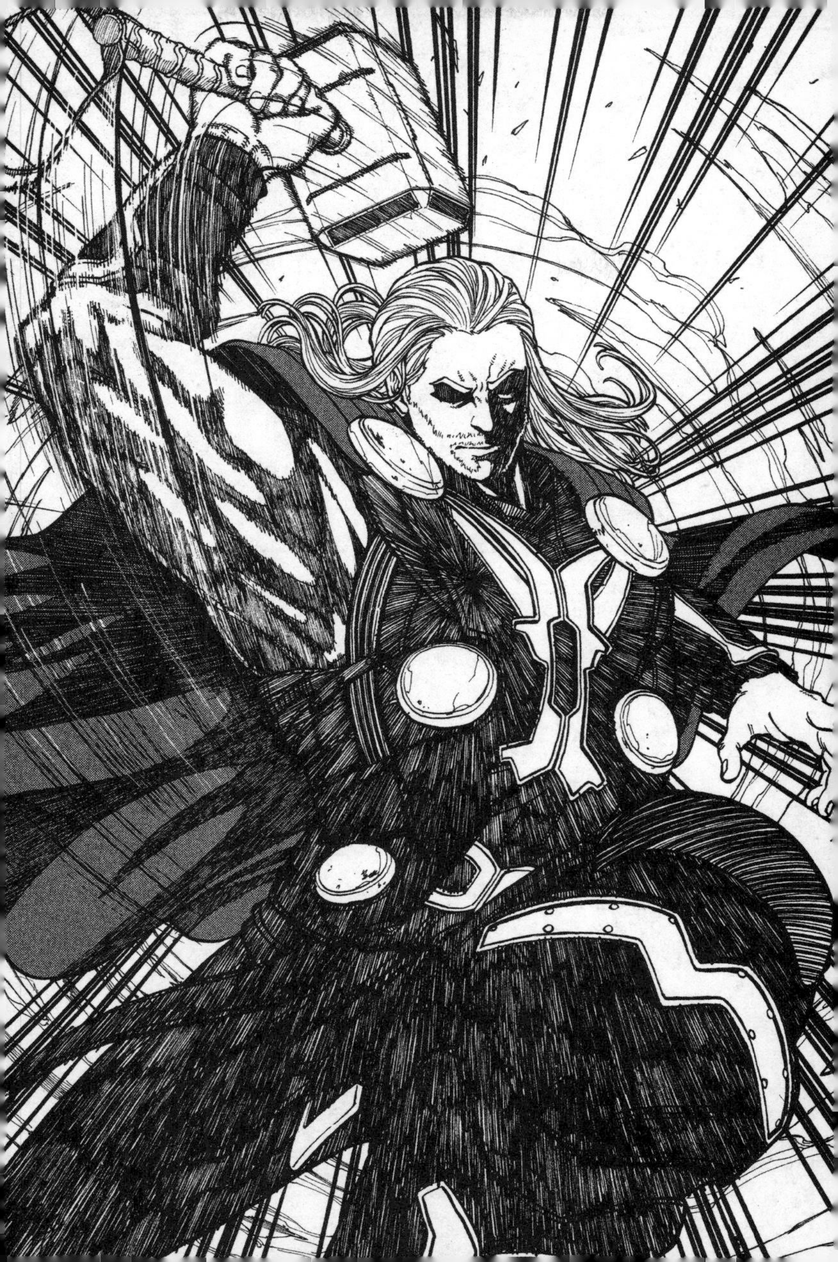

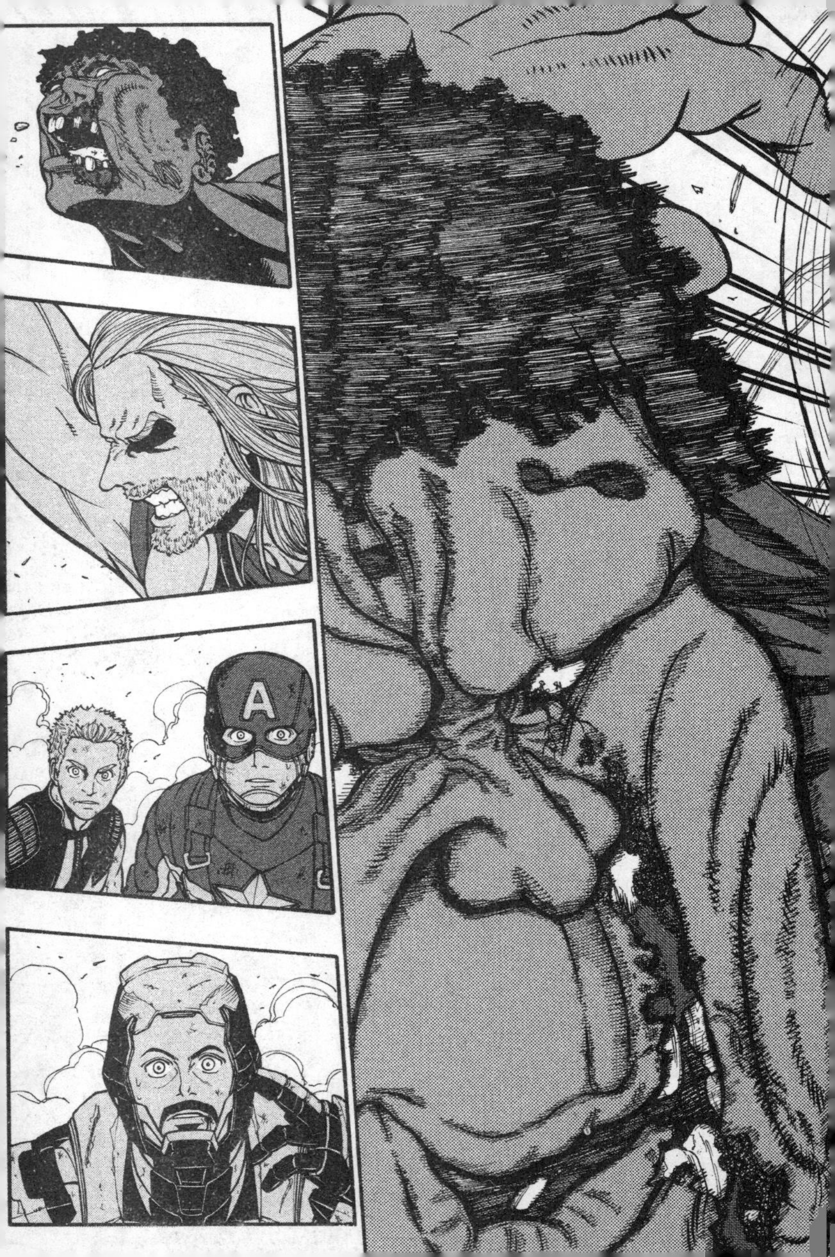

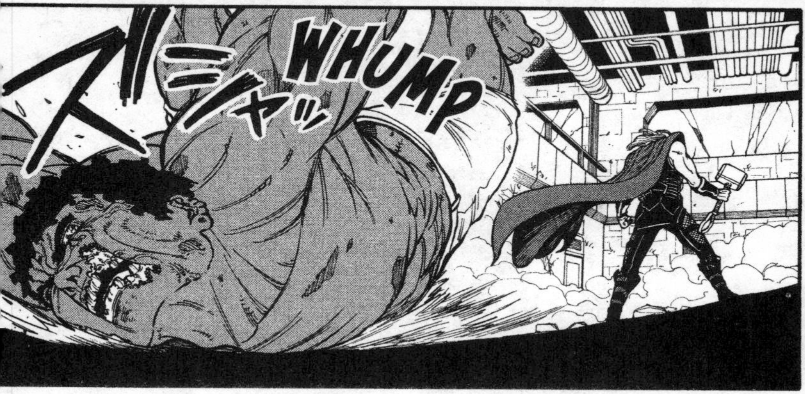
WHUMP
ズシャッ

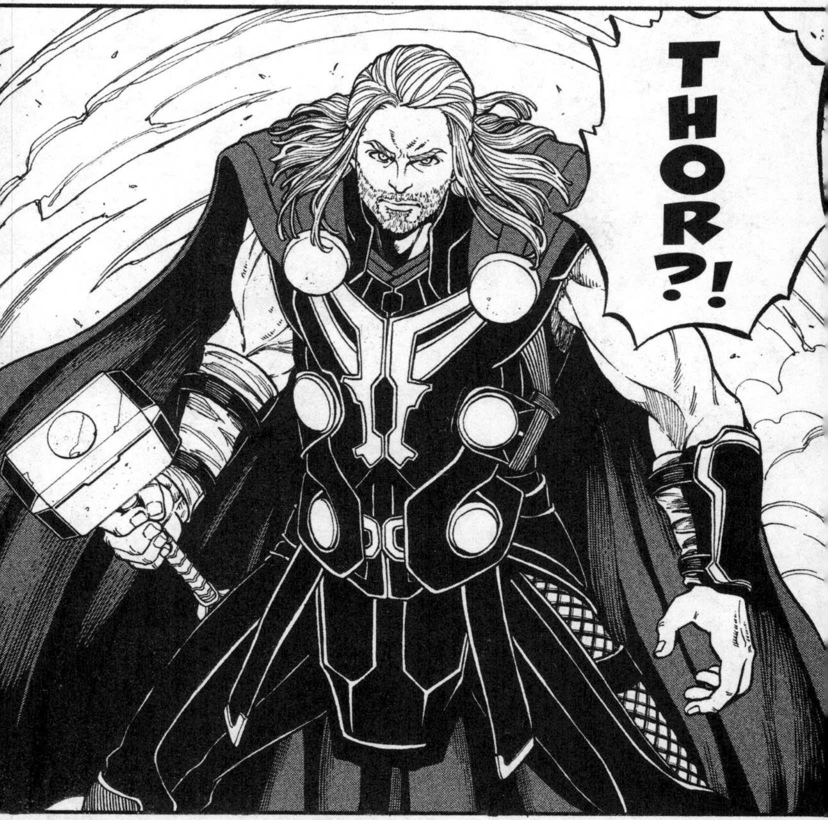
THOR?!

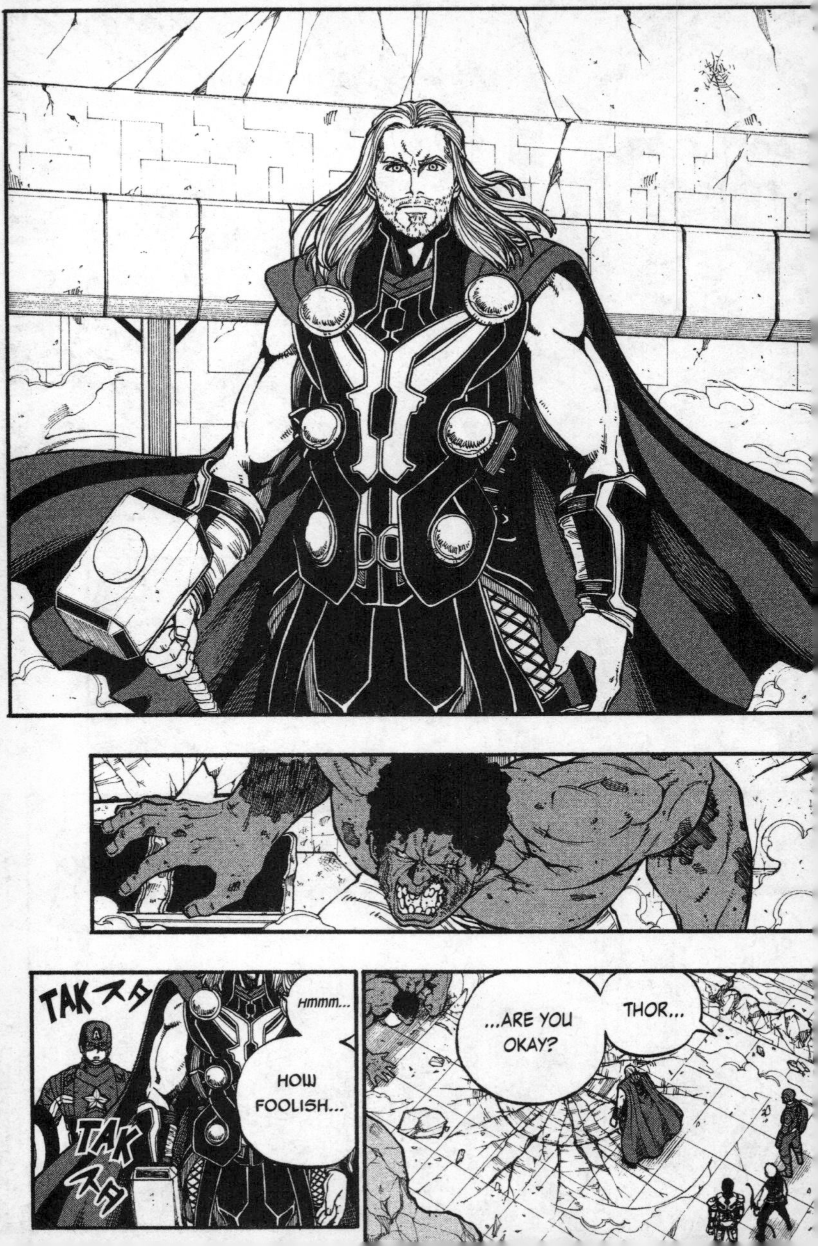
THOR...
...ARE YOU OKAY?
Hmmm...
TAK スタ
HOW FOOLISH...
TAK スタ

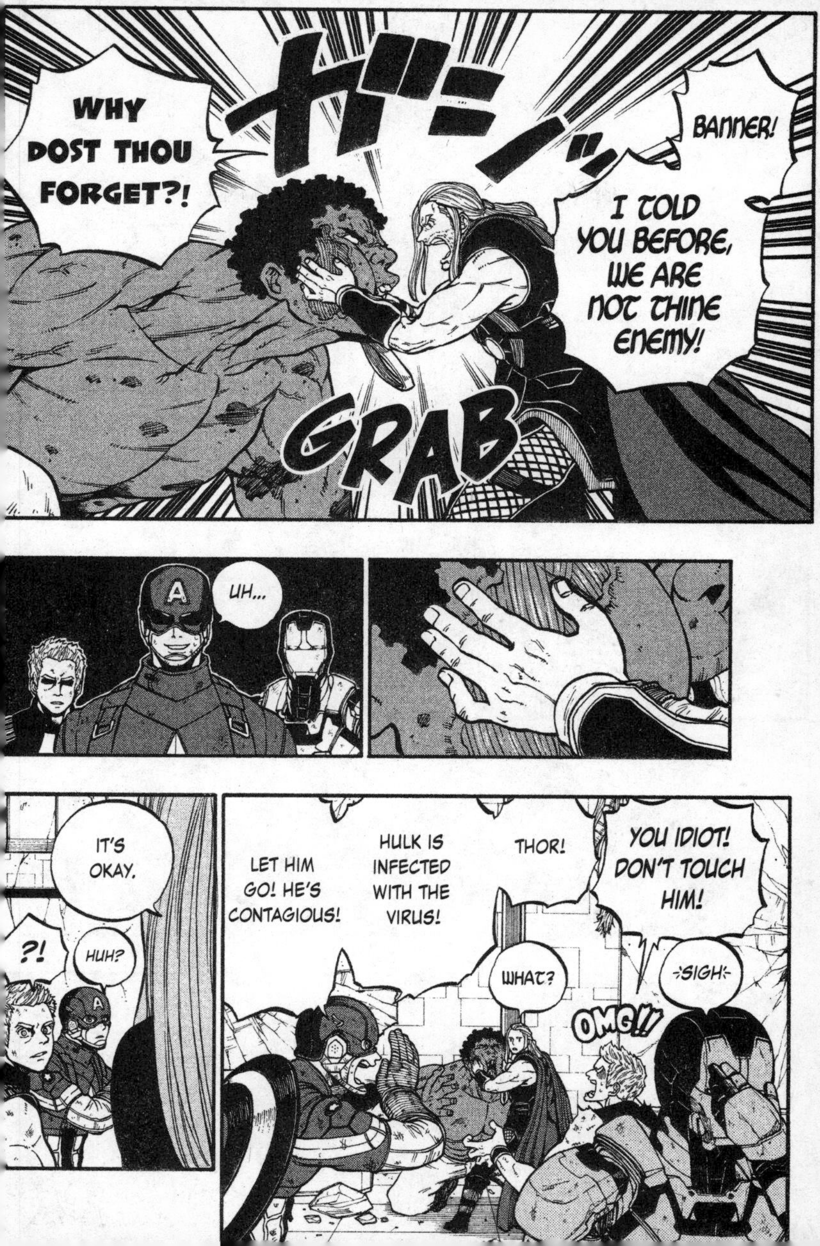
BANNER!
I TOLD YOU BEFORE, WE ARE NOT THINE ENEMY!
WHY DOST THOU FORGET?!
GRAB
UH...
YOU IDIOT! DON'T TOUCH HIM!
THOR!
HULK IS INFECTED WITH THE VIRUS!
LET HIM GO! HE'S CONTAGIOUS!
-SIGH-
OMG!!
WHAT?
IT'S OKAY.
HUH?
?!

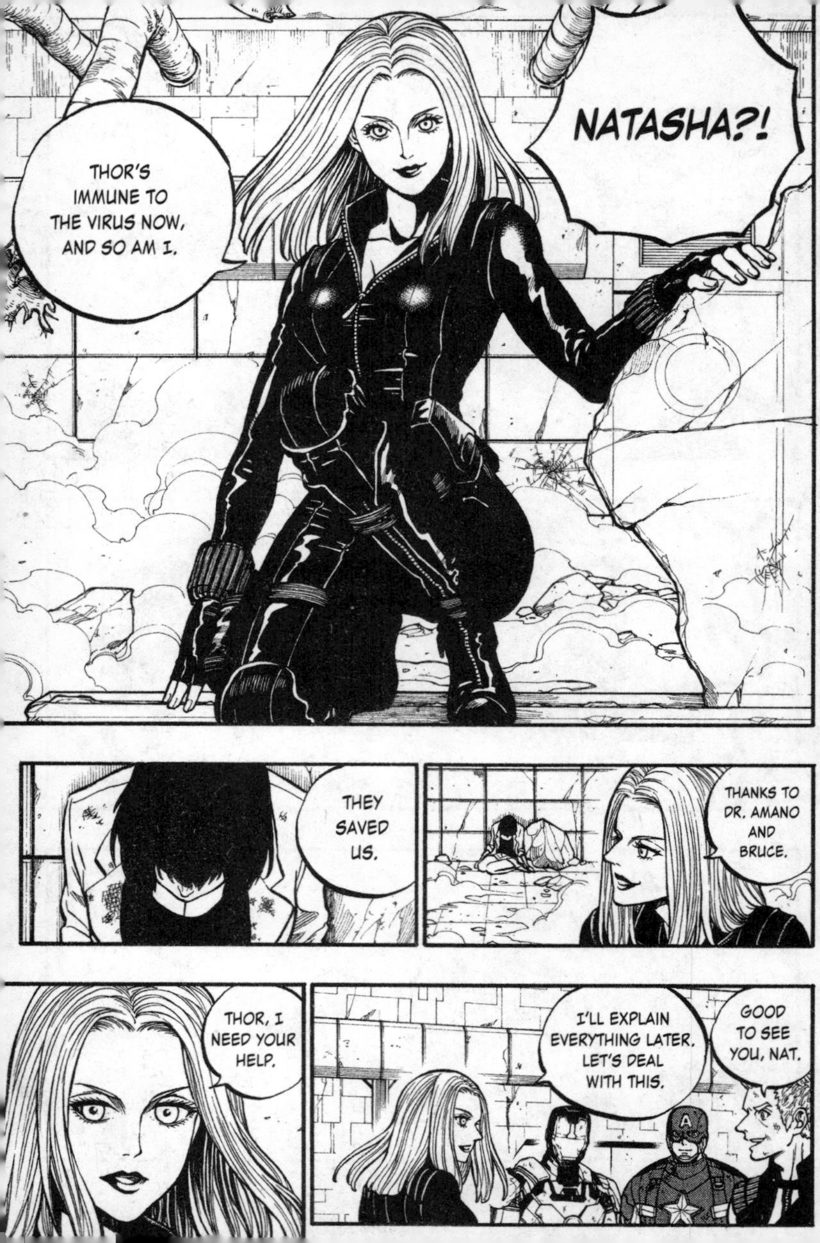
NATASHA?!
THOR'S IMMUNE TO THE VIRUS NOW, AND SO AM I.
THANKS TO DR. AMANO AND BRUCE.
THEY SAVED US.
GOOD TO SEE YOU, NAT.
I'LL EXPLAIN EVERYTHING LATER. LET'S DEAL WITH THIS.
THOR, I NEED YOUR HELP.

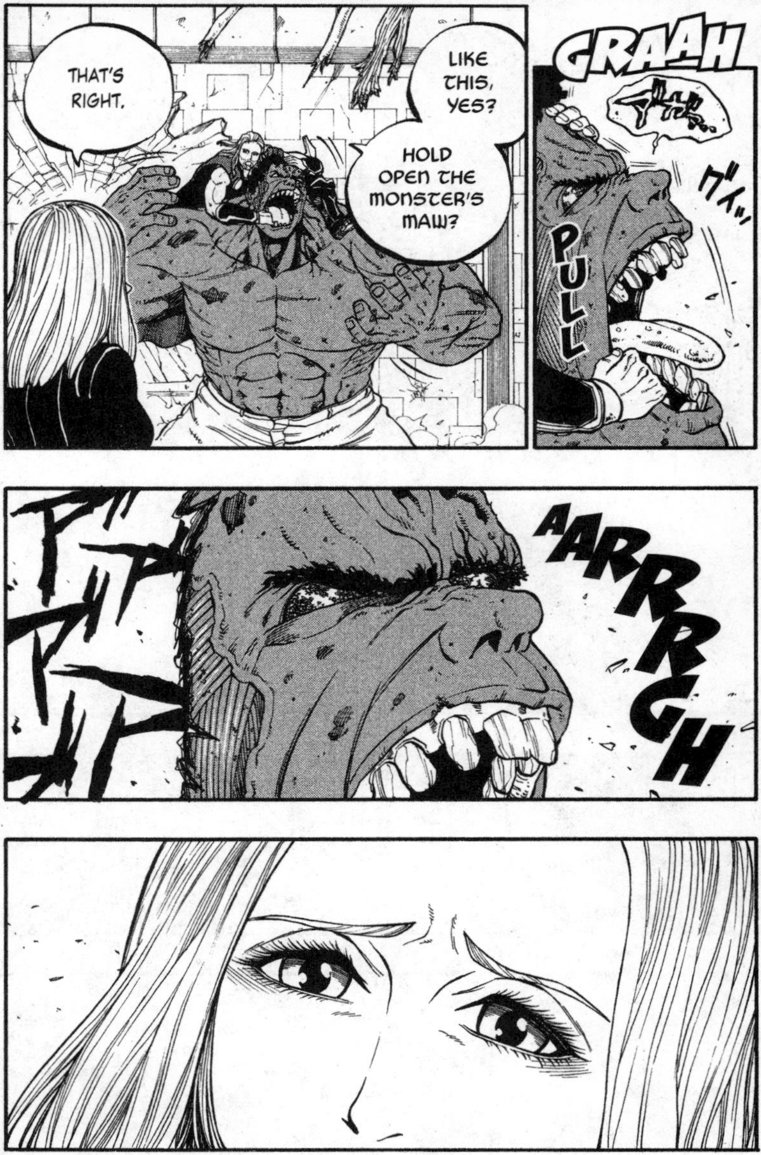
GRAAH
PULL
LIKE THIS, YES?
HOLD OPEN THE MONSTER'S MAW?
THAT'S RIGHT.
AARRRGH

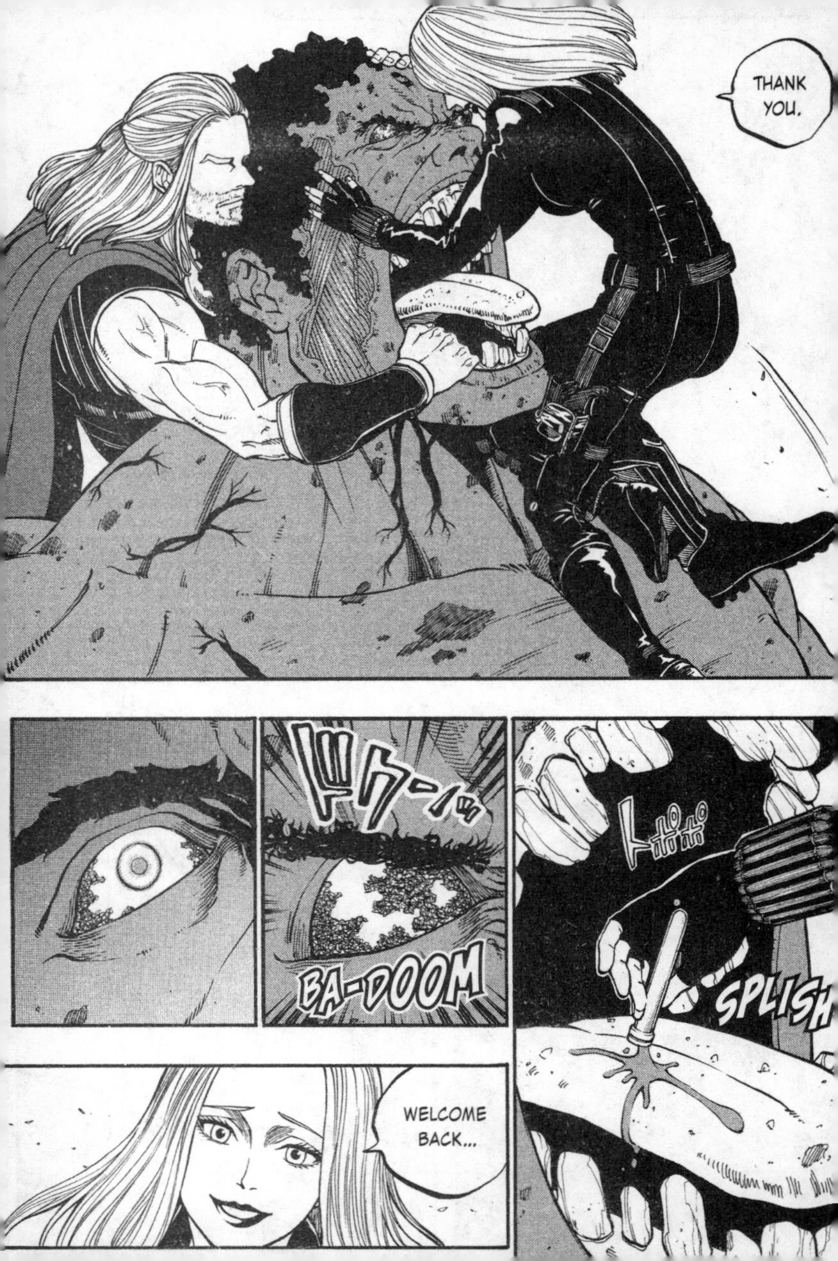

THANK YOU.
SPLISH
BA-DOOM
WELCOME BACK...

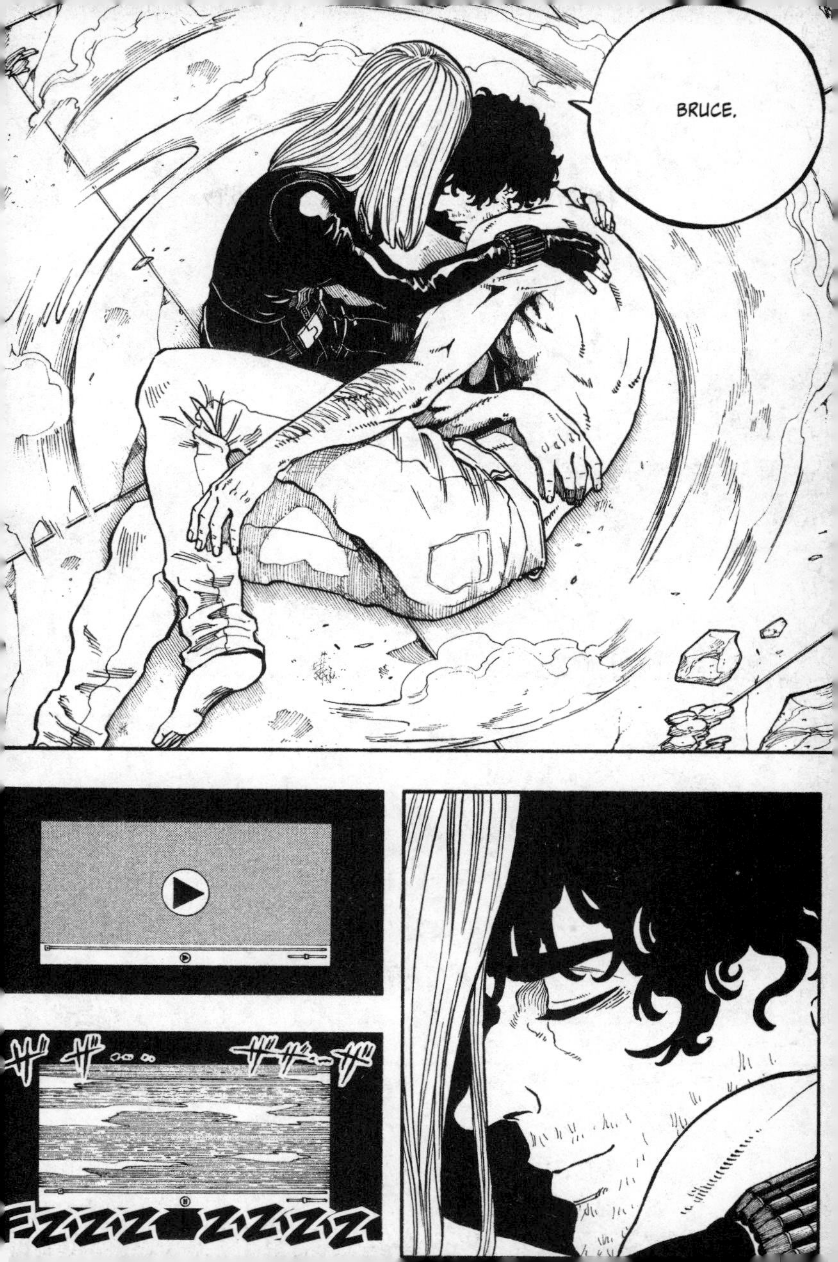
BRUCE.
FZZZ ZZZZZ

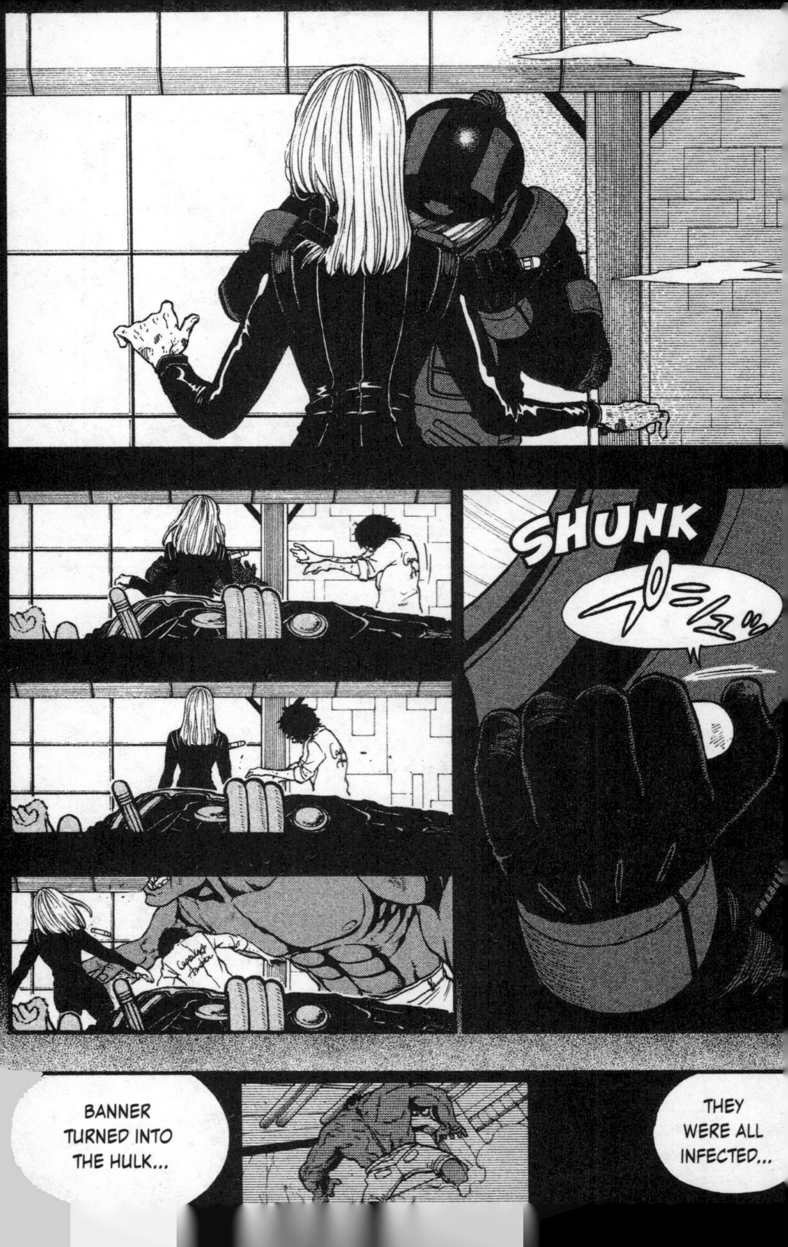
SHUNK
THEY WERE ALL INFECTED...
BANNER TURNED INTO THE HULK...

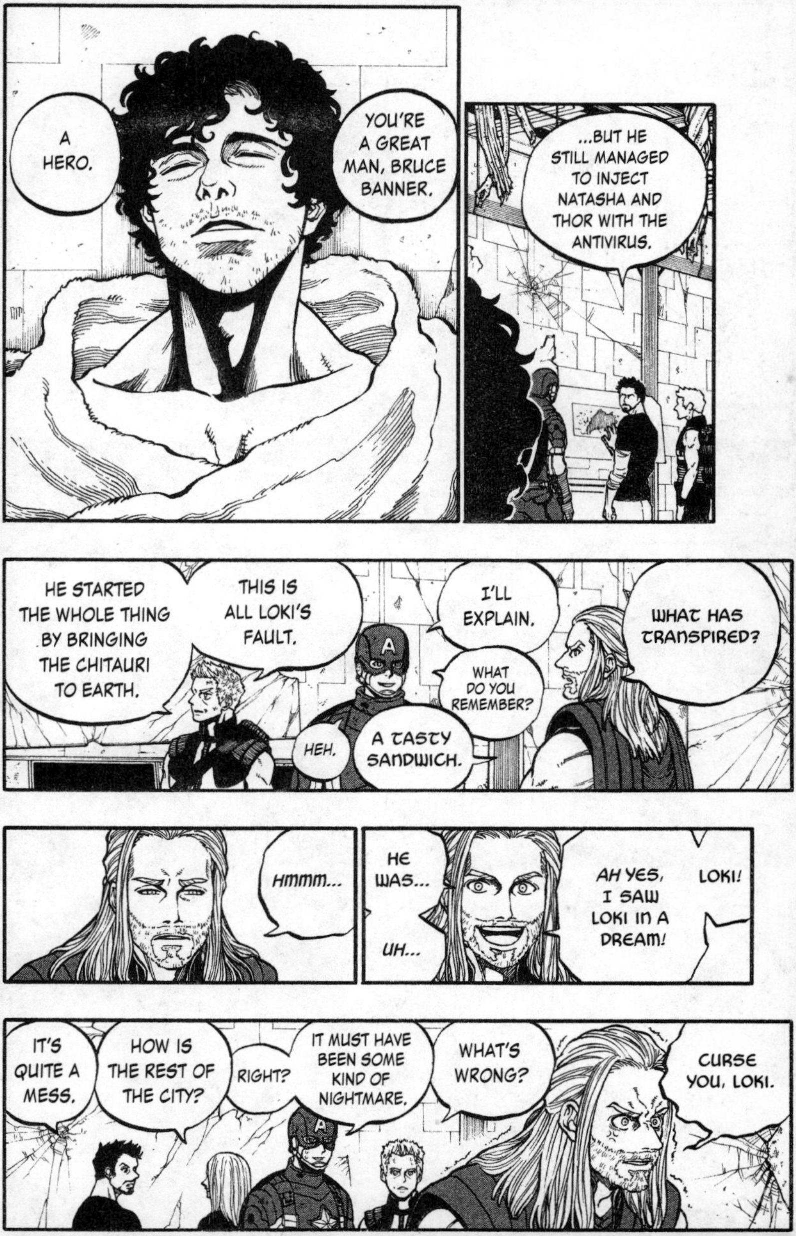
...BUT HE STILL MANAGED TO INJECT NATASHA AND THOR WITH THE ANTIVIRUS.
YOU'RE A GREAT MAN, BRUCE BANNER.
A HERO.
WHAT HAS TRANSPIRED?
I'LL EXPLAIN.
WHAT DO YOU REMEMBER?
THIS IS ALL LOKI'S FAULT.
HE STARTED THE WHOLE THING BY BRINGING THE CHITAURI TO EARTH.
A TASTY SANDWICH.
HEH.
LOKI!
AH YES, I SAW LOKI IN A DREAM!
HE WAS...
UH...
HMMM...
CURSE YOU, LOKI.
WHAT'S WRONG?
IT MUST HAVE BEEN SOME KIND OF NIGHTMARE.
RIGHT?
HOW IS THE REST OF THE CITY?
IT'S QUITE A MESS.

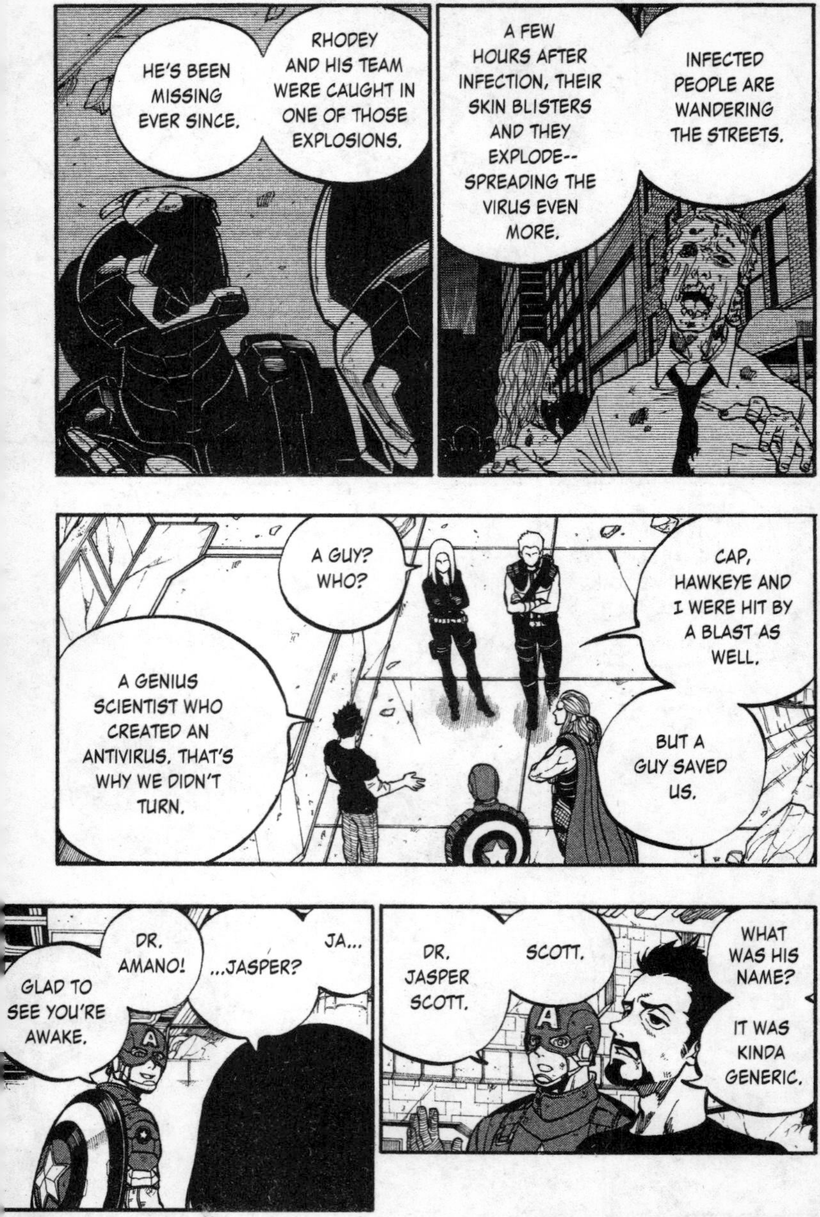
INFECTED PEOPLE ARE WANDERING THE STREETS.
A FEW HOURS AFTER INFECTION, THEIR SKIN BLISTERS AND THEY EXPLODE-- SPREADING THE VIRUS EVEN MORE.
RHODEY AND HIS TEAM WERE CAUGHT IN ONE OF THOSE EXPLOSIONS.
HE'S BEEN MISSING EVER SINCE.
CAP, HAWKEYE AND I WERE HIT BY A BLAST AS WELL.
BUT A GUY SAVED US.
A GUY? WHO?
A GENIUS SCIENTIST WHO CREATED AN ANTIVIRUS. THAT'S WHY WE DIDN'T TURN.
WHAT WAS HIS NAME?
IT WAS KINDA GENERIC.
SCOTT.
DR. JASPER SCOTT.
JA...
...JASPER?
DR. AMANO!
GLAD TO SEE YOU'RE AWAKE.

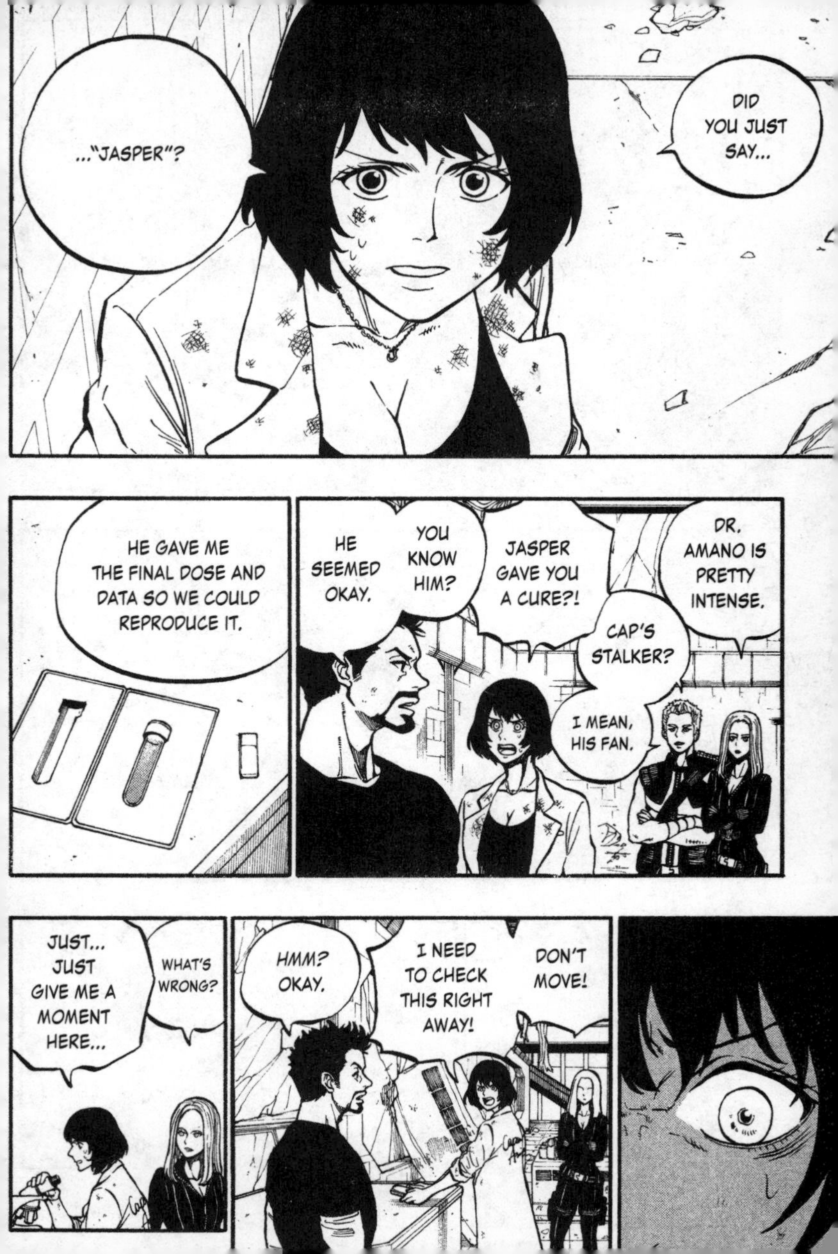
DID YOU JUST SAY...
..."JASPER"?
DR. AMANO IS PRETTY INTENSE.
CAP'S STALKER?
I MEAN, HIS FAN.
JASPER GAVE YOU A CURE?!
YOU KNOW HIM?
HE SEEMED OKAY.
HE GAVE ME THE FINAL DOSE AND DATA SO WE COULD REPRODUCE IT.
DON'T MOVE!
I NEED TO CHECK THIS RIGHT AWAY!
HMM? OKAY.
WHAT'S WRONG?
JUST... JUST GIVE ME A MOMENT HERE...

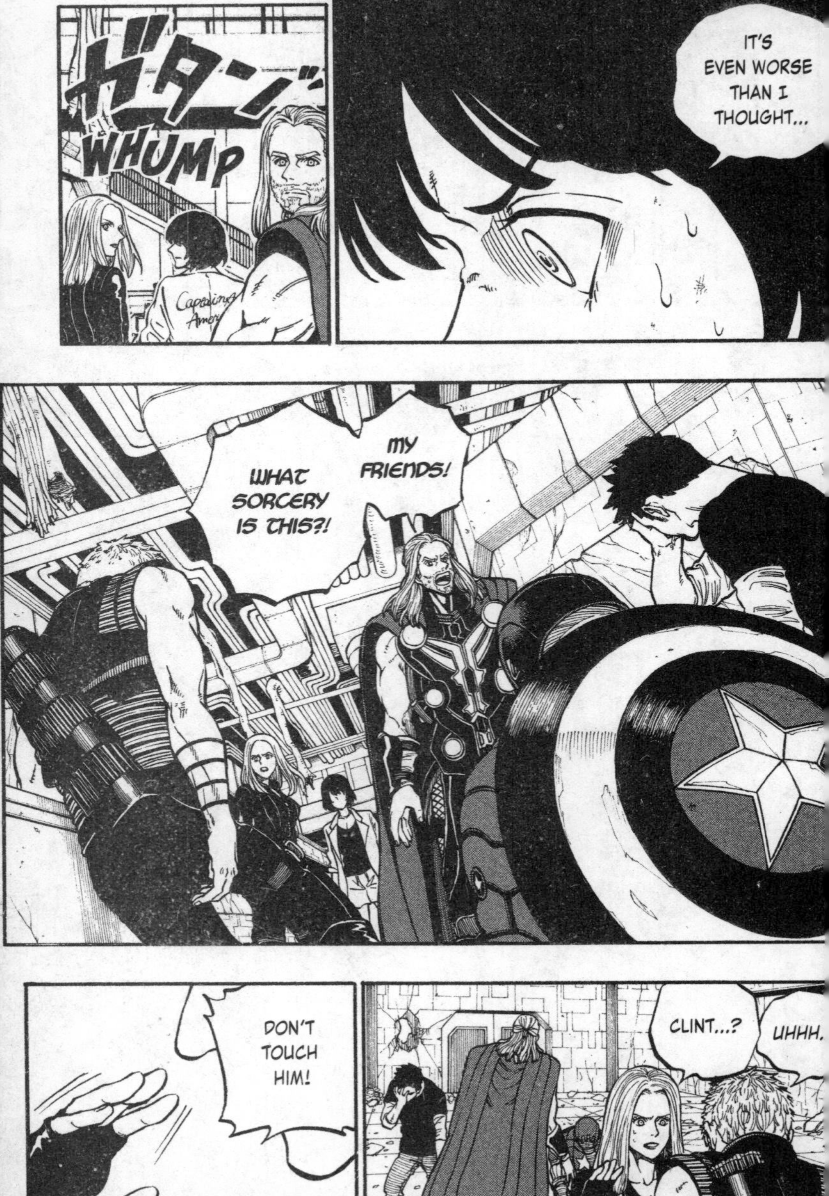
IT'S EVEN WORSE THAN I THOUGHT...
ガタン
WHUMP
MY FRIENDS!
WHAT SORCERY IS THIS?!
CLINT...?
UHHH.
DON'T TOUCH HIM!

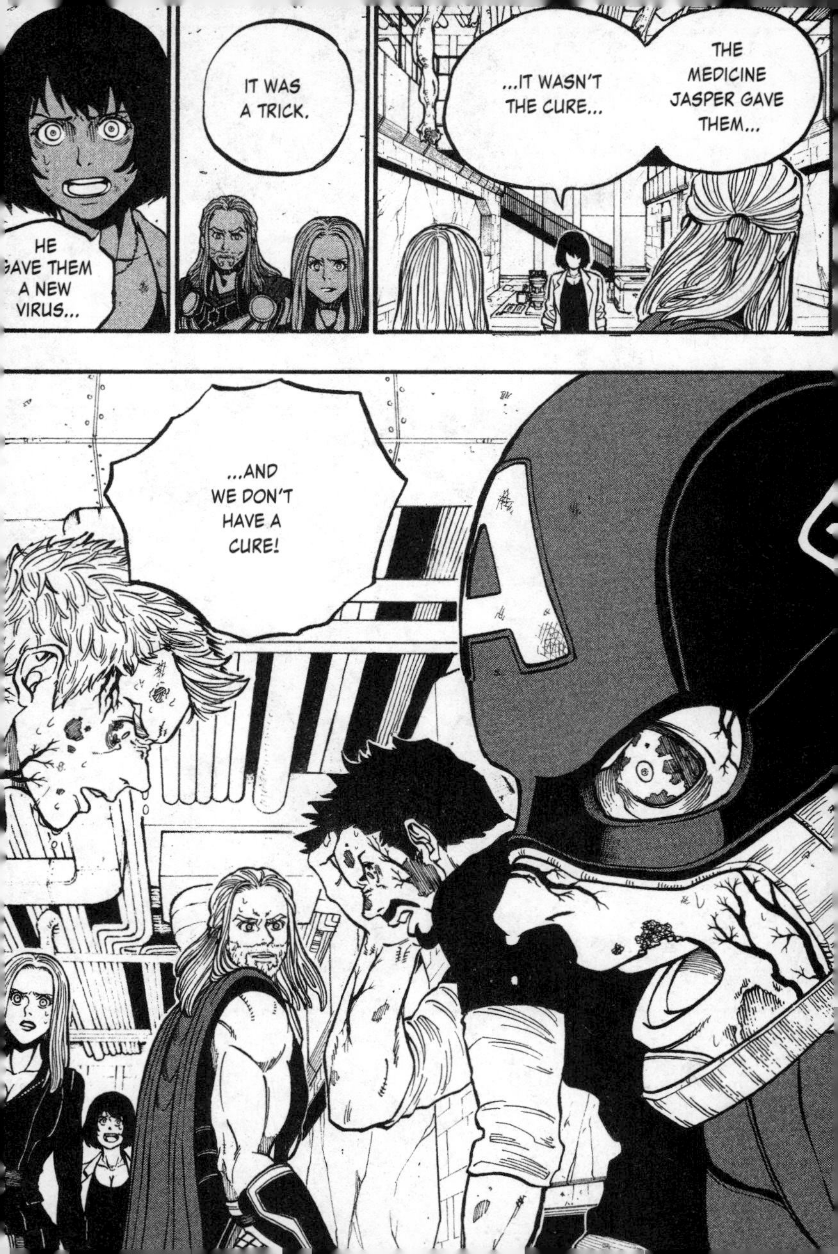
THE MEDICINE JASPER GAVE THEM...
...IT WASN'T THE CURE...
IT WAS A TRICK.
HE GAVE THEM A NEW VIRUS...
...AND WE DON'T HAVE A CURE!

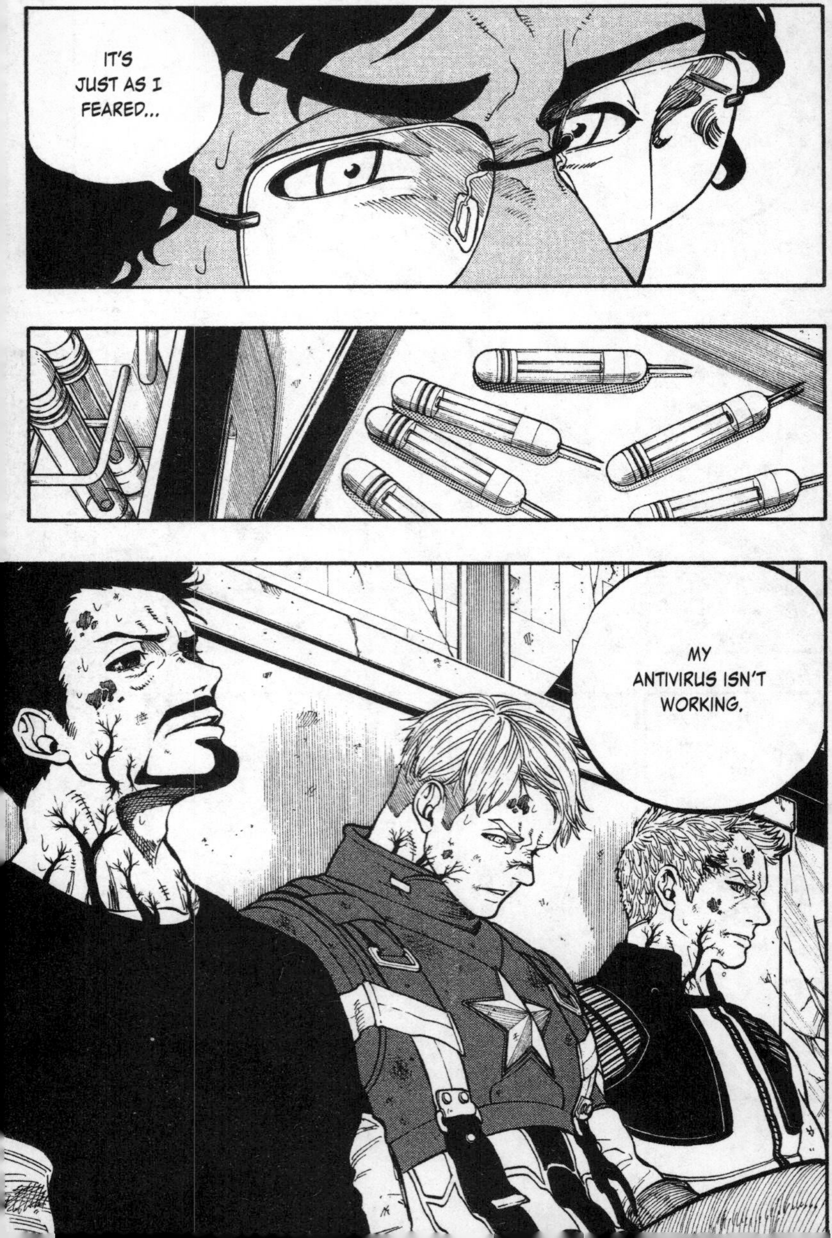
IT'S JUST AS I FEARED...
MY ANTIVIRUS ISN'T WORKING.

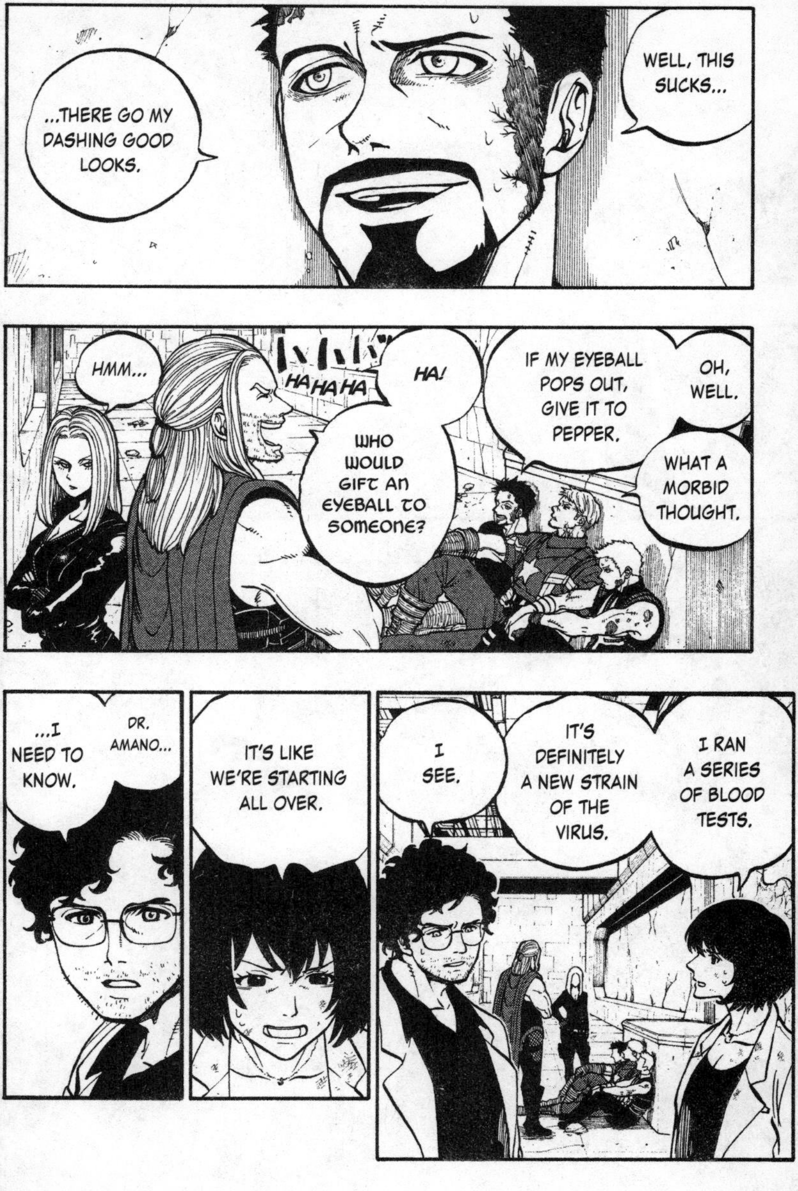
WELL, THIS SUCKS...
...THERE GO MY DASHING GOOD LOOKS.
OH, WELL.
IF MY EYEBALL POPS OUT, GIVE IT TO PEPPER.
WHAT A MORBID THOUGHT.
HA!
HA HA HA
WHO WOULD GIFT AN EYEBALL TO SOMEONE?
HMM...
I RAN A SERIES OF BLOOD TESTS.
IT'S DEFINITELY A NEW STRAIN OF THE VIRUS.
I SEE.
IT'S LIKE WE'RE STARTING ALL OVER.
DR. AMANO...
...I NEED TO KNOW.

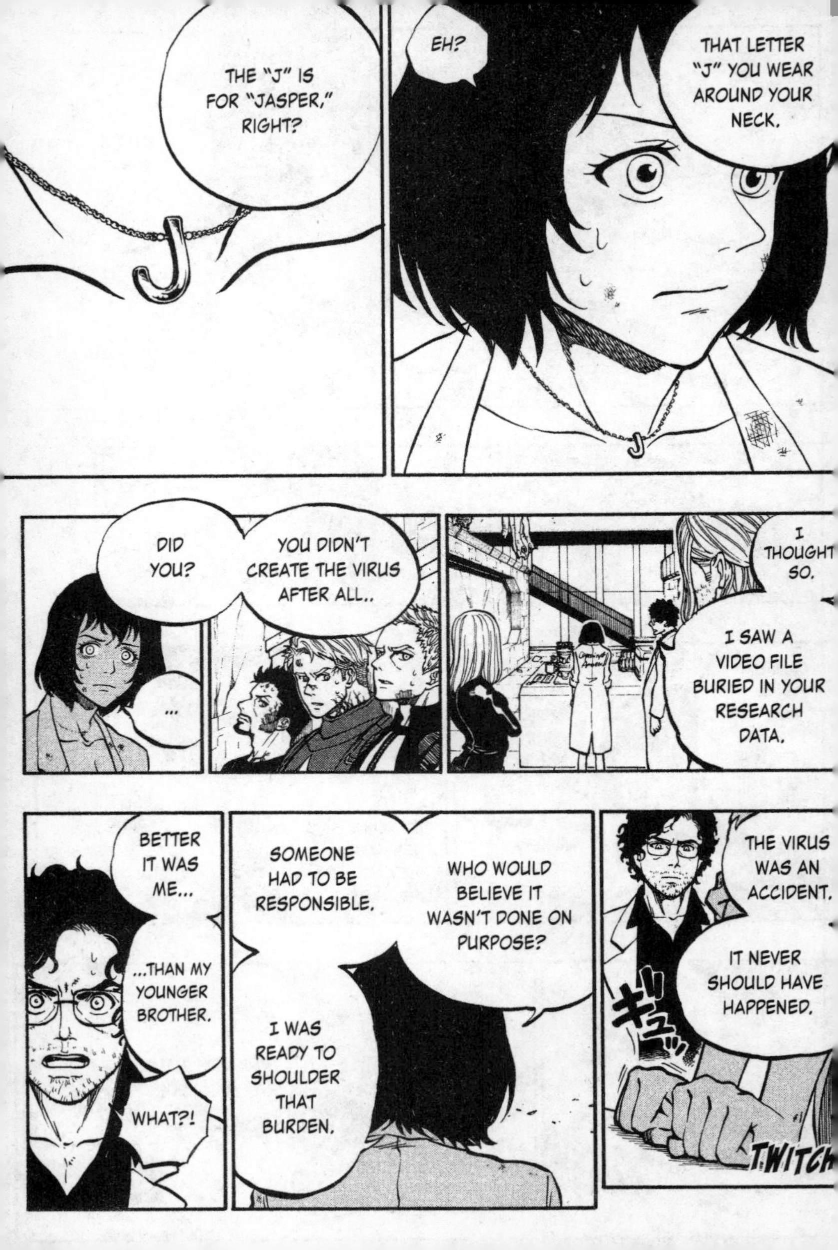

THAT LETTER "J" YOU WEAR AROUND YOUR NECK.
EH?
THE "J" IS FOR "JASPER," RIGHT?
I THOUGHT SO.
I SAW A VIDEO FILE BURIED IN YOUR RESEARCH DATA.
YOU DIDN'T CREATE THE VIRUS AFTER ALL..
DID YOU?
...
THE VIRUS WAS AN ACCIDENT.
IT NEVER SHOULD HAVE HAPPENED.
ギュッ
TWITCH
WHO WOULD BELIEVE IT WASN'T DONE ON PURPOSE?
SOMEONE HAD TO BE RESPONSIBLE.
I WAS READY TO SHOULDER THAT BURDEN.
BETTER IT WAS ME...
...THAN MY YOUNGER BROTHER.
WHAT?!

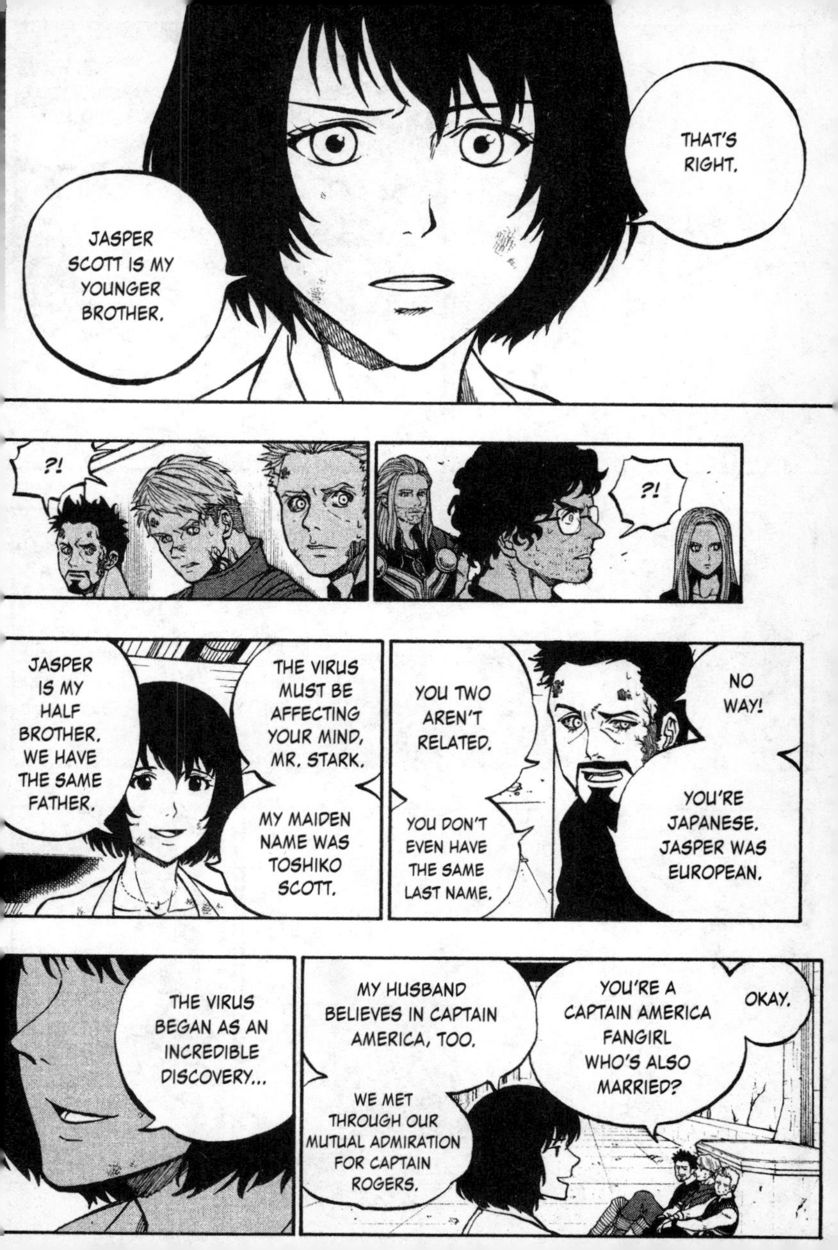
THAT'S RIGHT.
JASPER SCOTT IS MY YOUNGER BROTHER.
?!
?!
NO WAY!
YOU TWO AREN'T RELATED.
YOU'RE JAPANESE. JASPER WAS EUROPEAN.
YOU DON'T EVEN HAVE THE SAME LAST NAME.
THE VIRUS MUST BE AFFECTING YOUR MIND, MR. STARK.
JASPER IS MY HALF BROTHER. WE HAVE THE SAME FATHER.
MY MAIDEN NAME WAS TOSHIKO SCOTT.
OKAY.
YOU'RE A CAPTAIN AMERICA FANGIRL WHO'S ALSO MARRIED?
MY HUSBAND BELIEVES IN CAPTAIN AMERICA, TOO.
WE MET THROUGH OUR MUTUAL ADMIRATION FOR CAPTAIN ROGERS.
THE VIRUS BEGAN AS AN INCREDIBLE DISCOVERY...

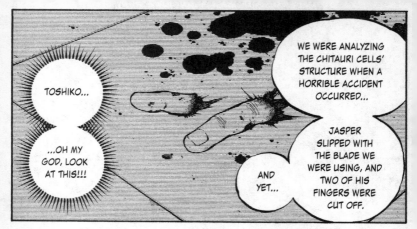

WE WERE ANALYZING THE CHITAURI CELLS' STRUCTURE WHEN A HORRIBLE ACCIDENT OCCURRED...
JASPER SLIPPED WITH THE BLADE WE WERE USING, AND TWO OF HIS FINGERS WERE CUT OFF.
AND YET...
TOSHIKO...
...OH MY GOD, LOOK AT THIS!!!
SOME OF THE CHITAURI CELLS HAD MIXED WITH HIS WOUND.
RIGHT BEFORE OUR EYES, HIS FINGERS BEGAN TO REGROW.
JASPER AND I HAD STUMBLED ACROSS AN INVENTION THAT COULD REGENERATE TISSUE!
A MEDICINE LIKE NO OTHER.
AT LEAST THAT'S WHAT WE THOUGHT...

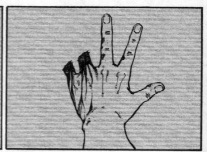

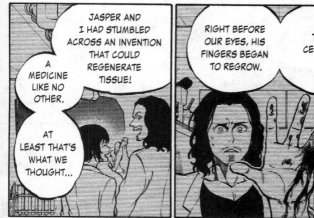

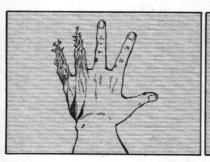

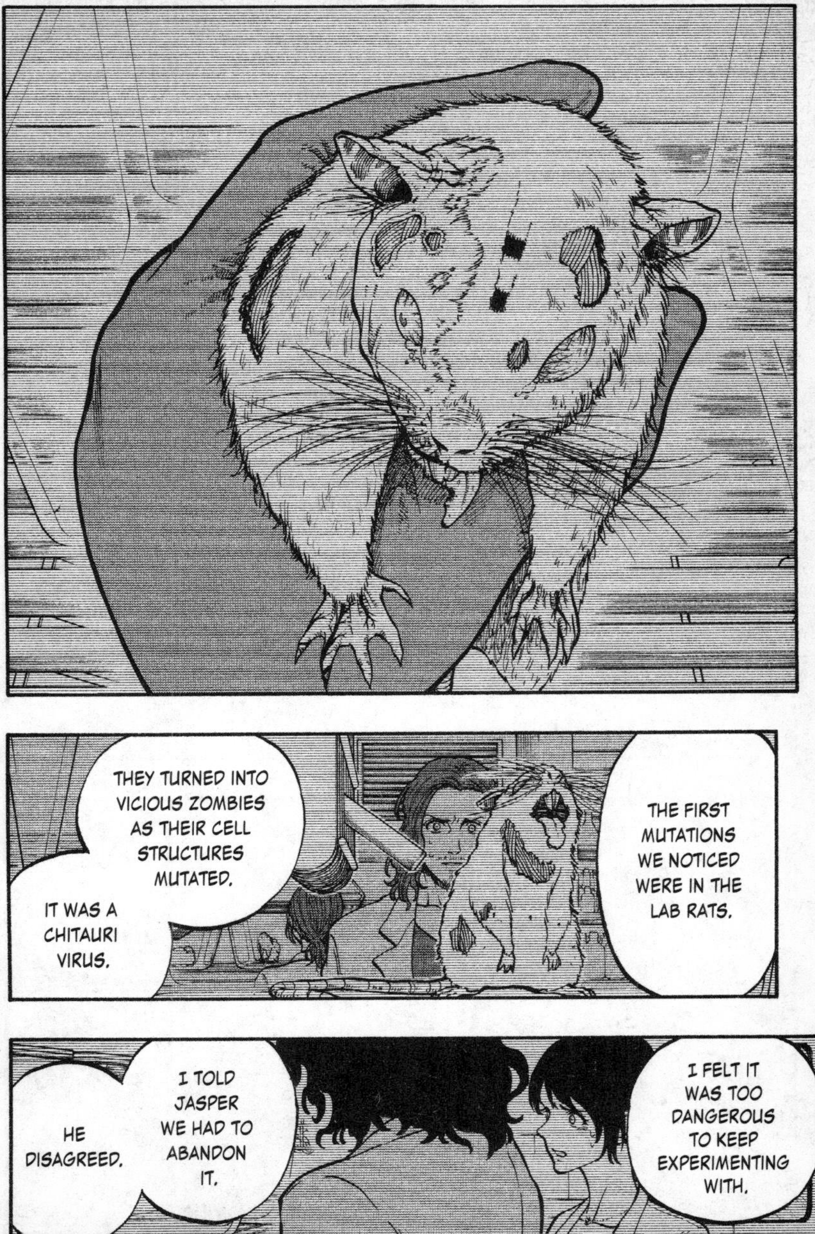
THE FIRST MUTATIONS WE NOTICED WERE IN THE LAB RATS.
THEY TURNED INTO VICIOUS ZOMBIES AS THEIR CELL STRUCTURES MUTATED.
IT WAS A CHITAURI VIRUS.
I FELT IT WAS TOO DANGEROUS TO KEEP EXPERIMENTING WITH.
I TOLD JASPER WE HAD TO ABANDON IT.
HE DISAGREED.

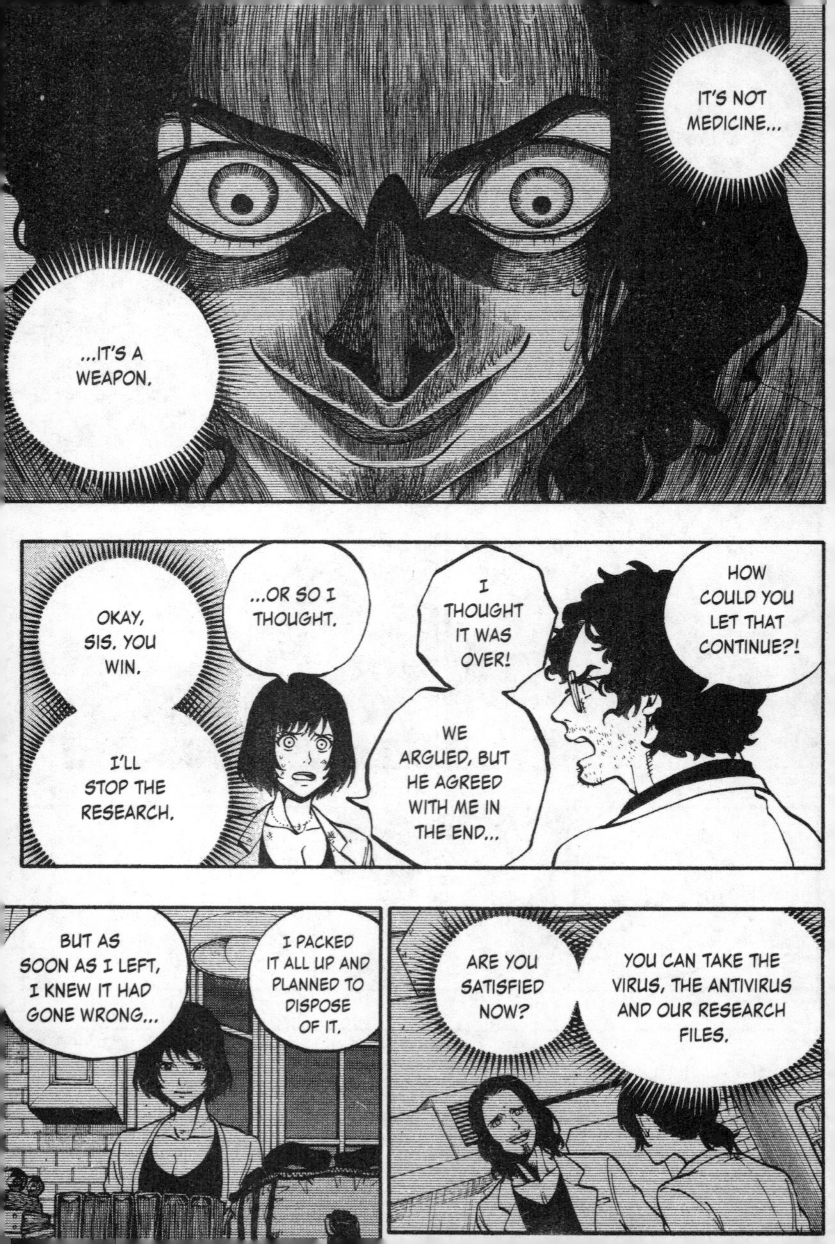
IT'S NOT MEDICINE...
...IT'S A WEAPON.
HOW COULD YOU LET THAT CONTINUE?!
I THOUGHT IT WAS OVER!
WE ARGUED, BUT HE AGREED WITH ME IN THE END...
OKAY, SIS. YOU WIN.
I'LL STOP THE RESEARCH.
...OR SO I THOUGHT.
YOU CAN TAKE THE VIRUS, THE ANTIVIRUS AND OUR RESEARCH FILES.
ARE YOU SATISFIED NOW?
I PACKED IT ALL UP AND PLANNED TO DISPOSE OF IT.
BUT AS SOON AS I LEFT, I KNEW IT HAD GONE WRONG...

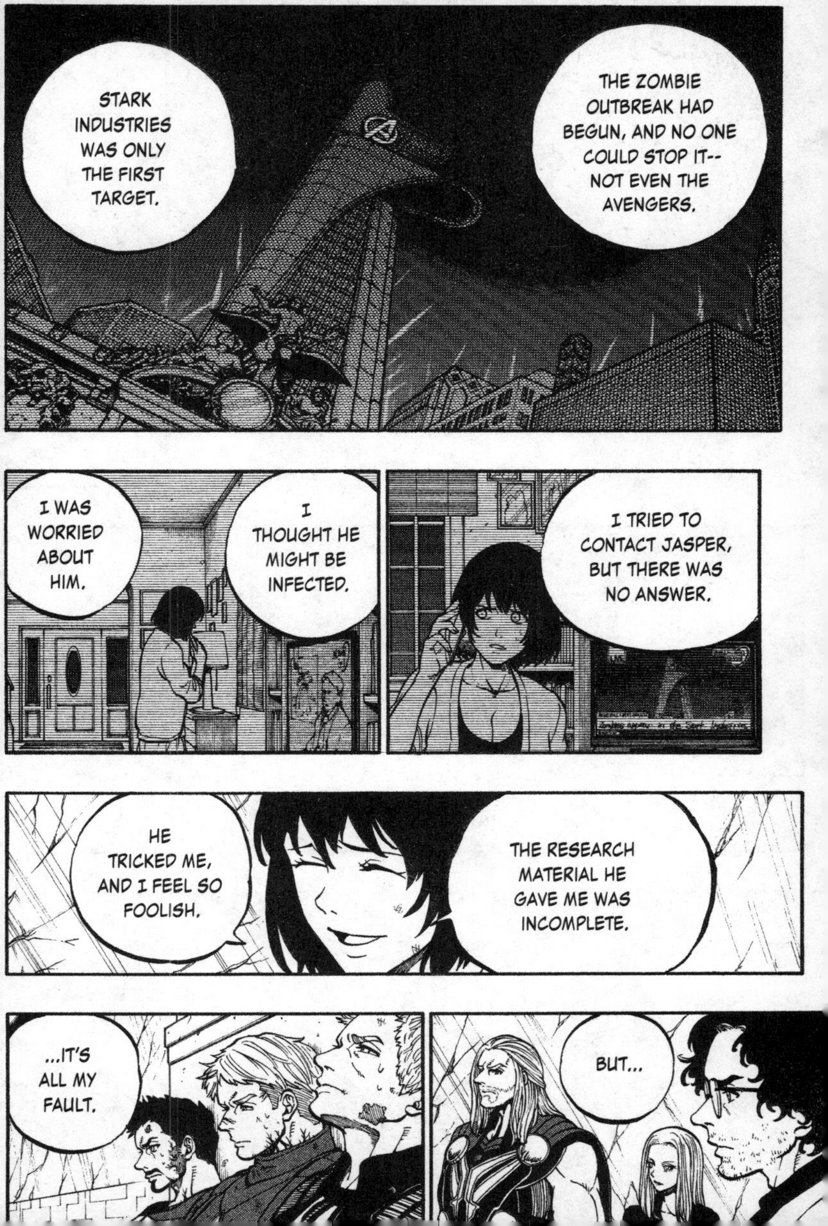
THE ZOMBIE OUTBREAK HAD BEGUN, AND NO ONE COULD STOP IT-- NOT EVEN THE AVENGERS.
STARK INDUSTRIES WAS ONLY THE FIRST TARGET.
I TRIED TO CONTACT JASPER, BUT THERE WAS NO ANSWER.
I THOUGHT HE MIGHT BE INFECTED.
I WAS WORRIED ABOUT HIM.
THE RESEARCH MATERIAL HE GAVE ME WAS INCOMPLETE.
HE TRICKED ME, AND I FEEL SO FOOLISH.
BUT...
...IT'S ALL MY FAULT.

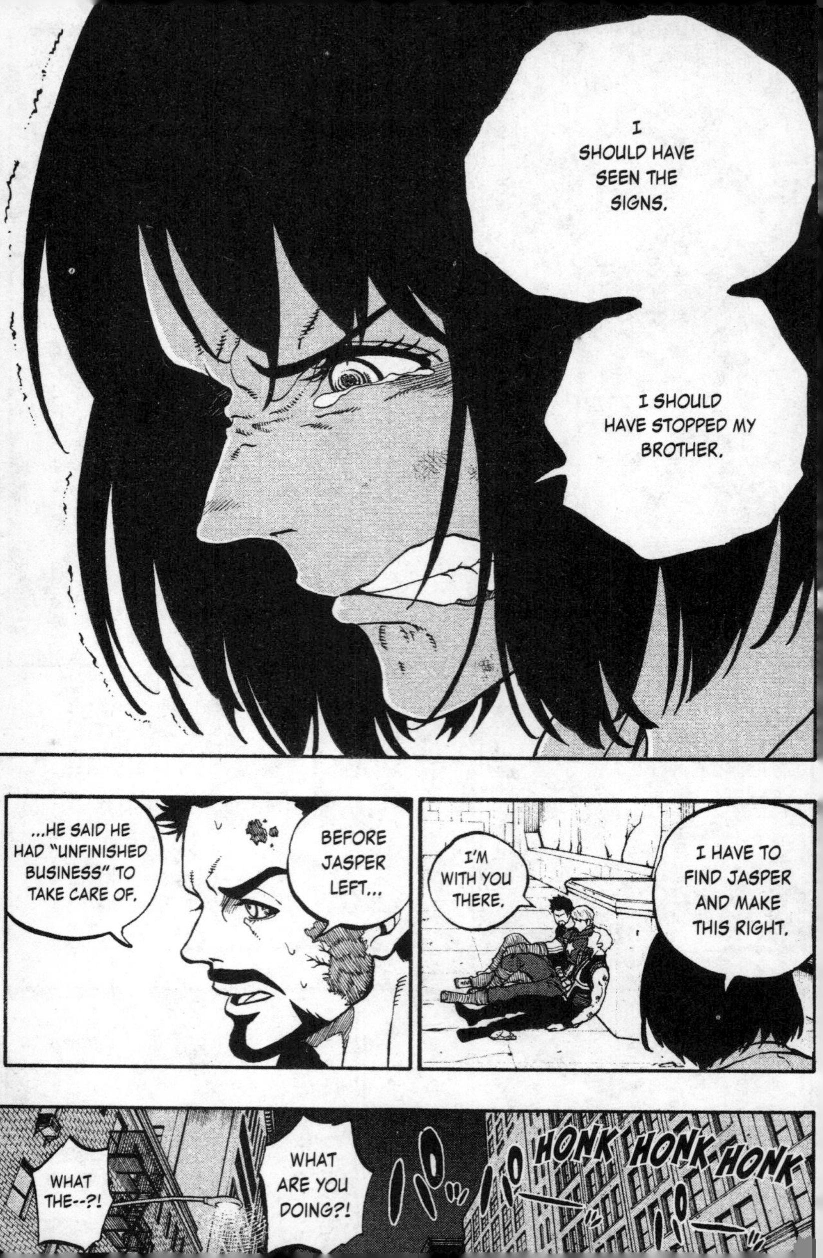

I SHOULD HAVE SEEN THE SIGNS.
I SHOULD HAVE STOPPED MY BROTHER.
I HAVE TO FIND JASPER AND MAKE THIS RIGHT.
I'M WITH YOU THERE.
BEFORE JASPER LEFT...
...HE SAID HE HAD "UNFINISHED BUSINESS" TO TAKE CARE OF.
HONK HONK HONK
WHAT ARE YOU DOING?!
WHAT THE--?!

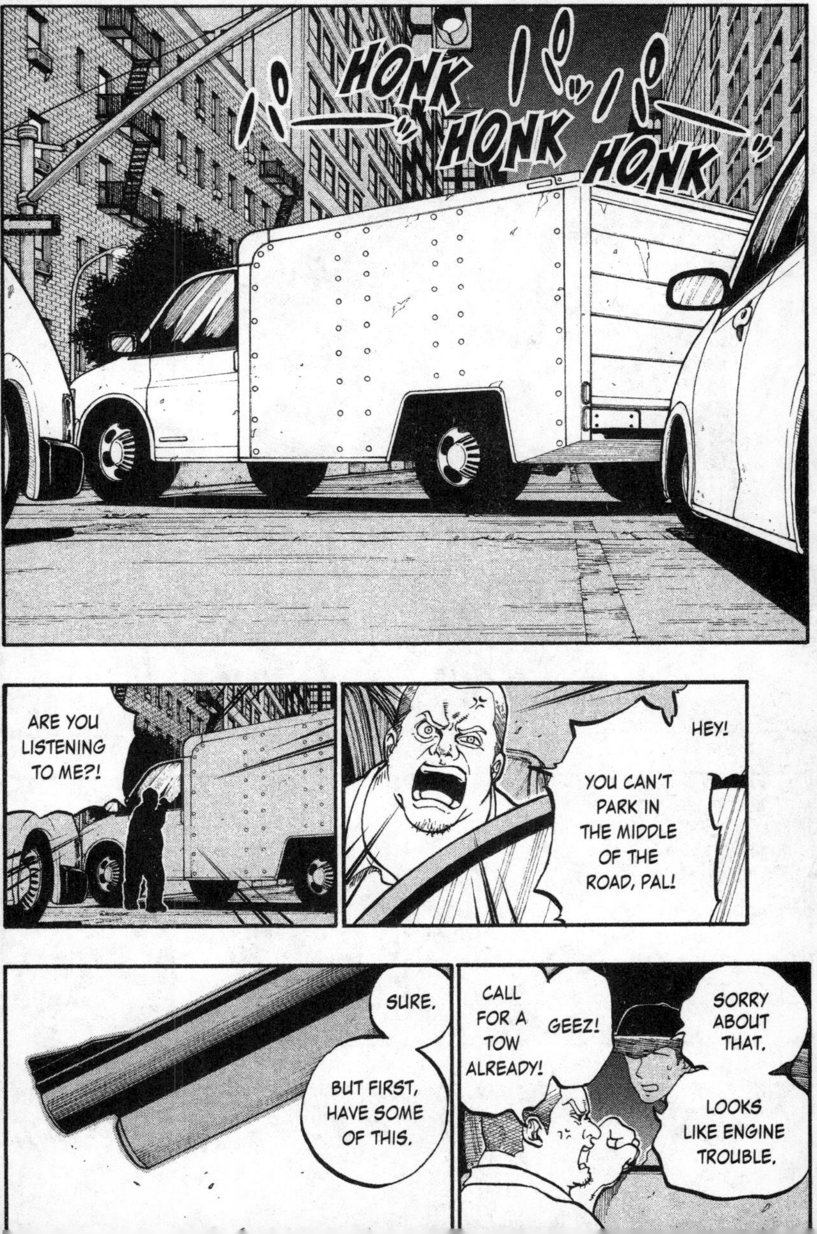
HONK
HONK
HONK
HEY!
YOU CAN'T PARK IN THE MIDDLE OF THE ROAD, PAL!
ARE YOU LISTENING TO ME?!
SORRY ABOUT THAT.
LOOKS LIKE ENGINE TROUBLE.
GEEZ!
CALL FOR A TOW ALREADY!
SURE.
BUT FIRST, HAVE SOME OF THIS.

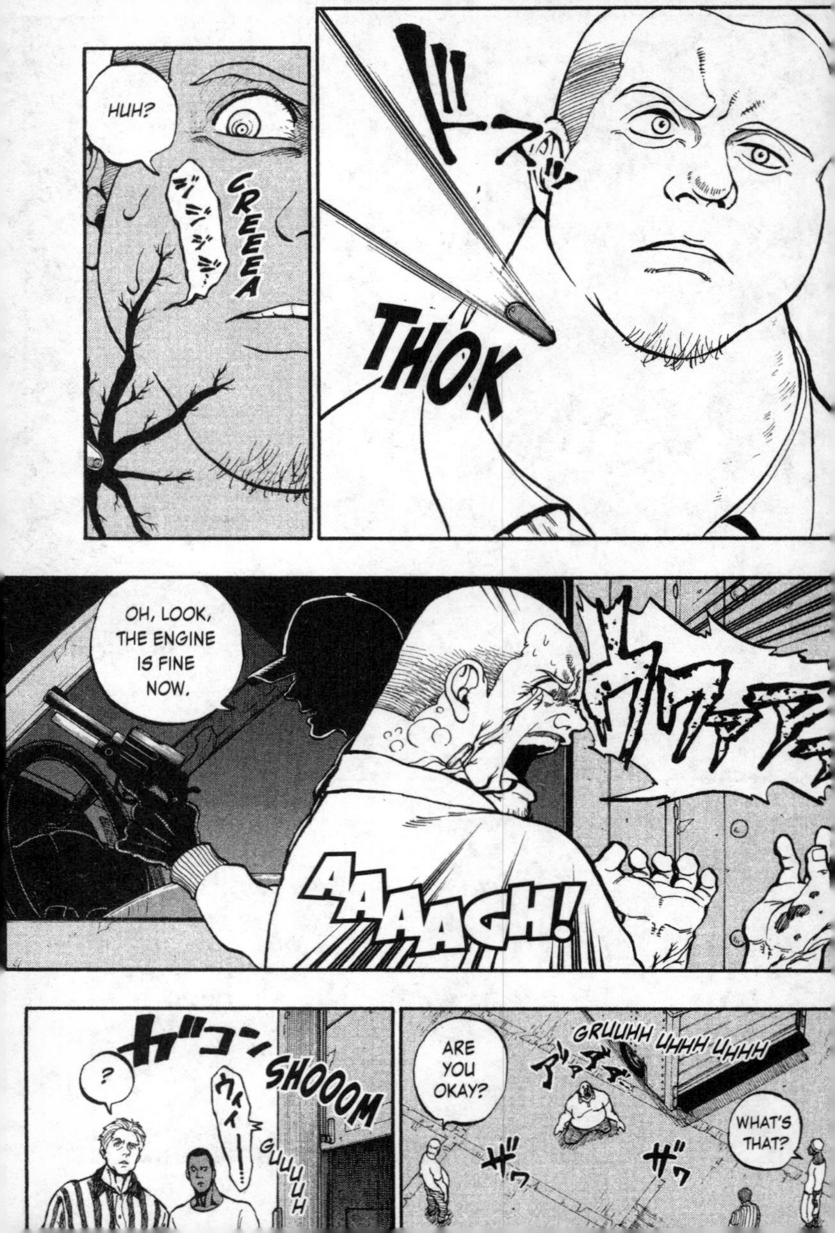
THOK
HUH?
CREEEA
AAAACH!
OH, LOOK, THE ENGINE IS FINE NOW.
GRUUHH UHHH UHHH
WHAT'S THAT?
ARE YOU OKAY?
SHOOOM
?
GUUUUH

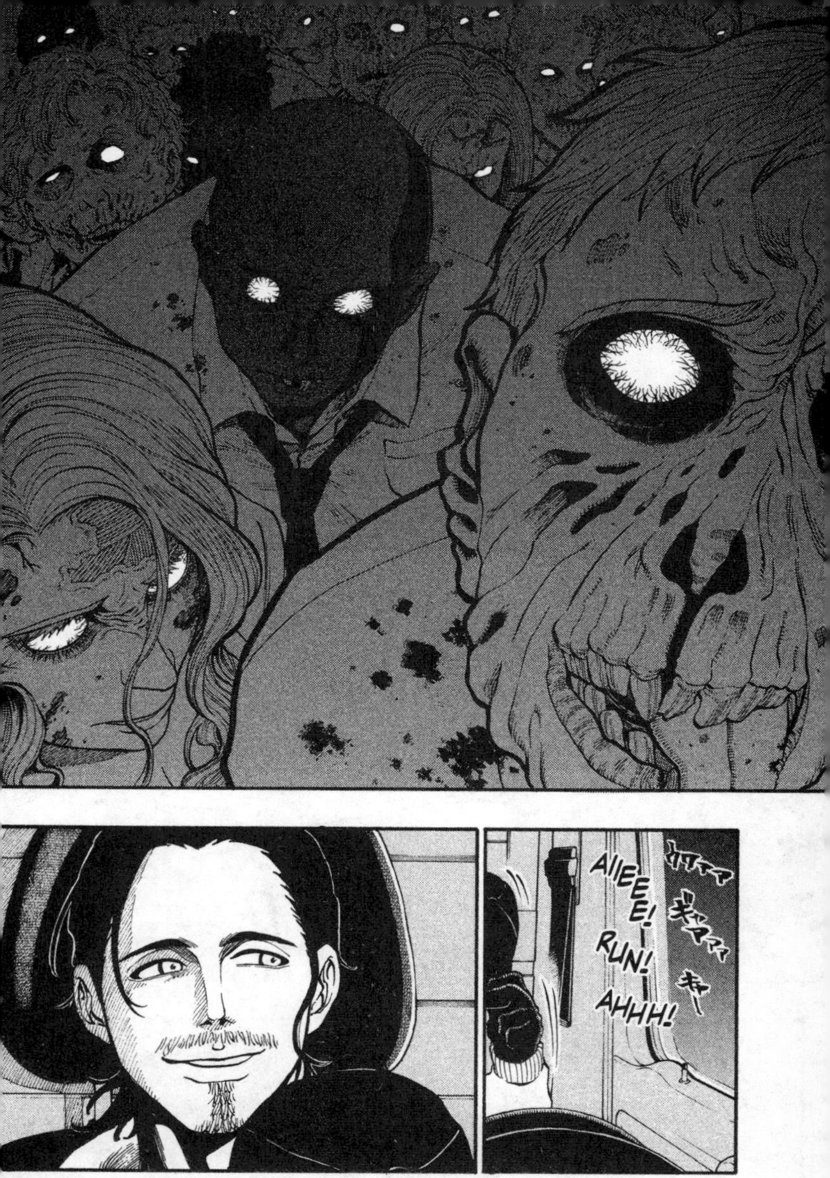
ギャアァァ
キャー
AIIEEEE!
RUN!
AHHH!

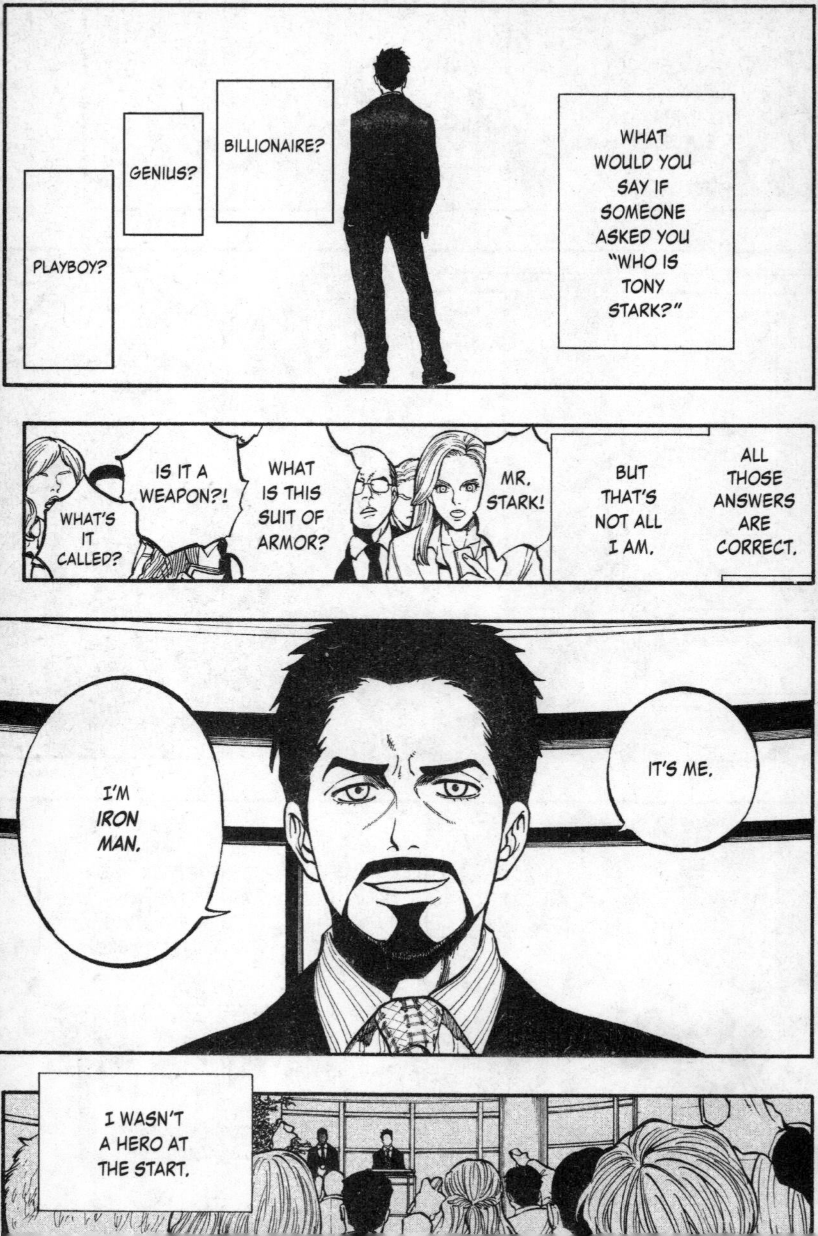
WHAT WOULD YOU SAY IF SOMEONE ASKED YOU "WHO IS TONY STARK?"
BILLIONAIRE?
GENIUS?
PLAYBOY?
ALL THOSE ANSWERS ARE CORRECT.
BUT THAT'S NOT ALL I AM.
MR. STARK!
WHAT IS THIS SUIT OF ARMOR?
IS IT A WEAPON?!
WHAT'S IT CALLED?
IT'S ME.
I'M *IRON MAN.*
I WASN'T A HERO AT THE START.

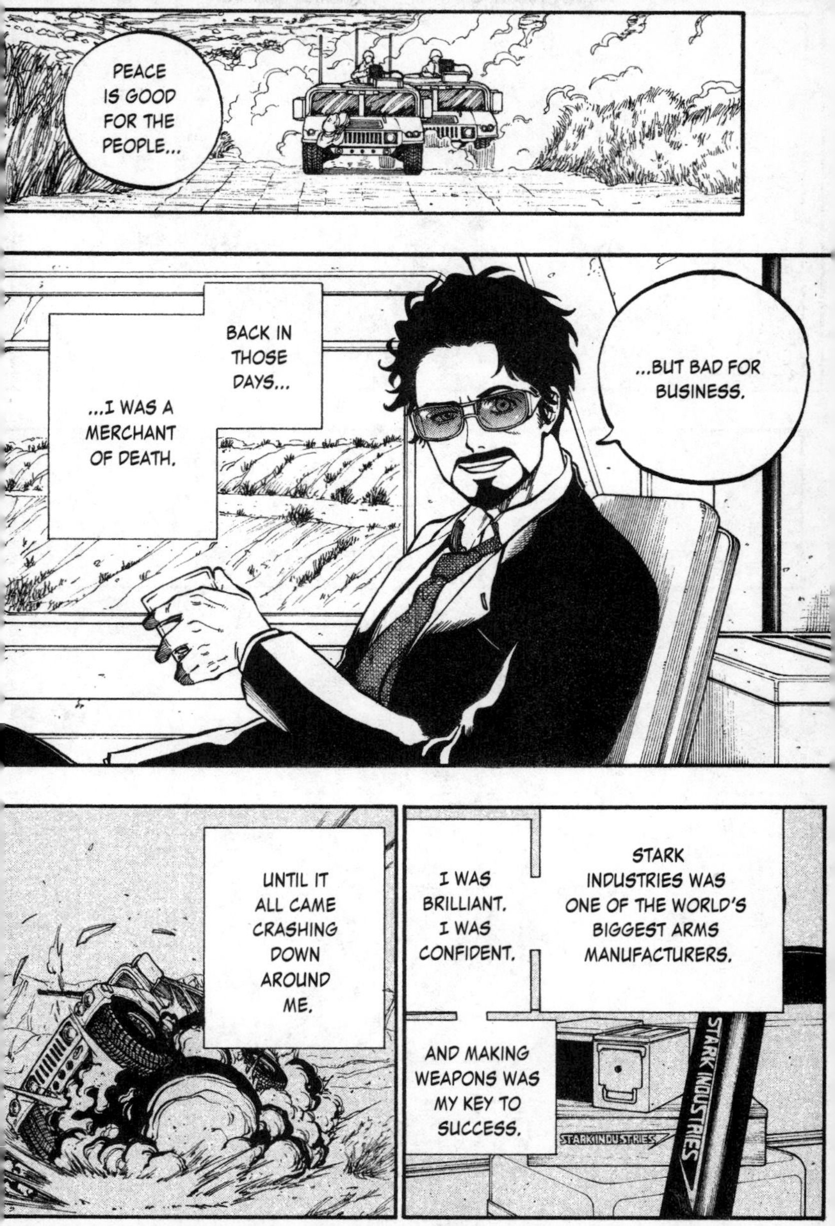
PEACE IS GOOD FOR THE PEOPLE...
...BUT BAD FOR BUSINESS.
BACK IN THOSE DAYS...
...I WAS A MERCHANT OF DEATH.
STARK INDUSTRIES WAS ONE OF THE WORLD'S BIGGEST ARMS MANUFACTURERS.
I WAS BRILLIANT. I WAS CONFIDENT.
AND MAKING WEAPONS WAS MY KEY TO SUCCESS.
STARK INDUSTRIES
STARK INDUSTRIES
UNTIL IT ALL CAME CRASHING DOWN AROUND ME.

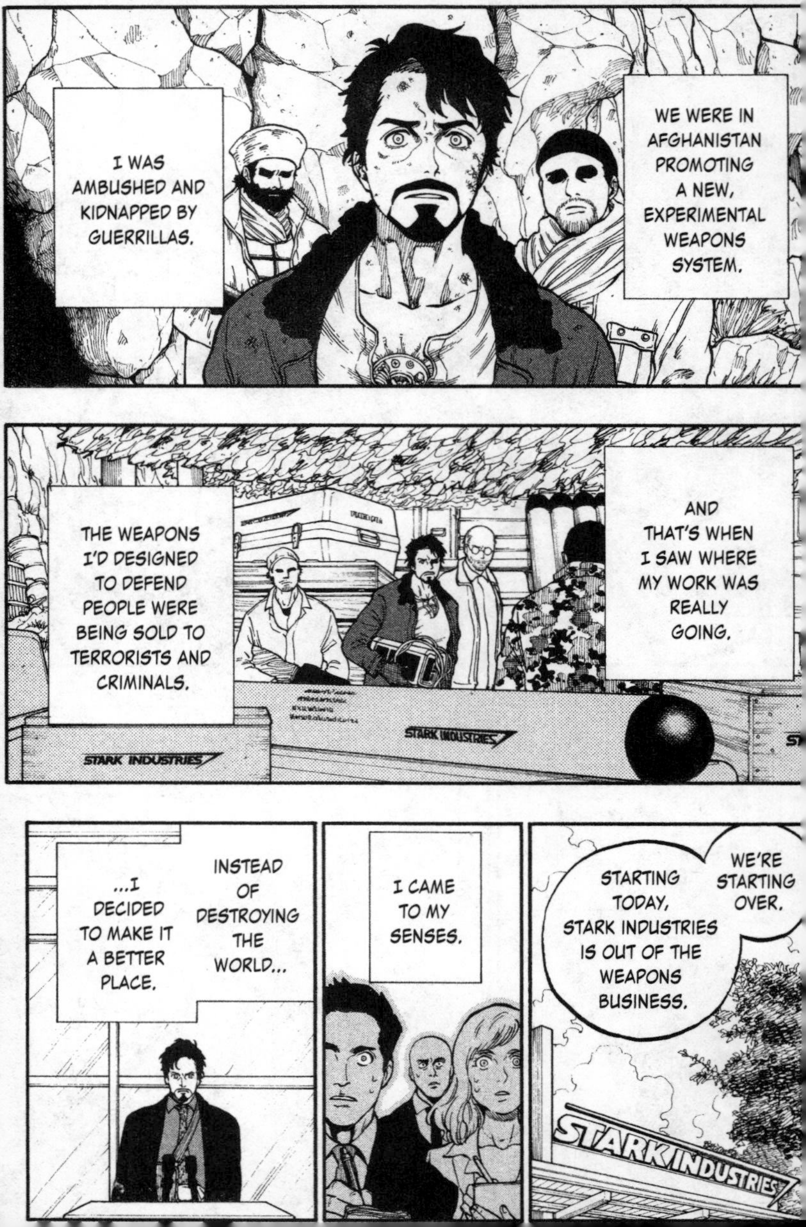
WE WERE IN AFGHANISTAN PROMOTING A NEW, EXPERIMENTAL WEAPONS SYSTEM.
I WAS AMBUSHED AND KIDNAPPED BY GUERRILLAS.
AND THAT'S WHEN I SAW WHERE MY WORK WAS REALLY GOING.
THE WEAPONS I'D DESIGNED TO DEFEND PEOPLE WERE BEING SOLD TO TERRORISTS AND CRIMINALS.
STARK INDUSTRIES
STARK INDUSTRIES
WE'RE STARTING OVER.
STARTING TODAY, STARK INDUSTRIES IS OUT OF THE WEAPONS BUSINESS.
STARK INDUSTRIES
I CAME TO MY SENSES.
INSTEAD OF DESTROYING THE WORLD...
...I DECIDED TO MAKE IT A BETTER PLACE.

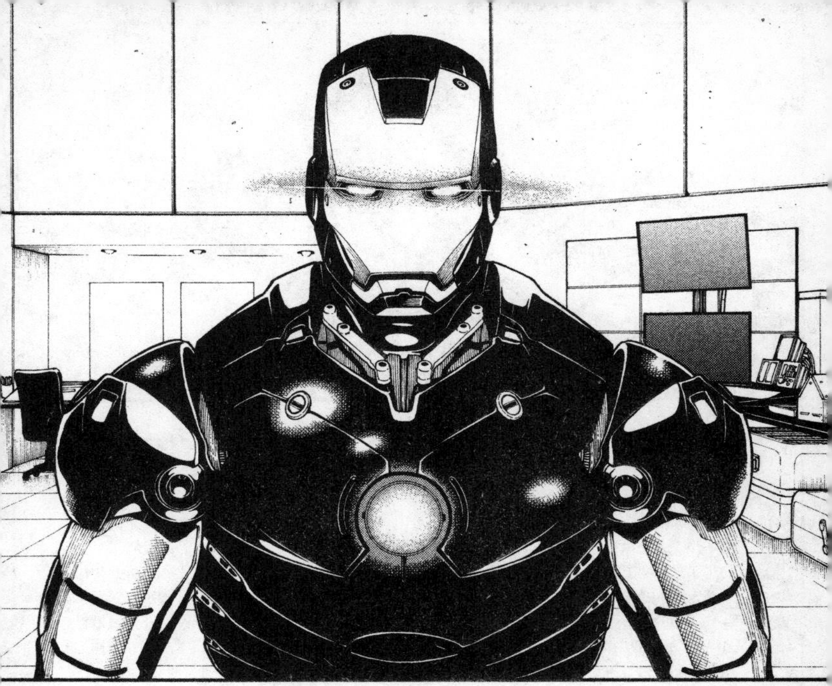

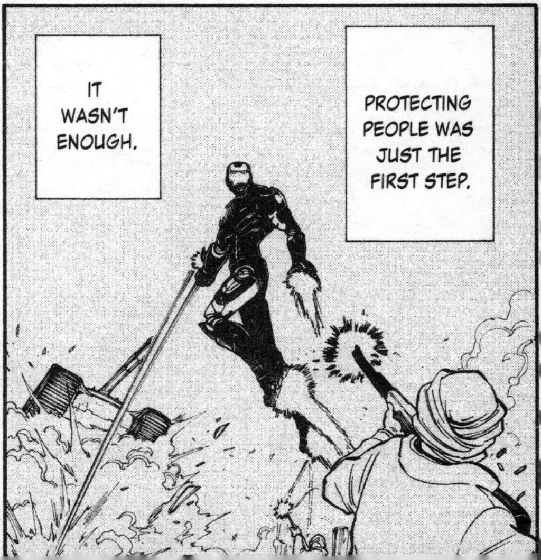
PROTECTING PEOPLE WAS JUST THE FIRST STEP.
IT WASN'T ENOUGH.

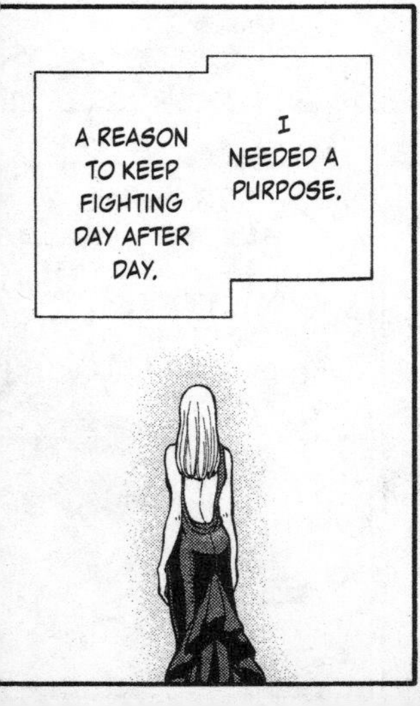
I NEEDED A PURPOSE.
A REASON TO KEEP FIGHTING DAY AFTER DAY.

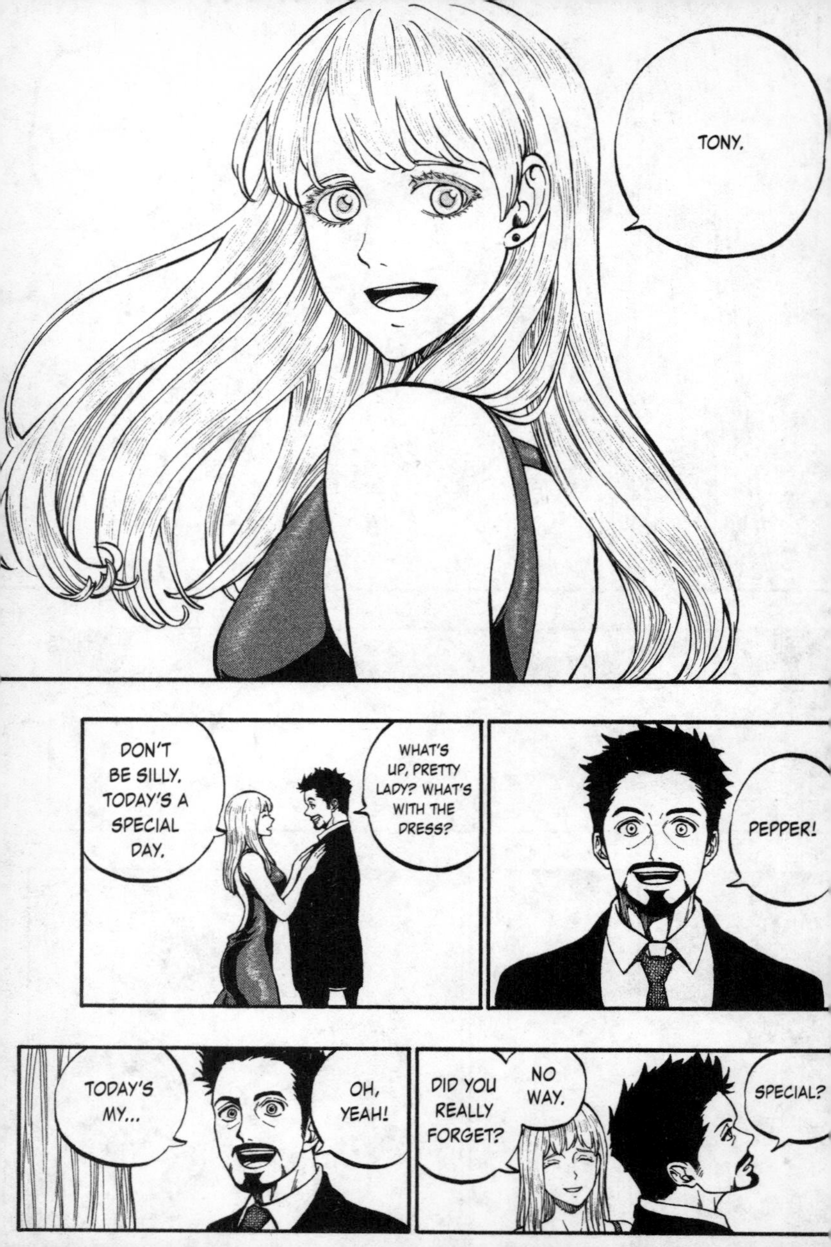
TONY.
PEPPER!
WHAT'S UP, PRETTY LADY? WHAT'S WITH THE DRESS?
DON'T BE SILLY. TODAY'S A SPECIAL DAY.
SPECIAL?
NO WAY.
DID YOU REALLY FORGET?
OH, YEAH!
TODAY'S MY...

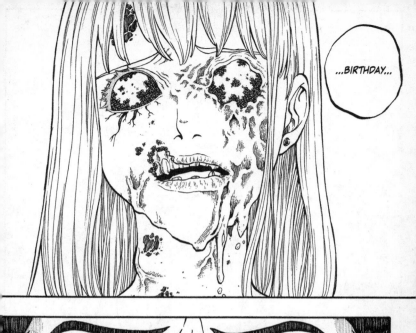

...BIRTHDAY...

PLEASE...

OH GOD, NO!

PEPPER!

GRUUUH

PEPPER!

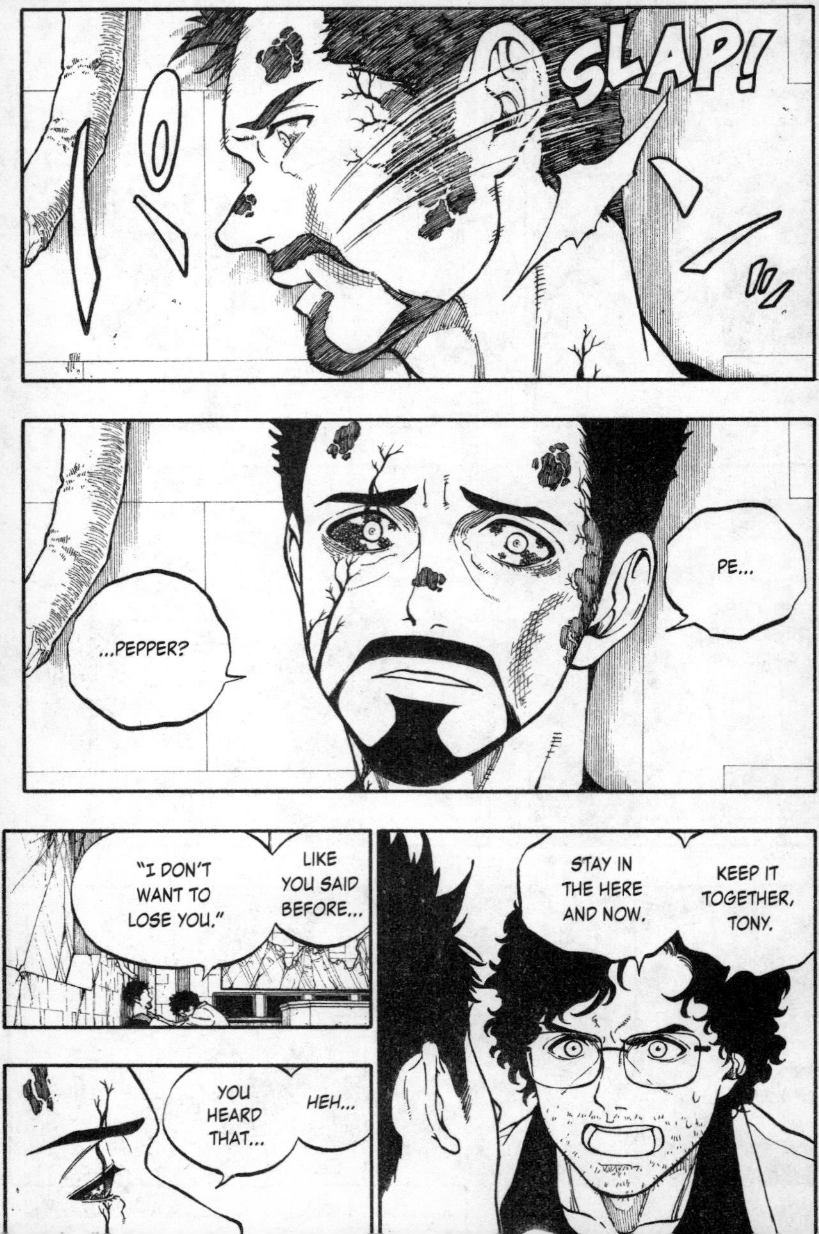
SLAP!
PE...
...PEPPER?
KEEP IT TOGETHER, TONY.
STAY IN THE HERE AND NOW.
LIKE YOU SAID BEFORE...
"I DON'T WANT TO LOSE YOU."
HEH...
YOU HEARD THAT...

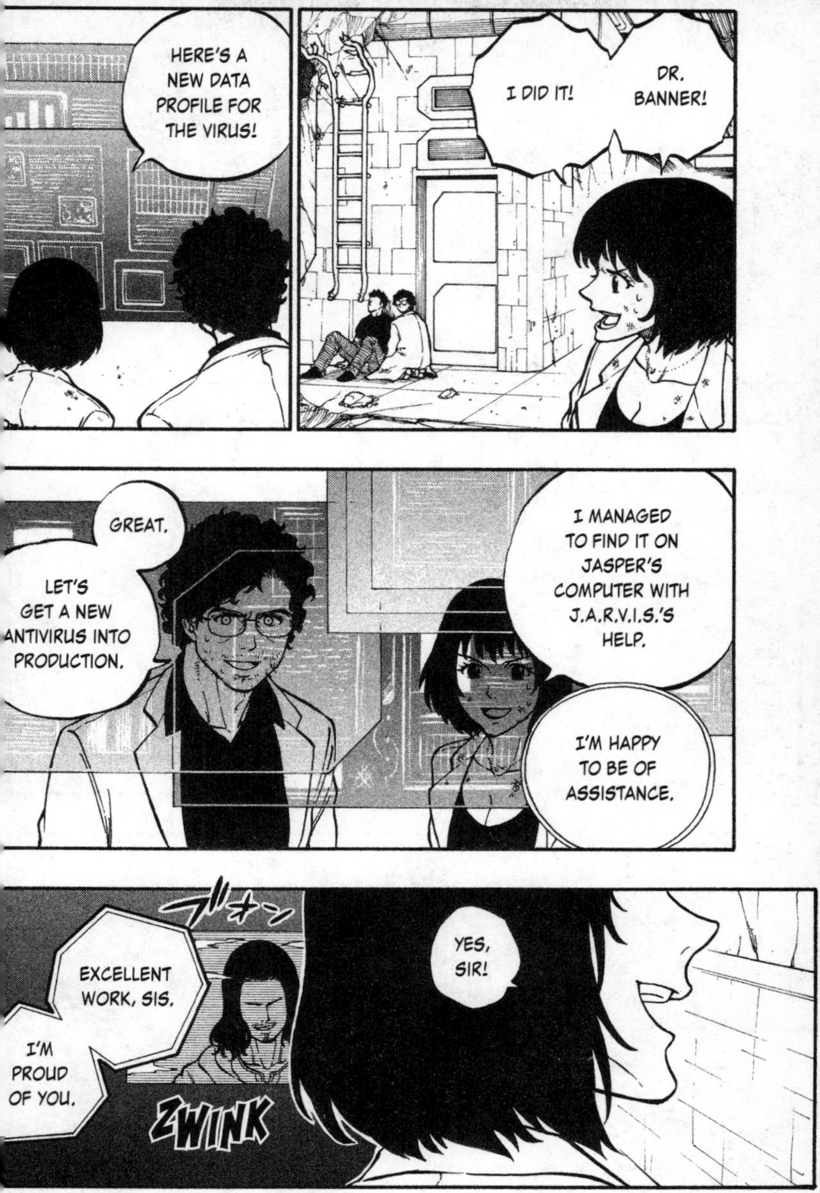
DR. BANNER!
I DID IT!
HERE'S A NEW DATA PROFILE FOR THE VIRUS!
I MANAGED TO FIND IT ON JASPER'S COMPUTER WITH J.A.R.V.I.S.'S HELP.
I'M HAPPY TO BE OF ASSISTANCE.
GREAT.
LET'S GET A NEW ANTIVIRUS INTO PRODUCTION.
ブォン
EXCELLENT WORK, SIS.
I'M PROUD OF YOU.
ZWINK
YES, SIR!

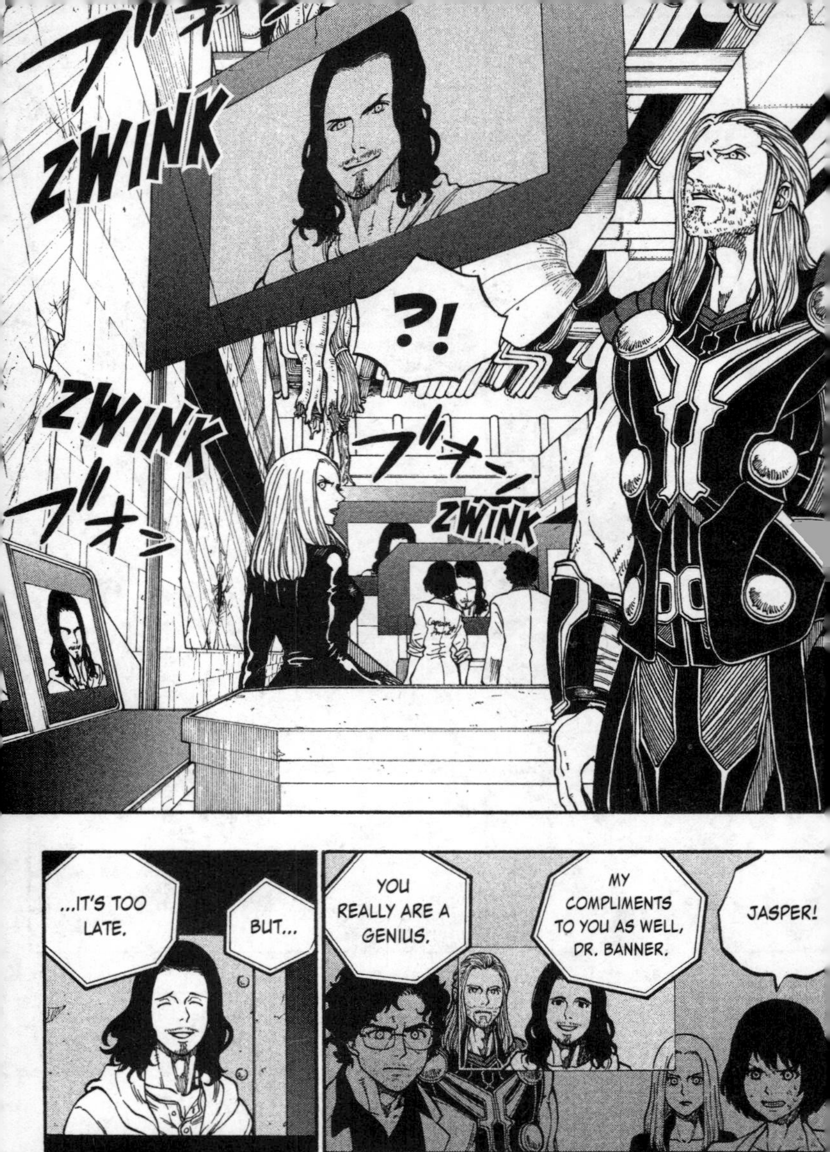

ブォ
ZWINK
?!
ブォーン
ZWINK
ZWINK
ブォン
JASPER!
MY COMPLIMENTS TO YOU AS WELL, DR. BANNER.
YOU REALLY ARE A GENIUS.
BUT...
...IT'S TOO LATE.

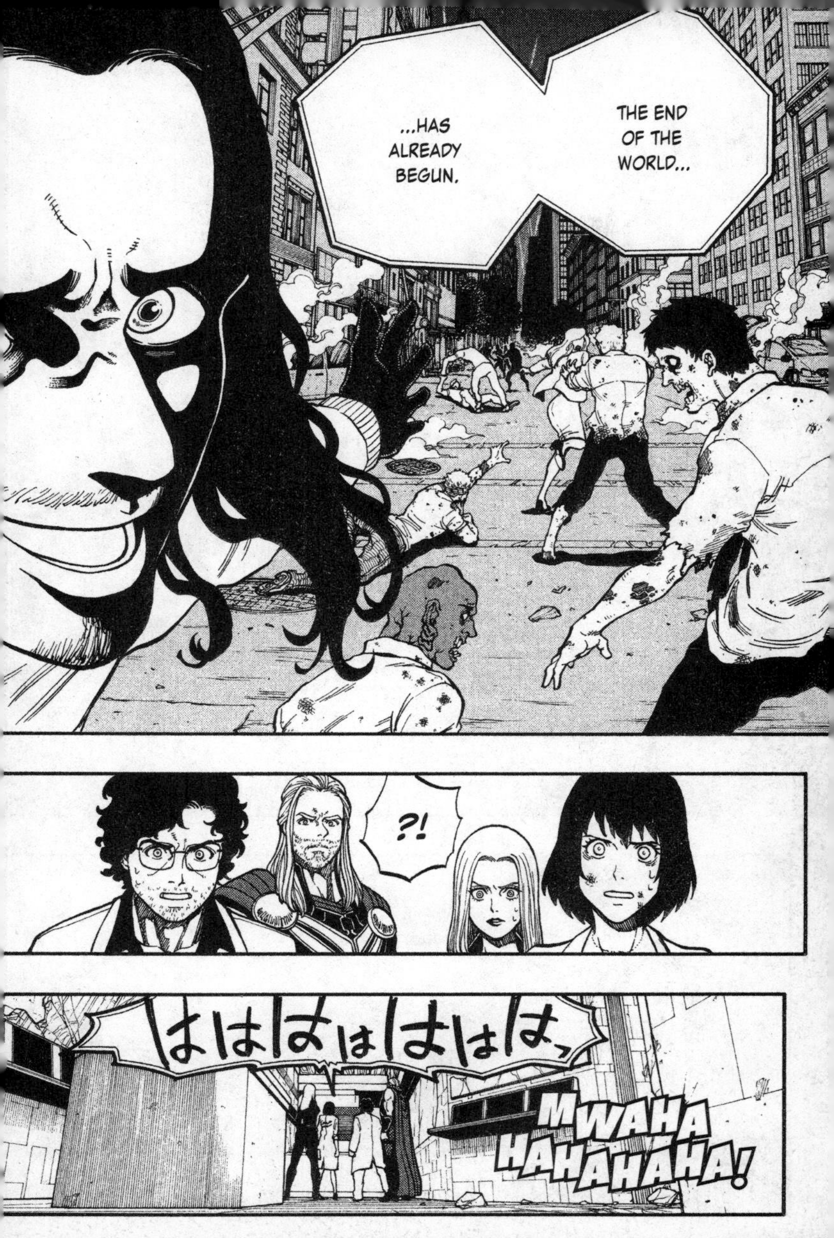
THE END OF THE WORLD...
...HAS ALREADY BEGUN.
?!
ははははははは
MWAHA HAHAHAHA!

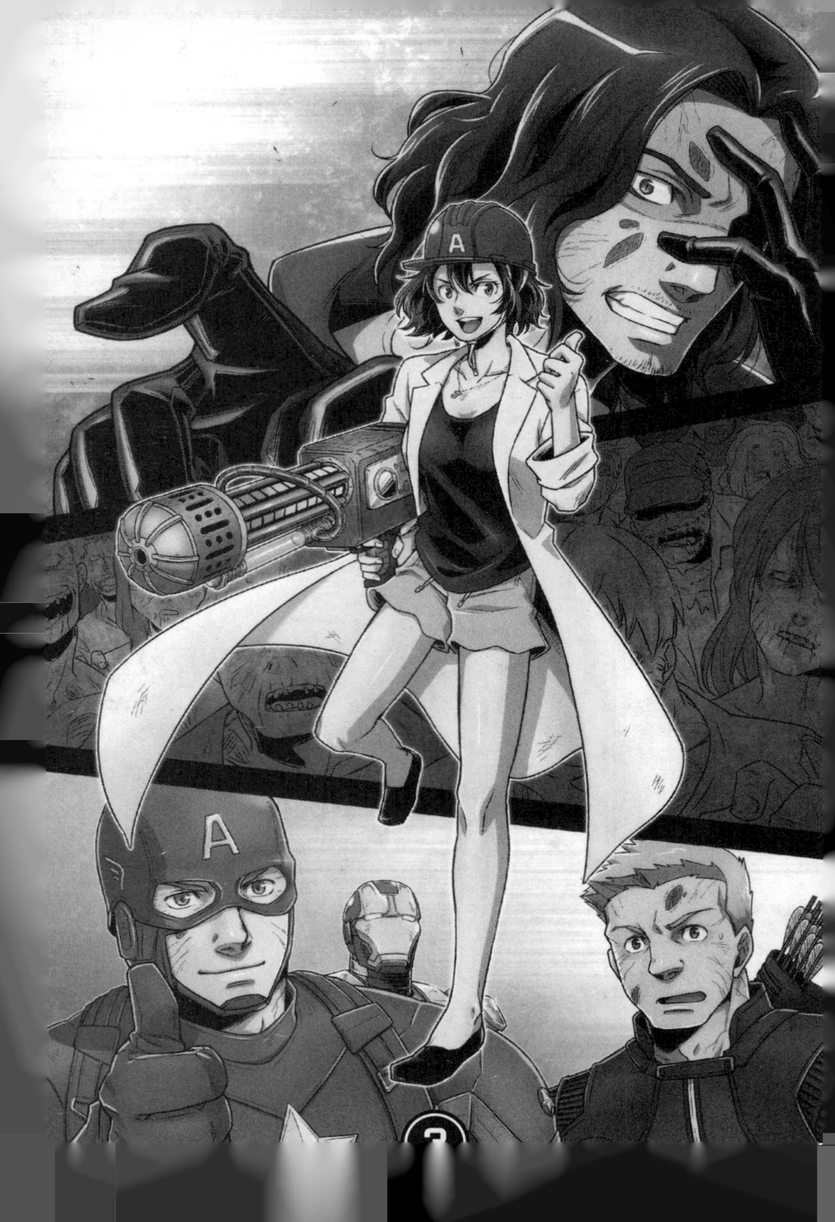

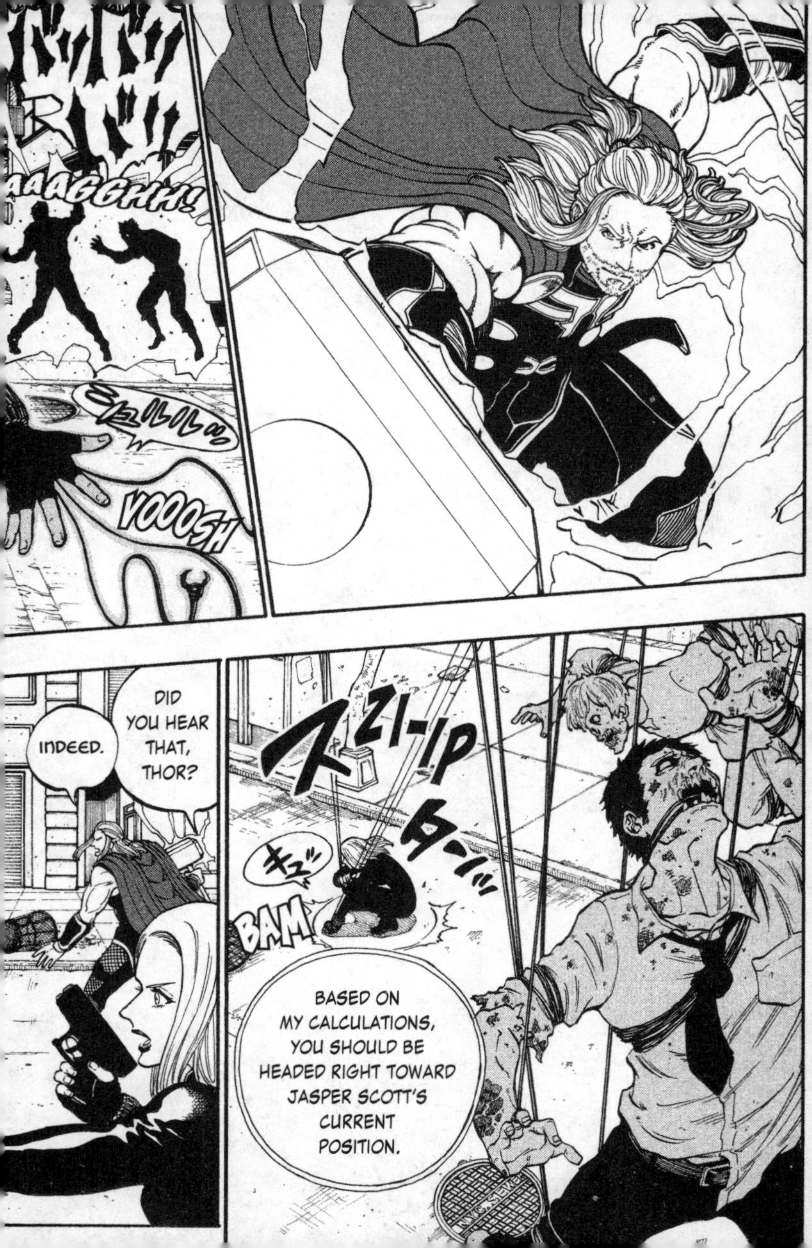
AAAAGGHH!
VOOOSH
ZI-IP
BAM
BASED ON MY CALCULATIONS, YOU SHOULD BE HEADED RIGHT TOWARD JASPER SCOTT'S CURRENT POSITION.
DID YOU HEAR THAT, THOR?
INDEED.

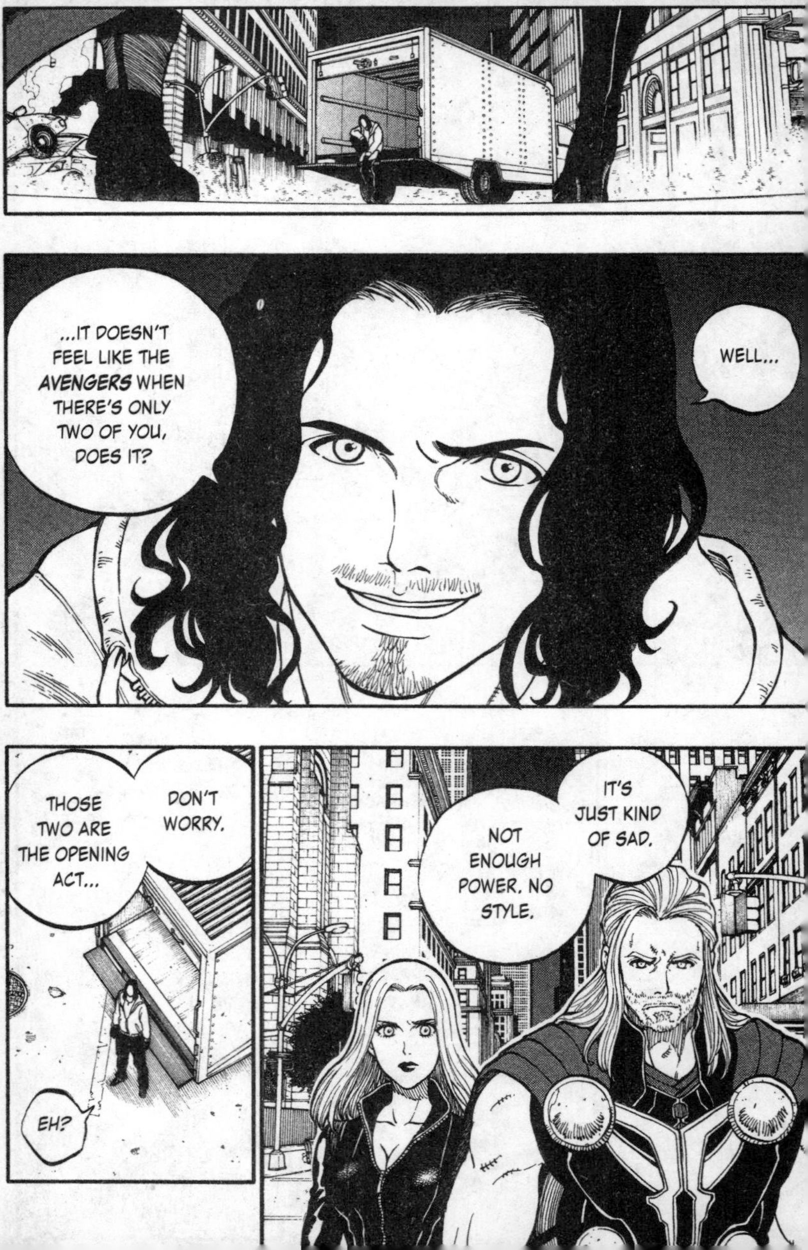
WELL...
...IT DOESN'T FEEL LIKE THE *AVENGERS* WHEN THERE'S ONLY TWO OF YOU, DOES IT?
IT'S JUST KIND OF SAD.
NOT ENOUGH POWER. NO STYLE.
DON'T WORRY.
THOSE TWO ARE THE OPENING ACT...
EH?

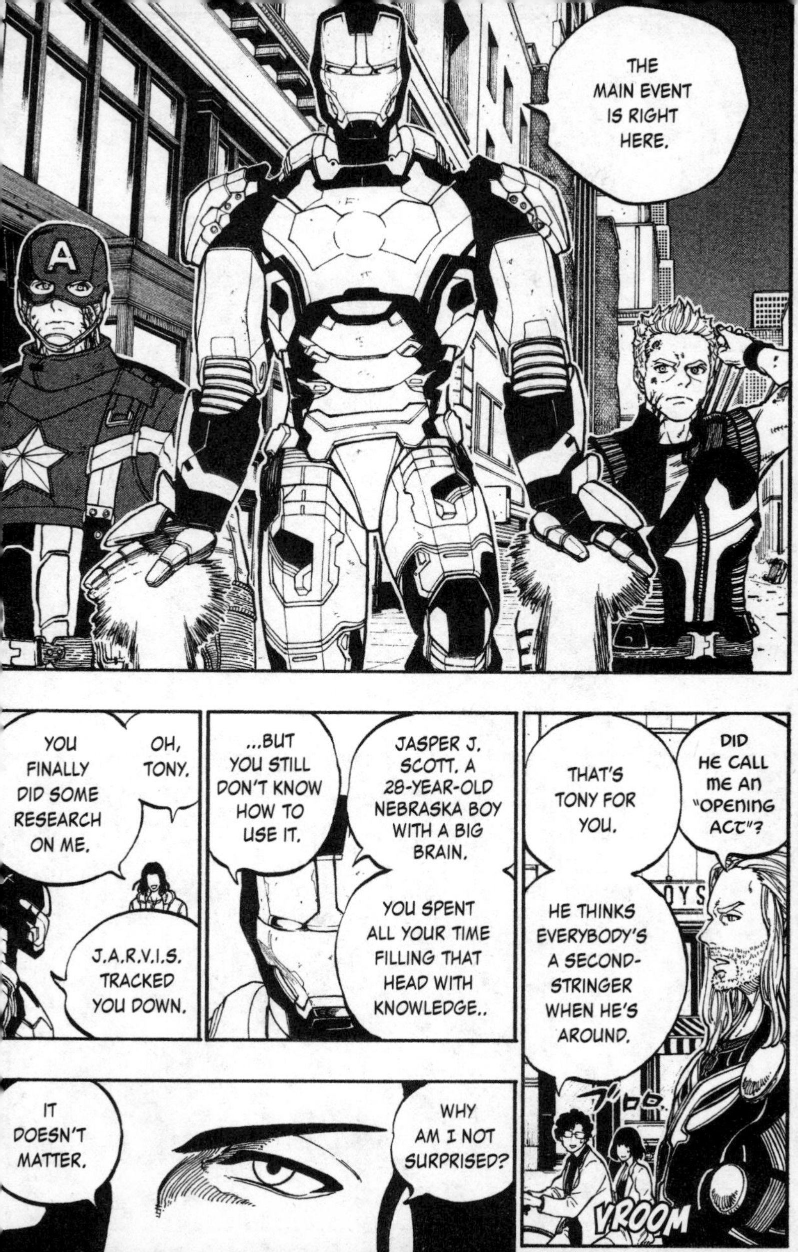
THE MAIN EVENT IS RIGHT HERE.
DID HE CALL ME AN "OPENING ACT"?
THAT'S TONY FOR YOU.
HE THINKS EVERYBODY'S A SECOND-STRINGER WHEN HE'S AROUND.
VROOM
JASPER J. SCOTT. A 28-YEAR-OLD NEBRASKA BOY WITH A BIG BRAIN.
YOU SPENT ALL YOUR TIME FILLING THAT HEAD WITH KNOWLEDGE..
...BUT YOU STILL DON'T KNOW HOW TO USE IT.
OH, TONY.
YOU FINALLY DID SOME RESEARCH ON ME.
J.A.R.V.I.S. TRACKED YOU DOWN.
WHY AM I NOT SURPRISED?
IT DOESN'T MATTER.

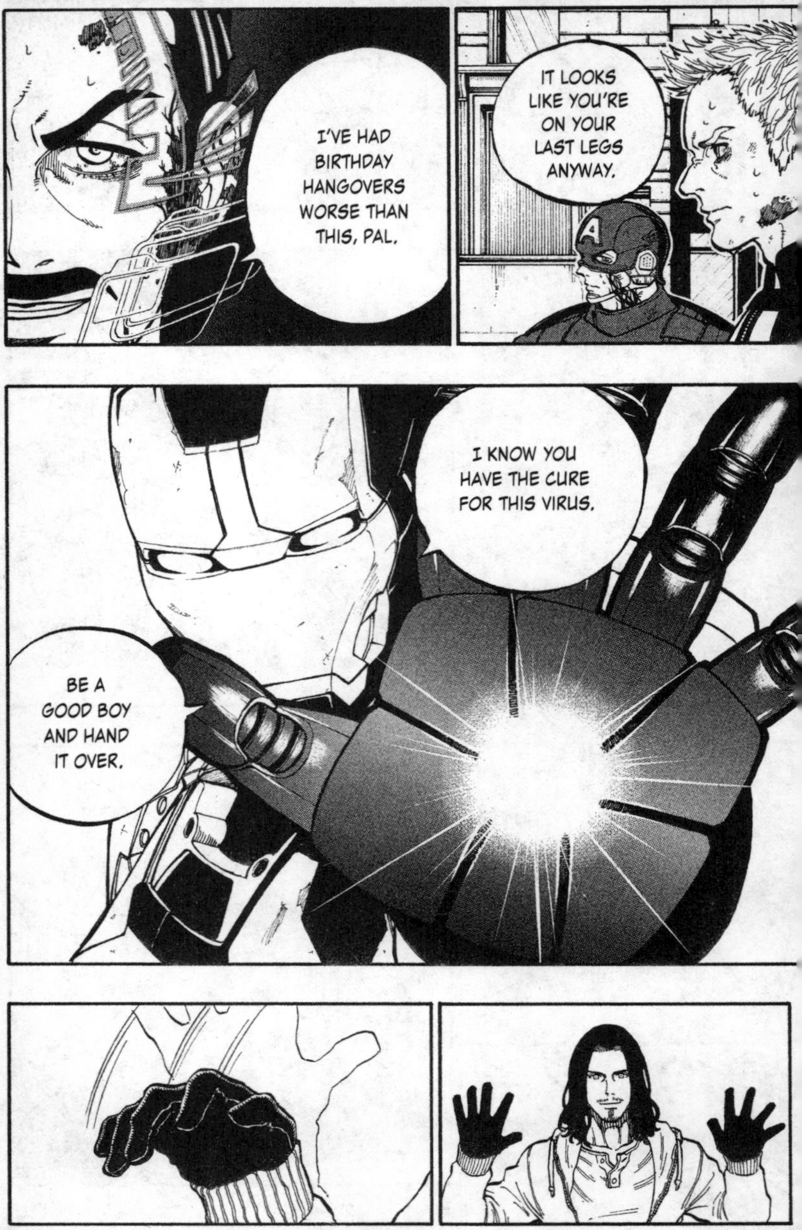
IT LOOKS LIKE YOU'RE ON YOUR LAST LEGS ANYWAY.
I'VE HAD BIRTHDAY HANGOVERS WORSE THAN THIS, PAL.
I KNOW YOU HAVE THE CURE FOR THIS VIRUS.
BE A GOOD BOY AND HAND IT OVER.

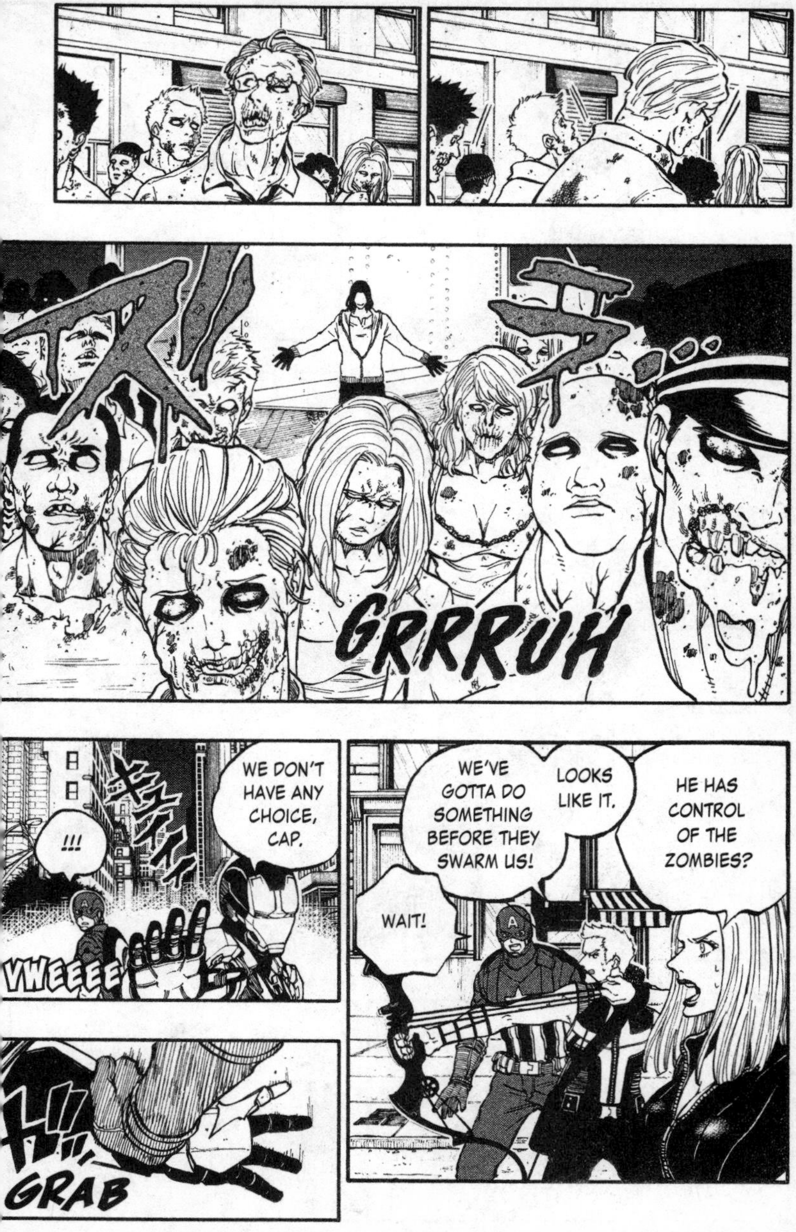
GRRRUH
HE HAS CONTROL OF THE ZOMBIES?
LOOKS LIKE IT.
WE'VE GOTTA DO SOMETHING BEFORE THEY SWARM US!
WAIT!
WE DON'T HAVE ANY CHOICE, CAP.
!!!
VWEEEE
GRAB

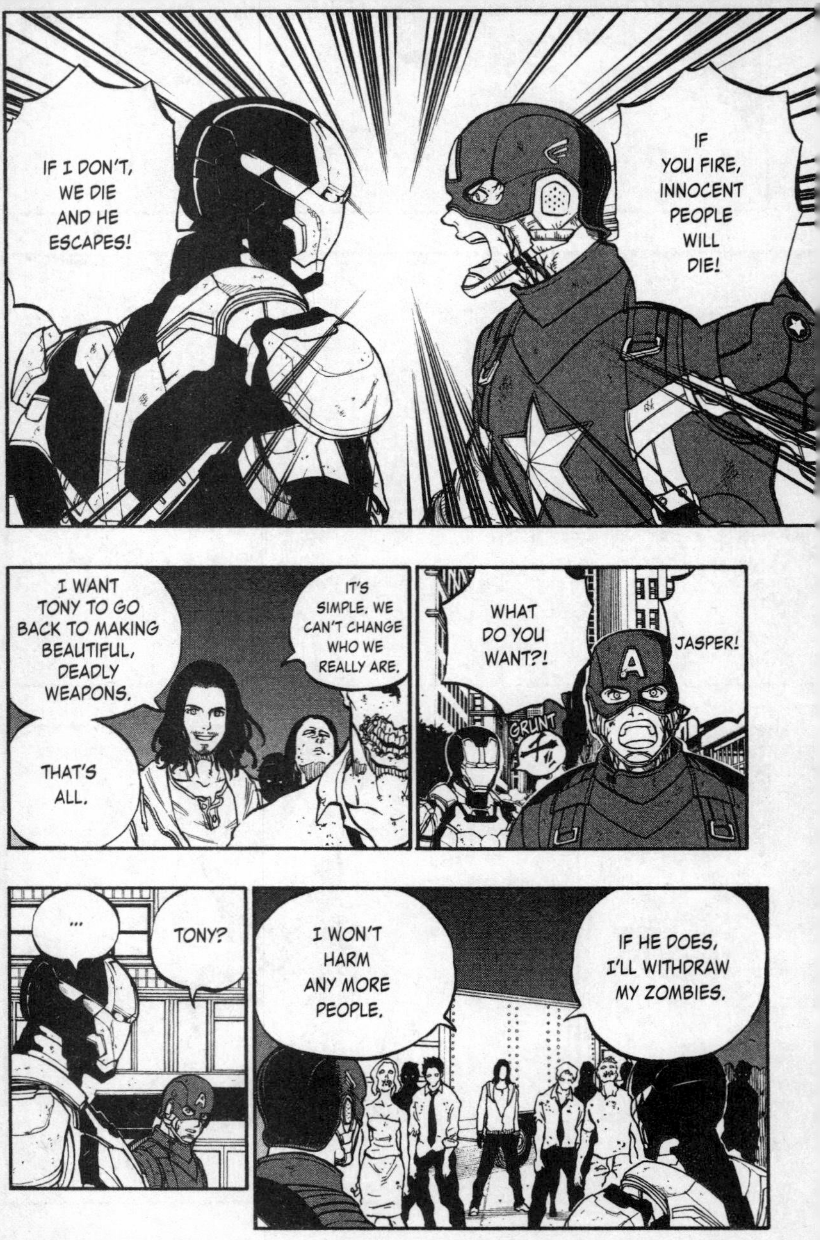
IF YOU FIRE, INNOCENT PEOPLE WILL DIE!
IF I DON'T, WE DIE AND HE ESCAPES!
JASPER!
WHAT DO YOU WANT?!
GRUNT
IT'S SIMPLE. WE CAN'T CHANGE WHO WE REALLY ARE.
I WANT TONY TO GO BACK TO MAKING BEAUTIFUL, DEADLY WEAPONS.
THAT'S ALL.
IF HE DOES, I'LL WITHDRAW MY ZOMBIES.
I WON'T HARM ANY MORE PEOPLE.
TONY?
...

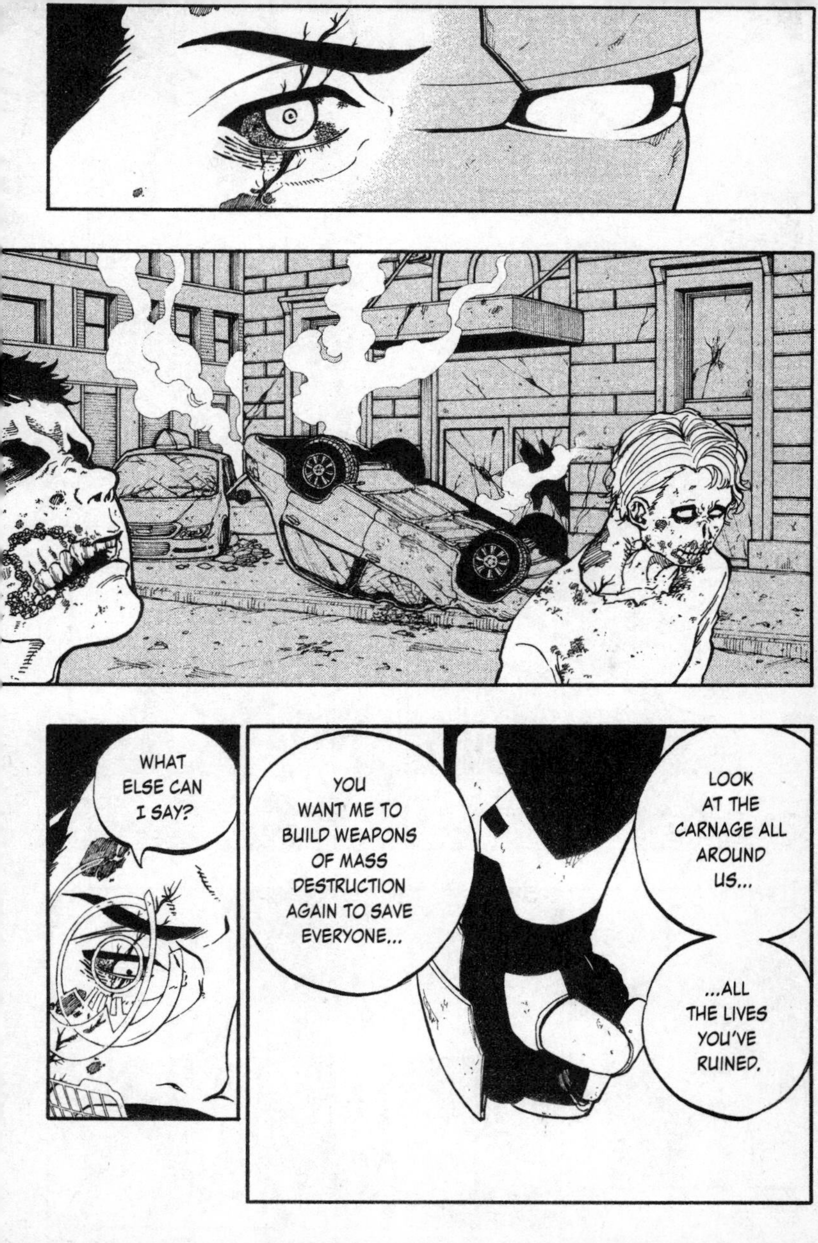
LOOK AT THE CARNAGE ALL AROUND US...
...ALL THE LIVES YOU'VE RUINED.
YOU WANT ME TO BUILD WEAPONS OF MASS DESTRUCTION AGAIN TO SAVE EVERYONE...
WHAT ELSE CAN I SAY?

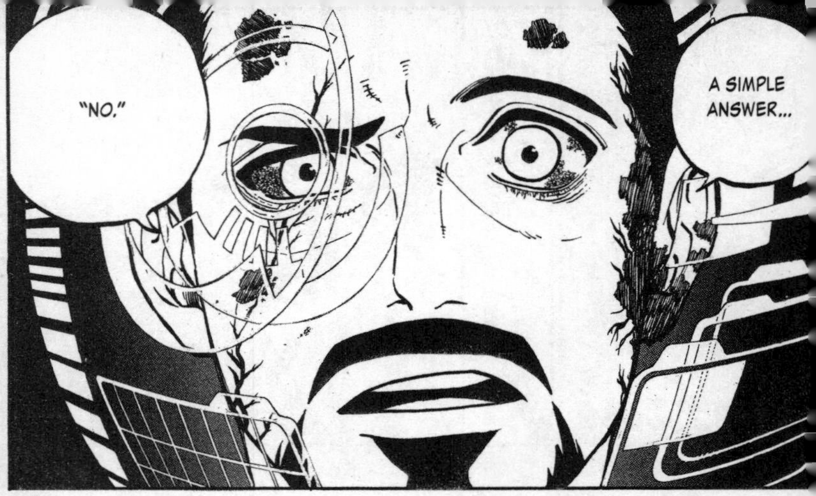
A SIMPLE ANSWER...
"NO."
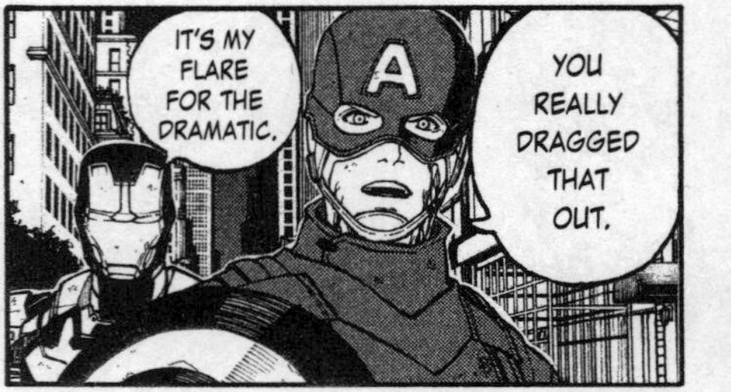
YOU REALLY DRAGGED THAT OUT.
IT'S MY FLARE FOR THE DRAMATIC.
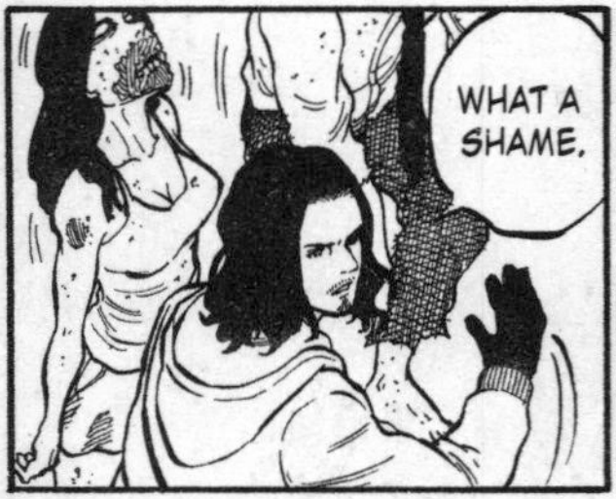
WHAT A SHAME.
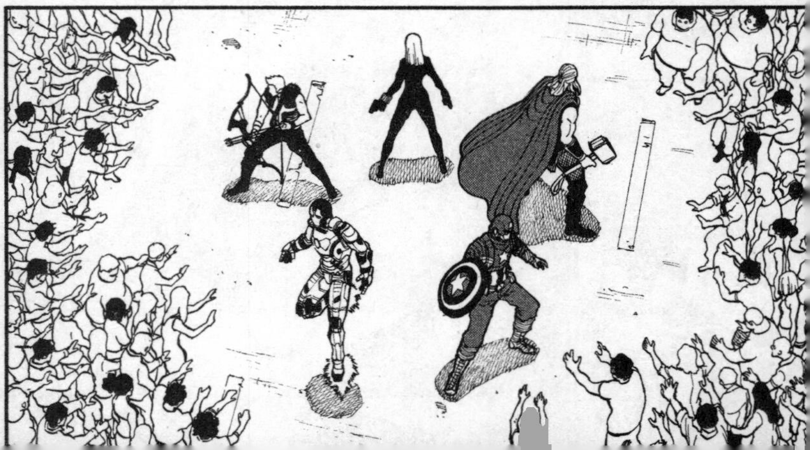

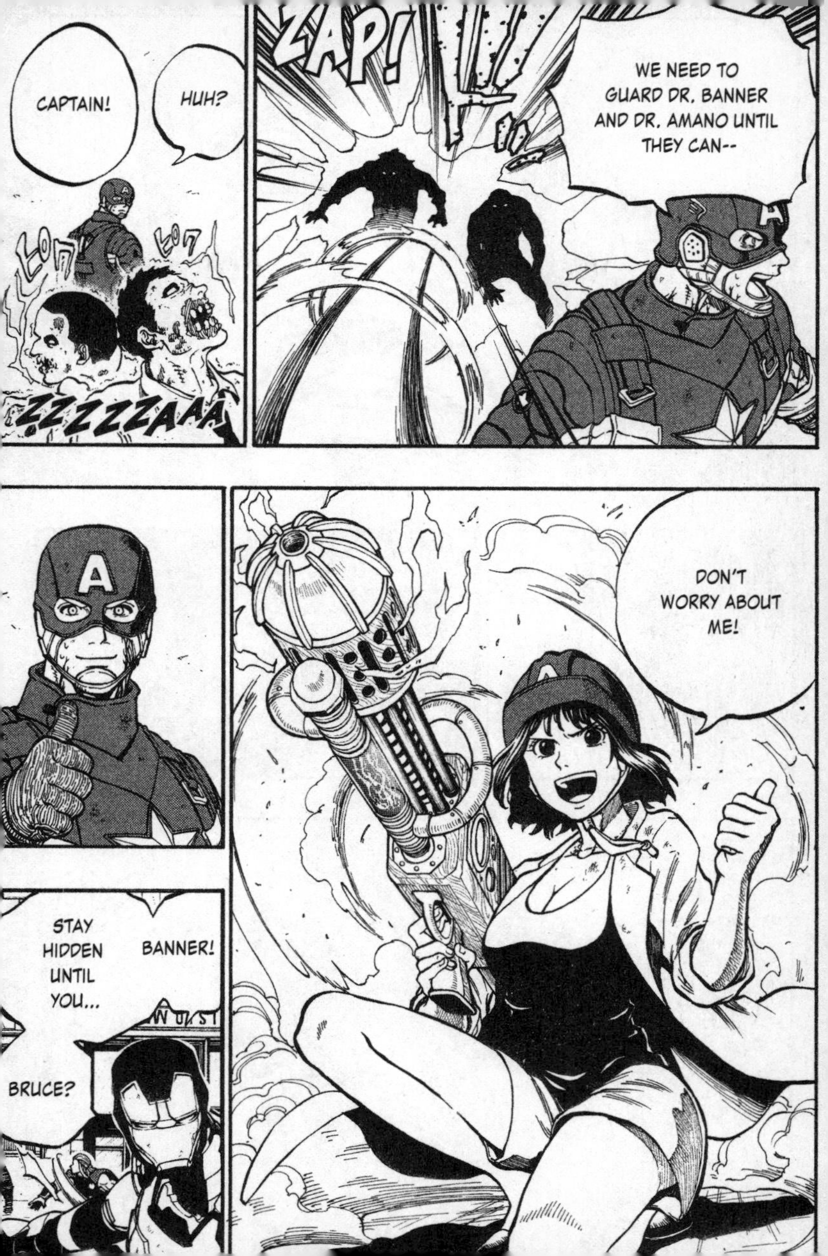
ZAP!
WE NEED TO GUARD DR. BANNER AND DR. AMANO UNTIL THEY CAN--
CAPTAIN!
HUH?
ZZZZZZAAA
DON'T WORRY ABOUT ME!
BANNER!
STAY HIDDEN UNTIL YOU...
BRUCE?

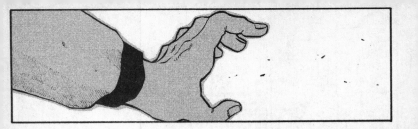

BRUCE!

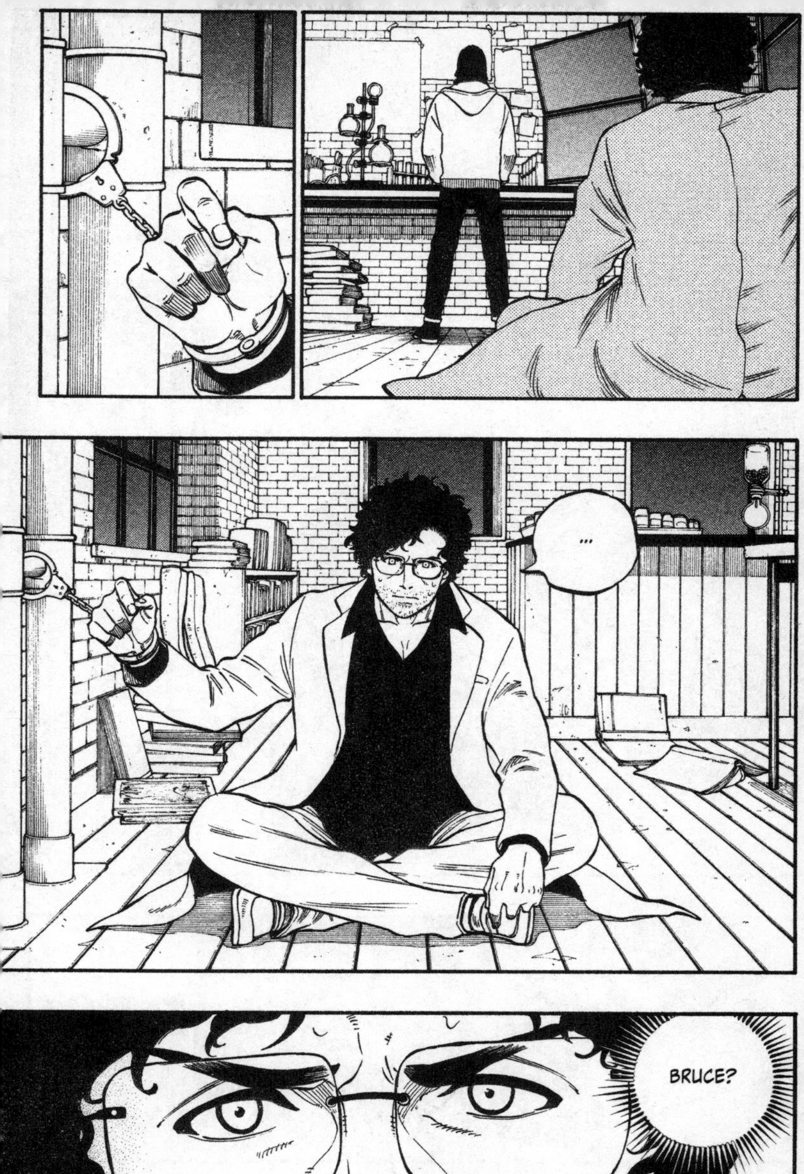
...
BRUCE?

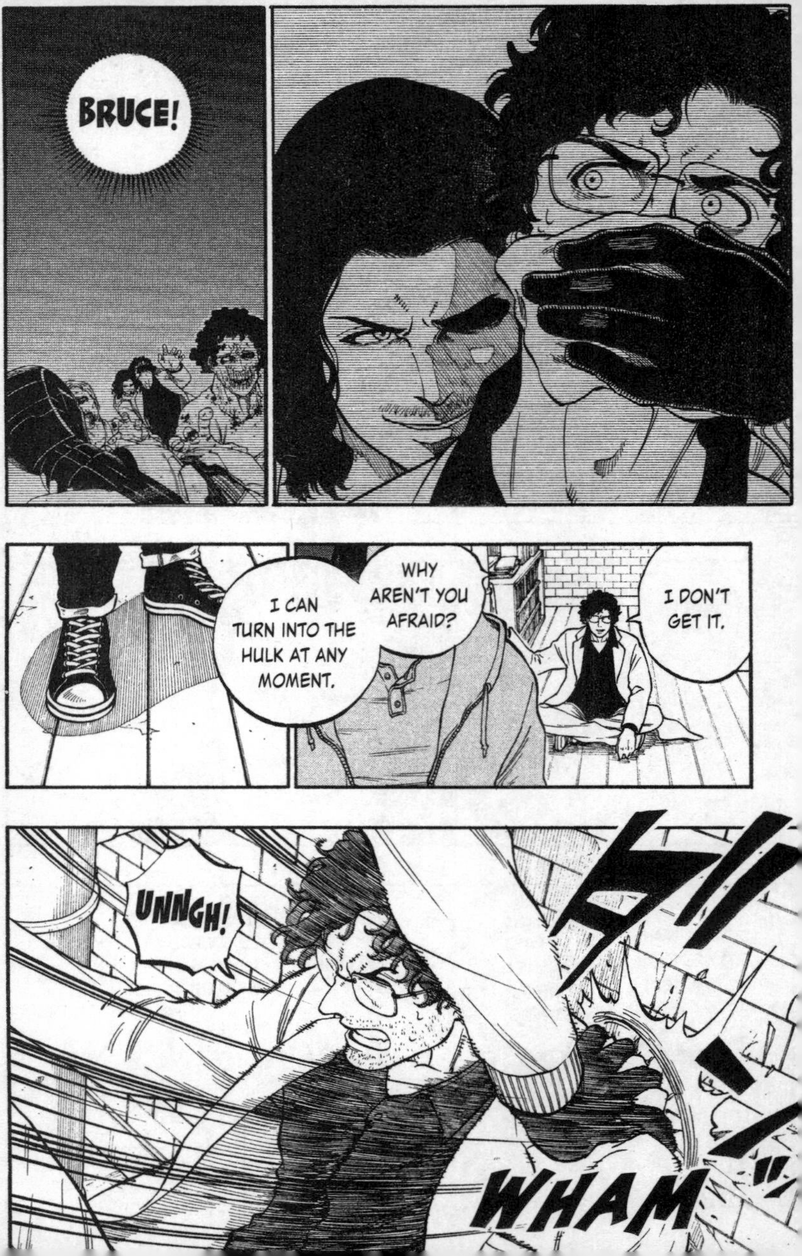

BRUCE!
I DON'T GET IT.
WHY AREN'T YOU AFRAID?
I CAN TURN INTO THE HULK AT ANY MOMENT.
UNNGH!
WHAM

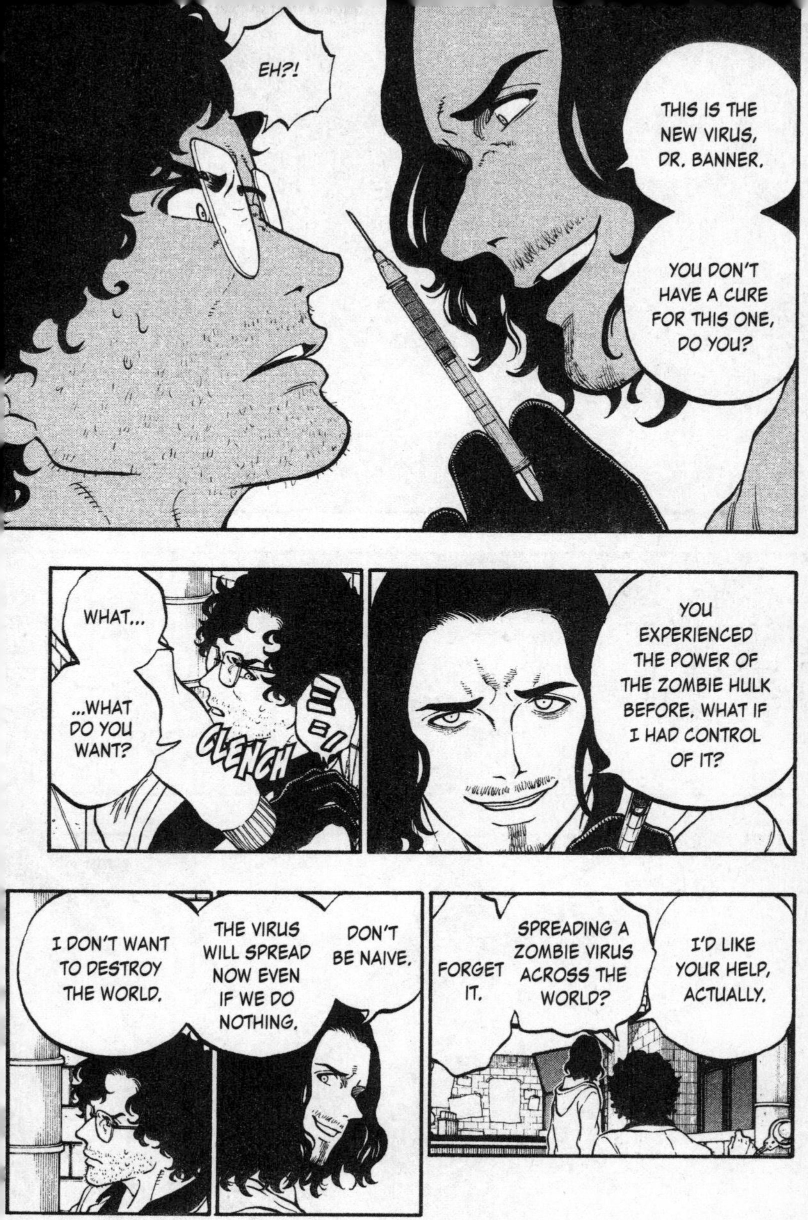
THIS IS THE NEW VIRUS, DR. BANNER.
YOU DON'T HAVE A CURE FOR THIS ONE, DO YOU?
EH?!
YOU EXPERIENCED THE POWER OF THE ZOMBIE HULK BEFORE. WHAT IF I HAD CONTROL OF IT?
WHAT...
...WHAT DO YOU WANT?
CLENCH
I'D LIKE YOUR HELP, ACTUALLY.
SPREADING A ZOMBIE VIRUS ACROSS THE WORLD?
FORGET IT.
DON'T BE NAIVE.
THE VIRUS WILL SPREAD NOW EVEN IF WE DO NOTHING.
I DON'T WANT TO DESTROY THE WORLD.

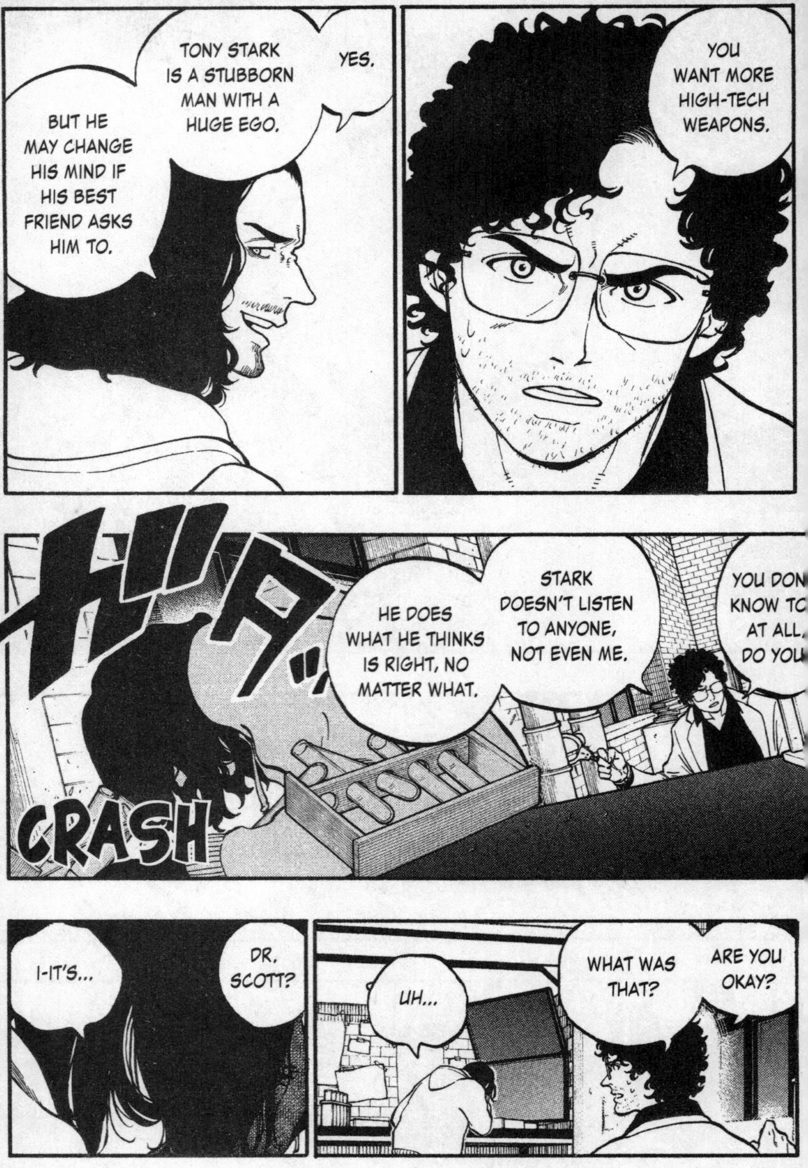
YOU WANT MORE HIGH-TECH WEAPONS.
YES.
TONY STARK IS A STUBBORN MAN WITH A HUGE EGO.
BUT HE MAY CHANGE HIS MIND IF HIS BEST FRIEND ASKS HIM TO.
YOU DON KNOW TO AT ALL, DO YOU
STARK DOESN'T LISTEN TO ANYONE, NOT EVEN ME.
HE DOES WHAT HE THINKS IS RIGHT, NO MATTER WHAT.
CRASH
ARE YOU OKAY?
WHAT WAS THAT?
UH...
DR. SCOTT?
I-IT'S...

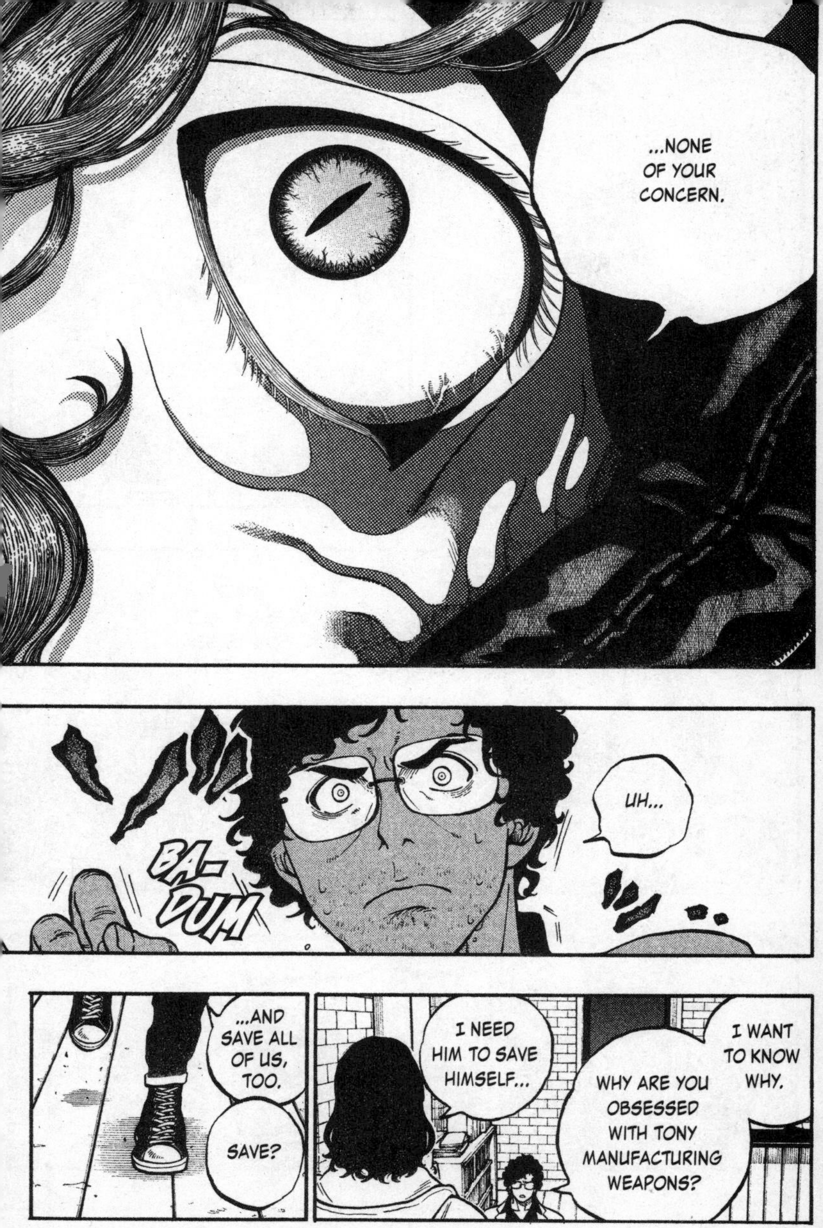
...NONE OF YOUR CONCERN.
UH...
BA-DUM
I WANT TO KNOW WHY.
WHY ARE YOU OBSESSED WITH TONY MANUFACTURING WEAPONS?
I NEED HIM TO SAVE HIMSELF...
...AND SAVE ALL OF US, TOO.
SAVE?

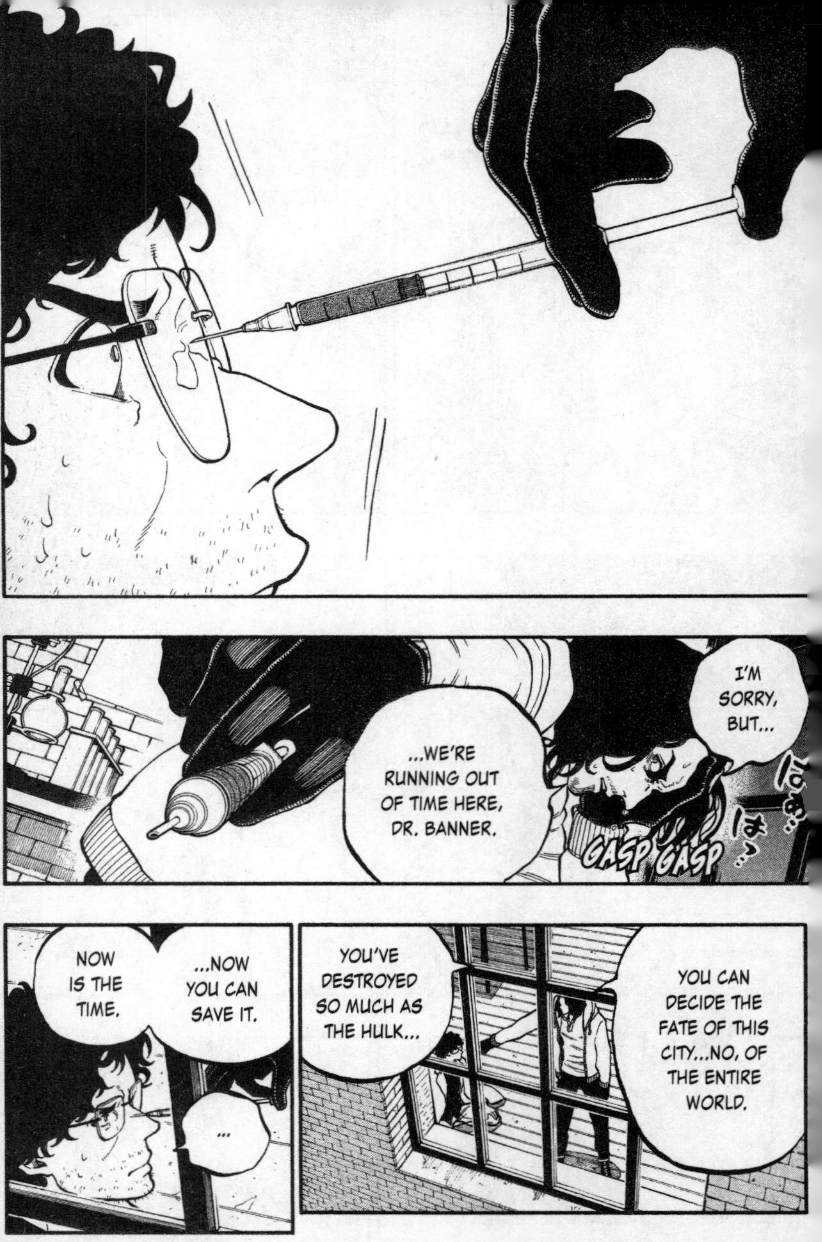
I'M SORRY, BUT...
GASP GASP
...WE'RE RUNNING OUT OF TIME HERE, DR. BANNER.
YOU CAN DECIDE THE FATE OF THIS CITY...NO, OF THE ENTIRE WORLD.
YOU'VE DESTROYED SO MUCH AS THE HULK...
...NOW YOU CAN SAVE IT.
NOW IS THE TIME.
...

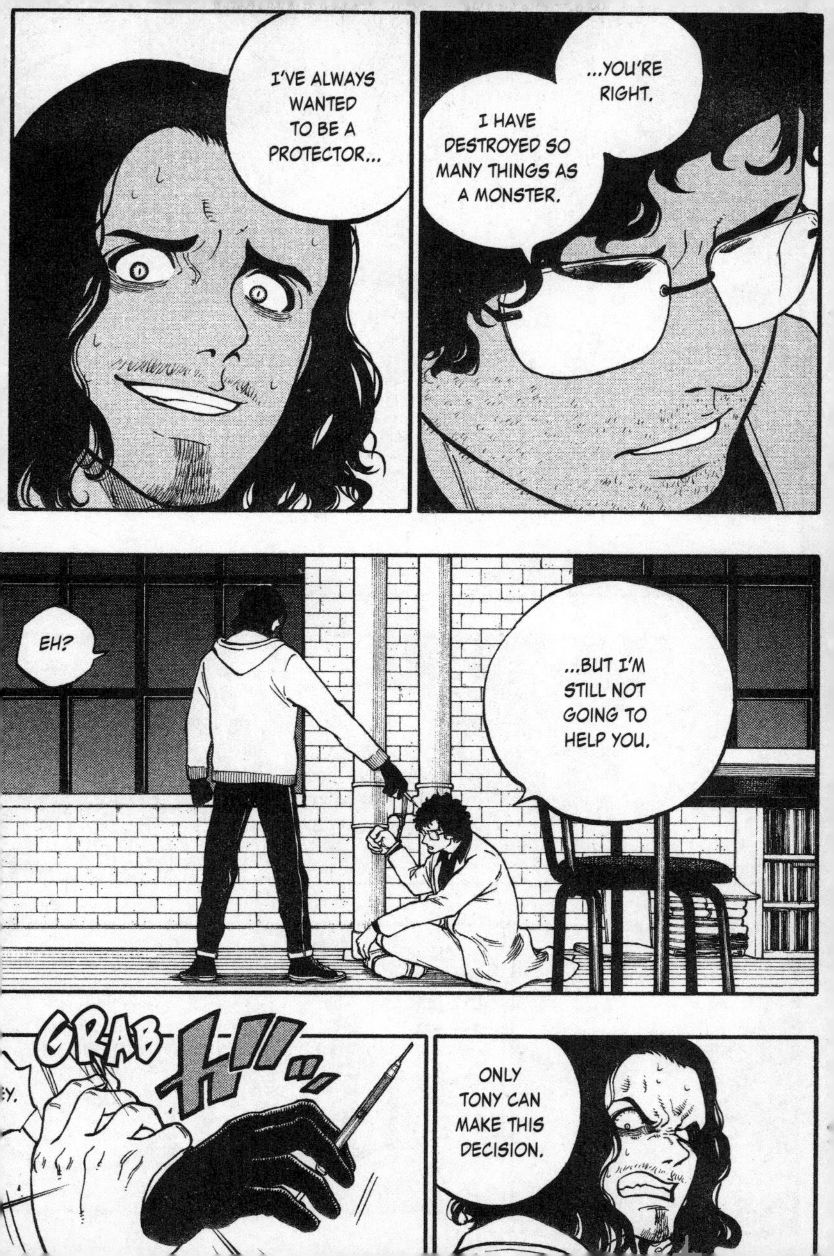
...YOU'RE RIGHT.
I HAVE DESTROYED SO MANY THINGS AS A MONSTER.
I'VE ALWAYS WANTED TO BE A PROTECTOR...
...BUT I'M STILL NOT GOING TO HELP YOU.
EH?
ONLY TONY CAN MAKE THIS DECISION.
GRAB

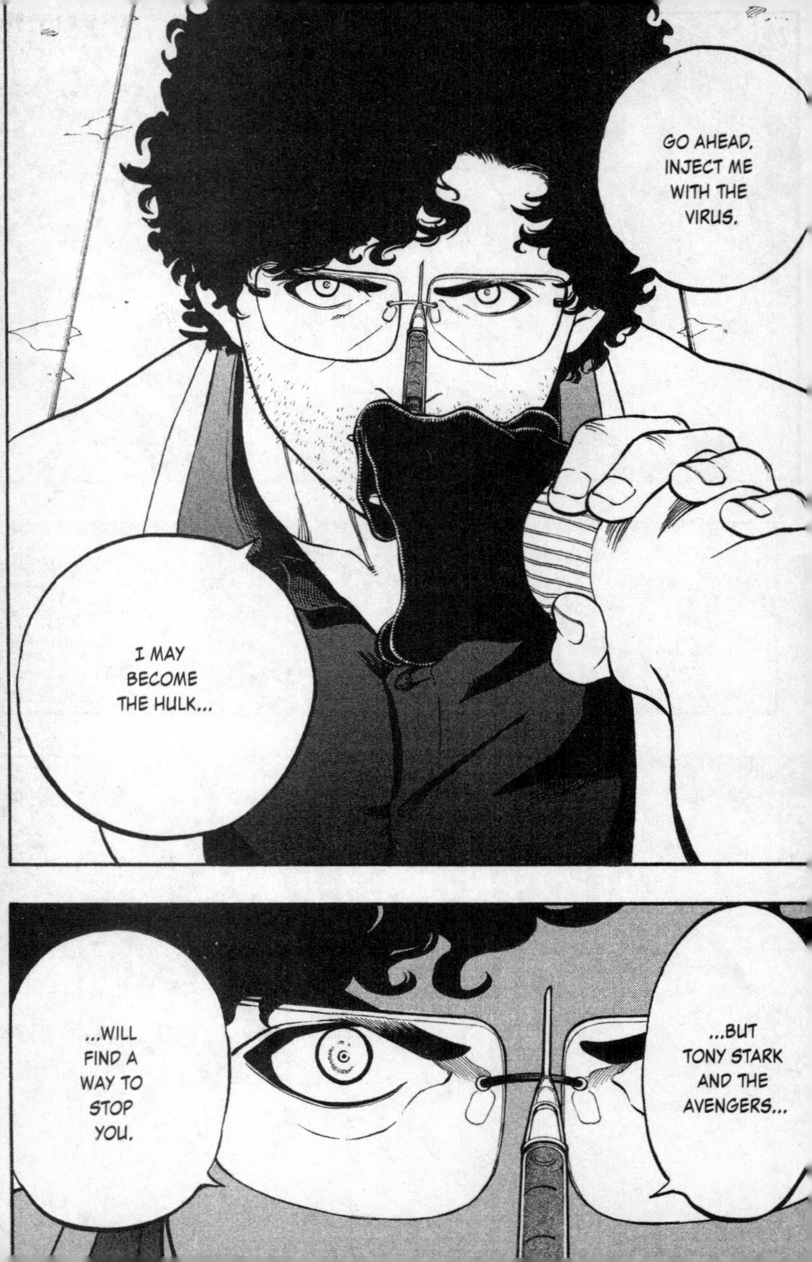
GO AHEAD. INJECT ME WITH THE VIRUS.
I MAY BECOME THE HULK...
...BUT TONY STARK AND THE AVENGERS...
...WILL FIND A WAY TO STOP YOU.

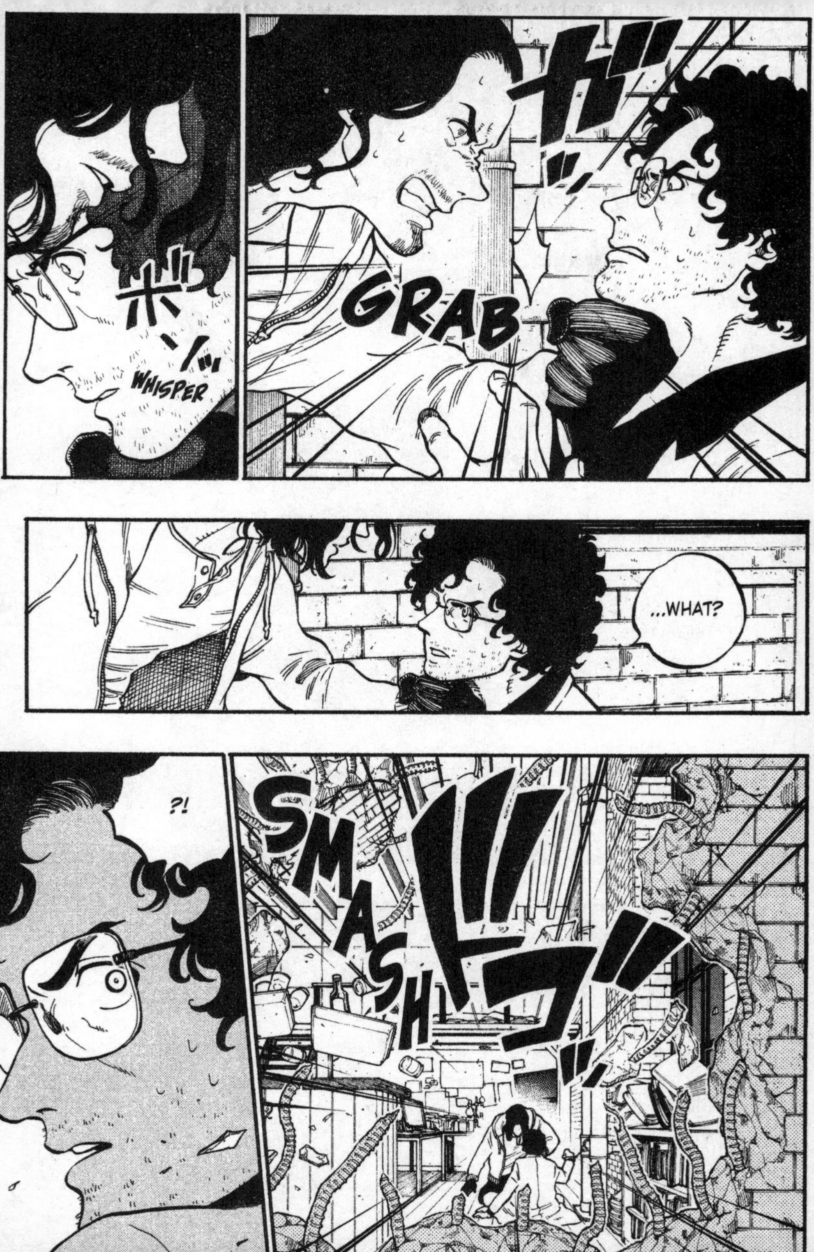
GRAB
WHISPER
...WHAT?
SMASH
?!

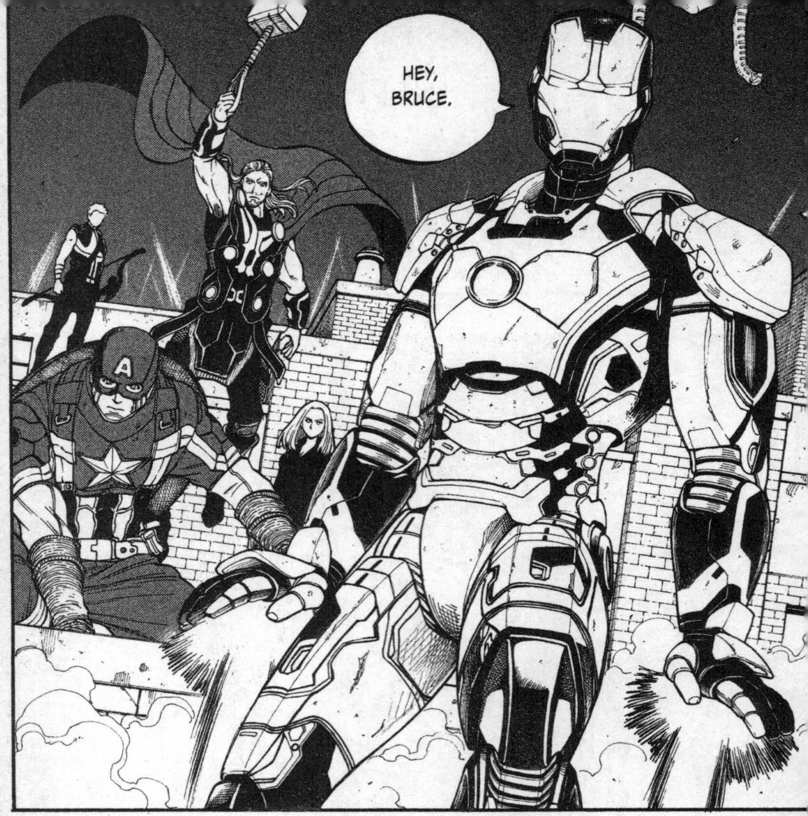
HEY, BRUCE.
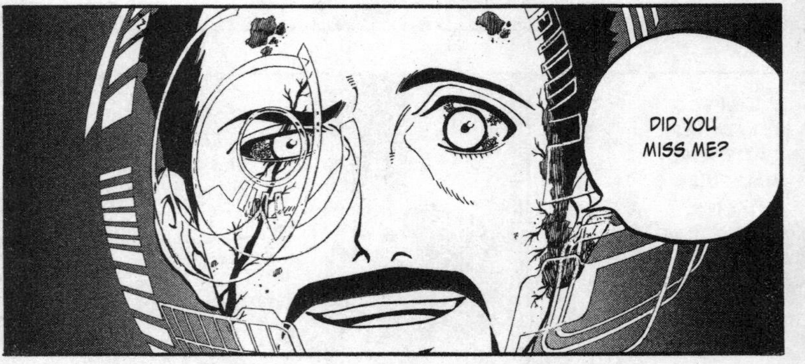
DID YOU MISS ME?

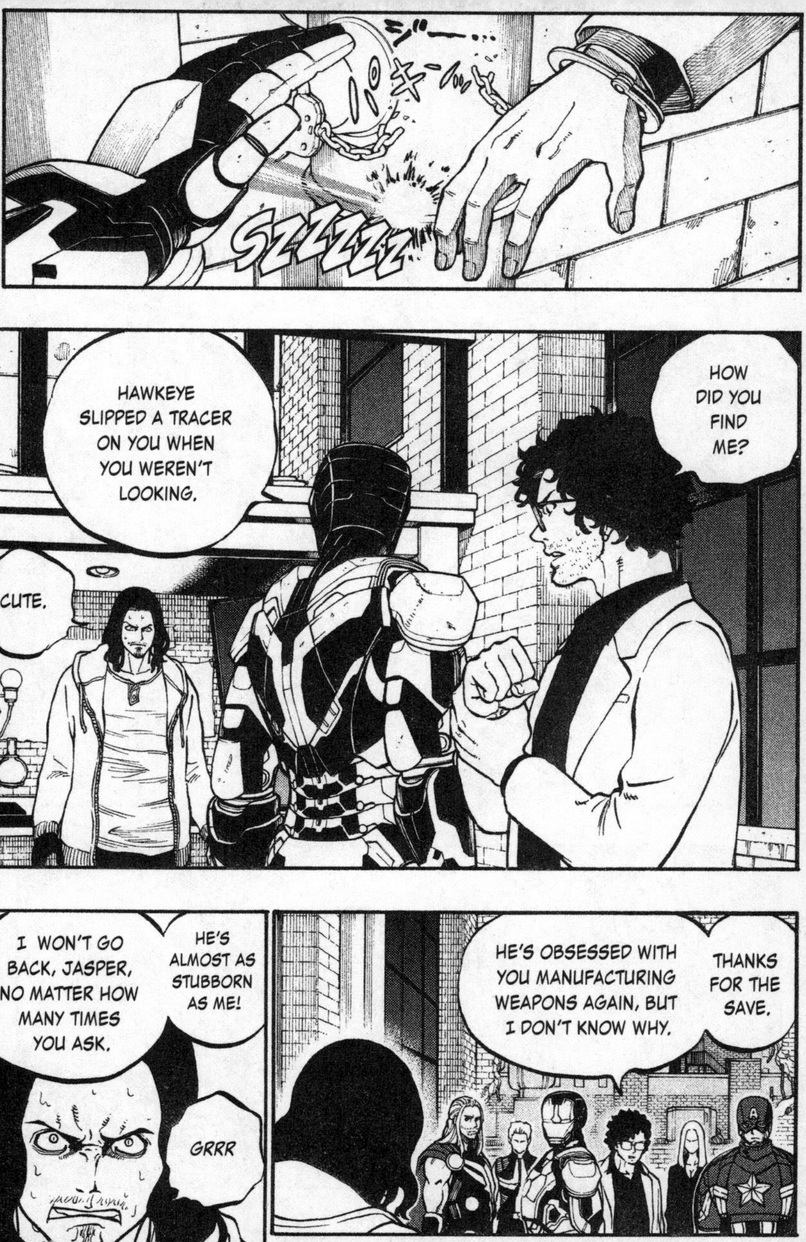
SZZZZZ
HOW DID YOU FIND ME?
HAWKEYE SLIPPED A TRACER ON YOU WHEN YOU WEREN'T LOOKING.
CUTE.
THANKS FOR THE SAVE.
HE'S OBSESSED WITH YOU MANUFACTURING WEAPONS AGAIN, BUT I DON'T KNOW WHY.
HE'S ALMOST AS STUBBORN AS ME!
I WON'T GO BACK, JASPER, NO MATTER HOW MANY TIMES YOU ASK.
GRRR

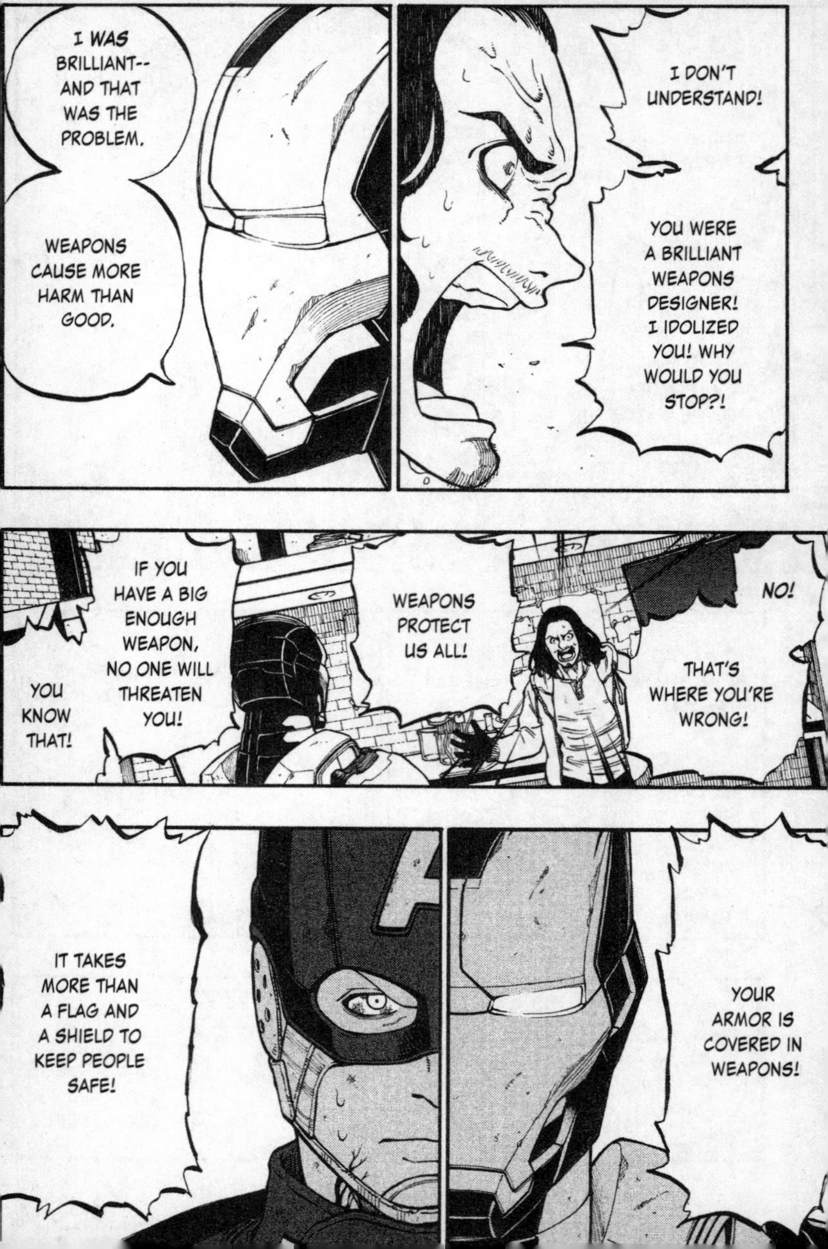
I DON'T UNDERSTAND!
YOU WERE A BRILLIANT WEAPONS DESIGNER! I IDOLIZED YOU! WHY WOULD YOU STOP?!
I WAS BRILLIANT-- AND THAT WAS THE PROBLEM.
WEAPONS CAUSE MORE HARM THAN GOOD.
NO!
THAT'S WHERE YOU'RE WRONG!
WEAPONS PROTECT US ALL!
IF YOU HAVE A BIG ENOUGH WEAPON, NO ONE WILL THREATEN YOU!
YOU KNOW THAT!
YOUR ARMOR IS COVERED IN WEAPONS!
IT TAKES MORE THAN A FLAG AND A SHIELD TO KEEP PEOPLE SAFE!

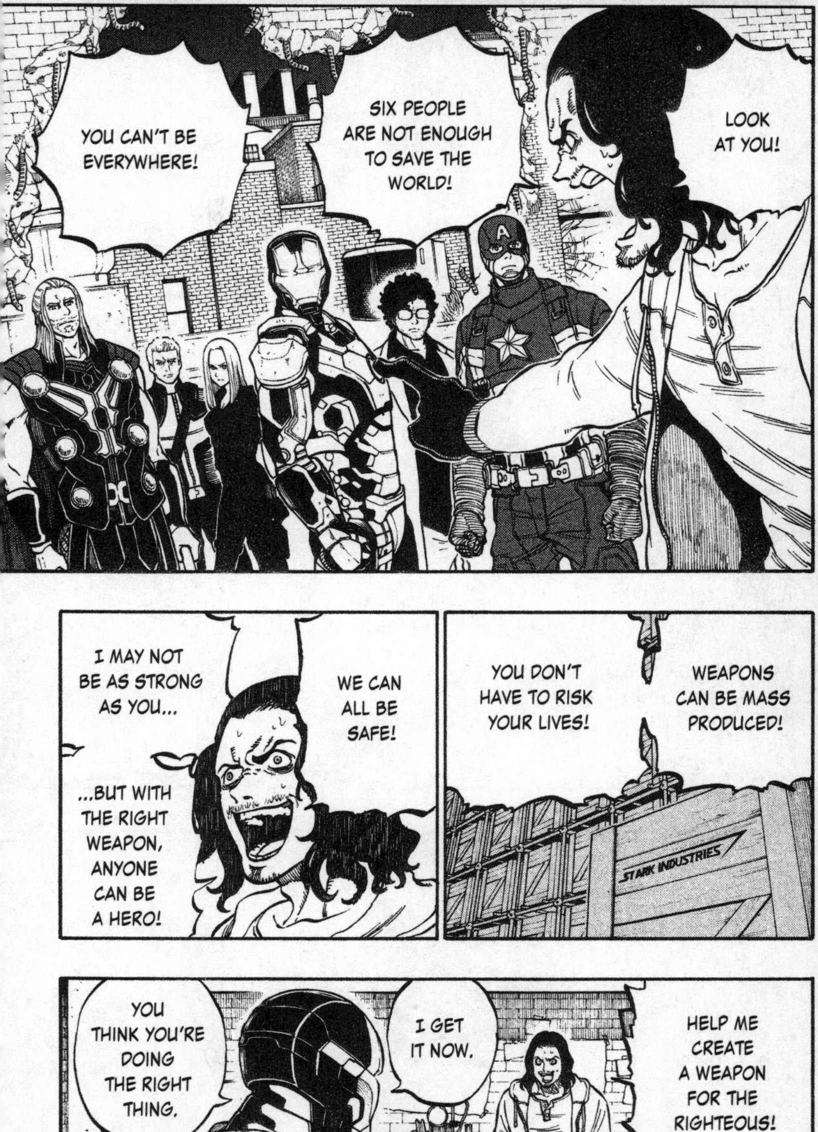
LOOK AT YOU!
SIX PEOPLE ARE NOT ENOUGH TO SAVE THE WORLD!
YOU CAN'T BE EVERYWHERE!
WEAPONS CAN BE MASS PRODUCED!
YOU DON'T HAVE TO RISK YOUR LIVES!
STARK INDUSTRIES
WE CAN ALL BE SAFE!
I MAY NOT BE AS STRONG AS YOU...
...BUT WITH THE RIGHT WEAPON, ANYONE CAN BE A HERO!
HELP ME CREATE A WEAPON FOR THE RIGHTEOUS!
I GET IT NOW.
YOU THINK YOU'RE DOING THE RIGHT THING.

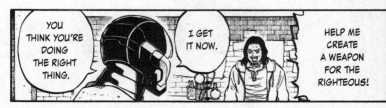

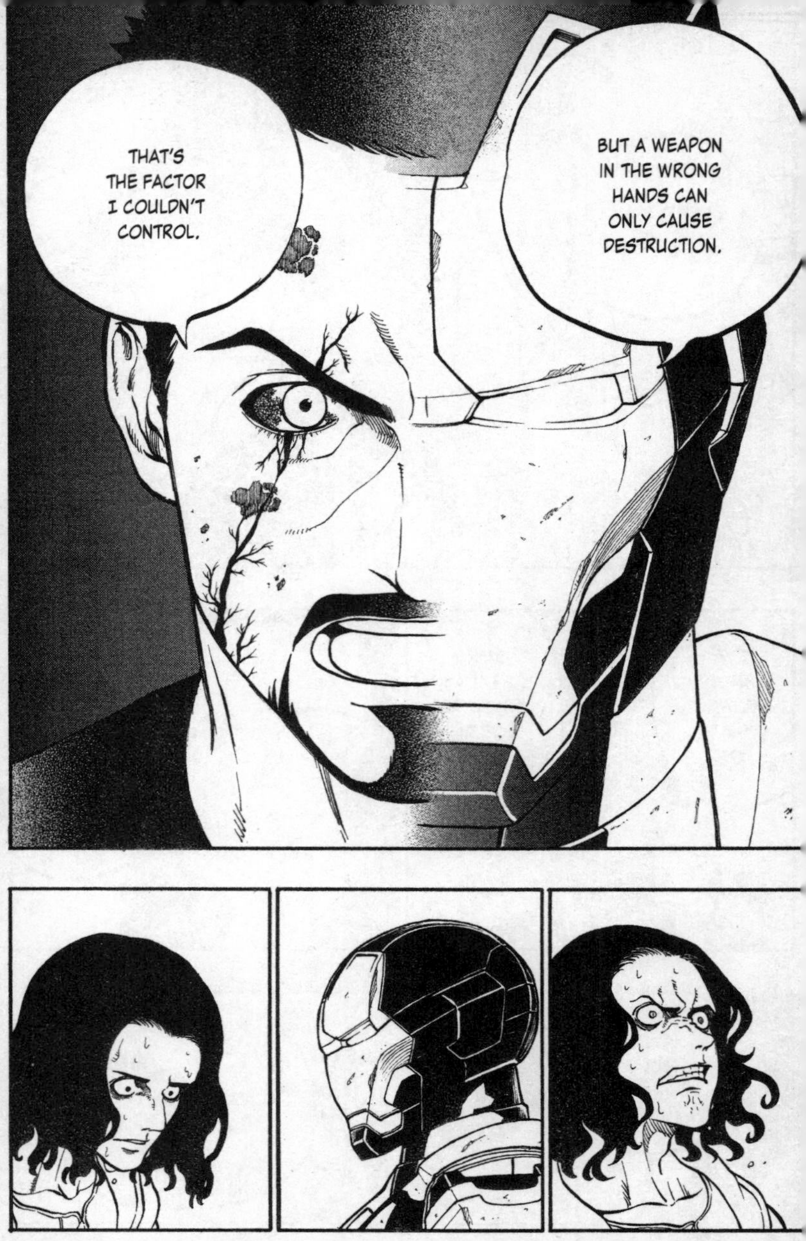
BUT A WEAPON IN THE WRONG HANDS CAN ONLY CAUSE DESTRUCTION.
THAT'S THE FACTOR I COULDN'T CONTROL.

SUCH A SILLY MISTAKE.

I KNEW THAT.

YES...

...THAT'S TRUE, OF COURSE.

I'VE BEEN DOWN THAT ROAD.

BEING SMART AND CONFIDENT DOESN'T MAKE YOU RIGHT.

I'M SORRY, TONY.

I MISJUDGED YOU.

I...I CAN'T DO THAT.

SO...

...IF YOU REALLY UNDERSTAND, HELP US FIX THIS.

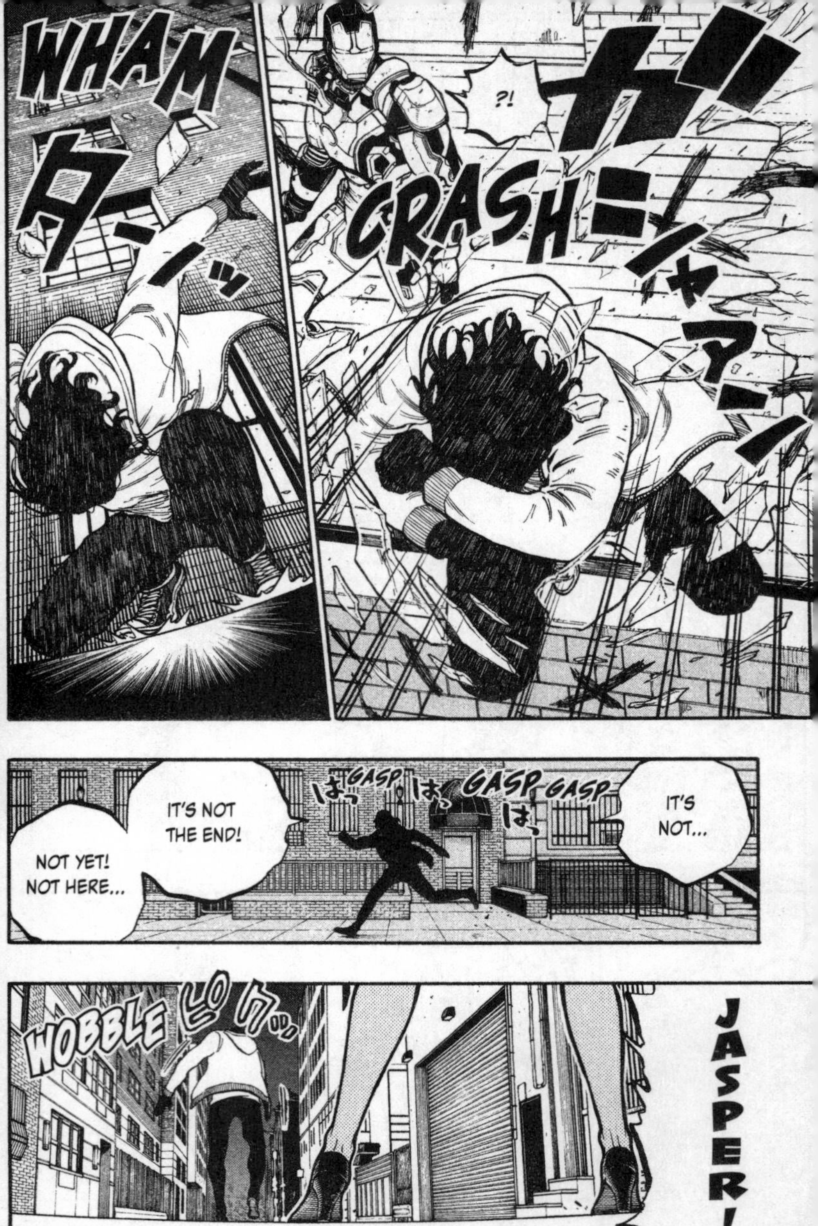
?!
CRASH
WHAM
IT'S NOT...
GASP GASP GASP
IT'S NOT THE END!
NOT YET! NOT HERE...
JASPER!
WOBBLE

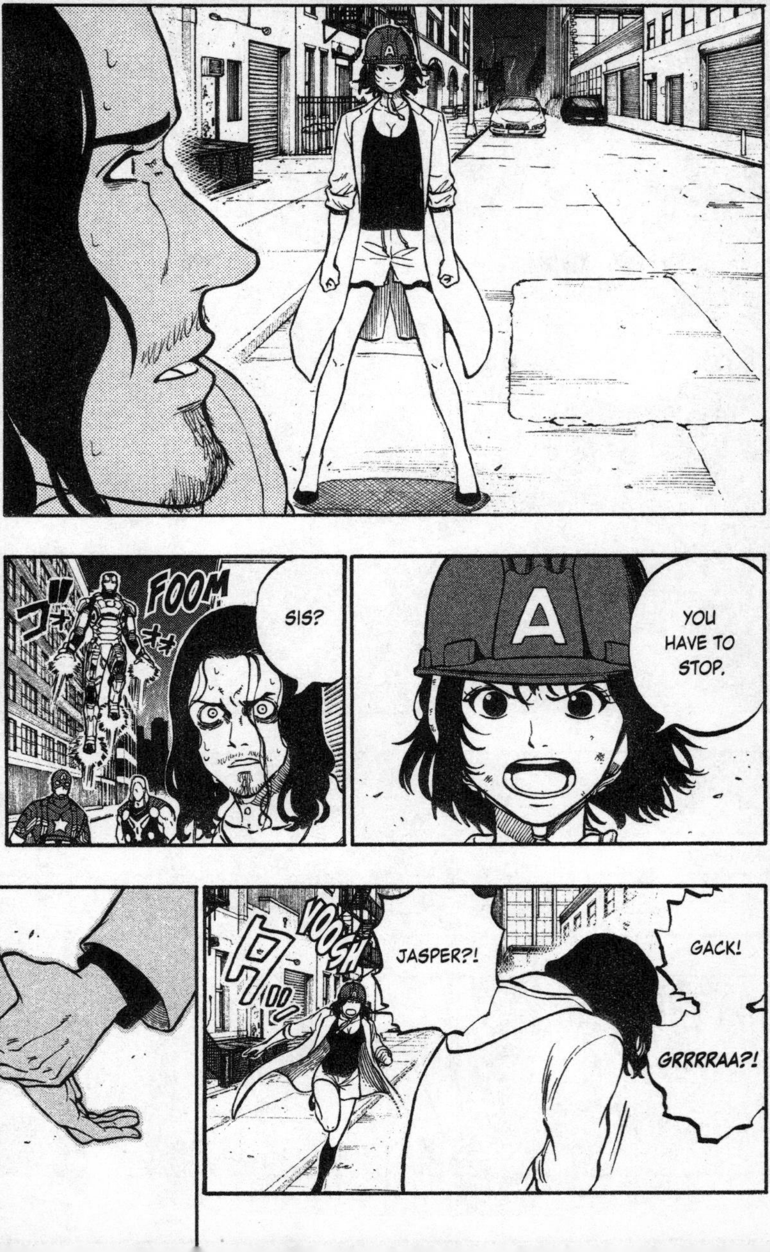
YOU HAVE TO STOP.
SIS?
FOOM
GACK!
JASPER?!
VOOSH
GRRRAA?!

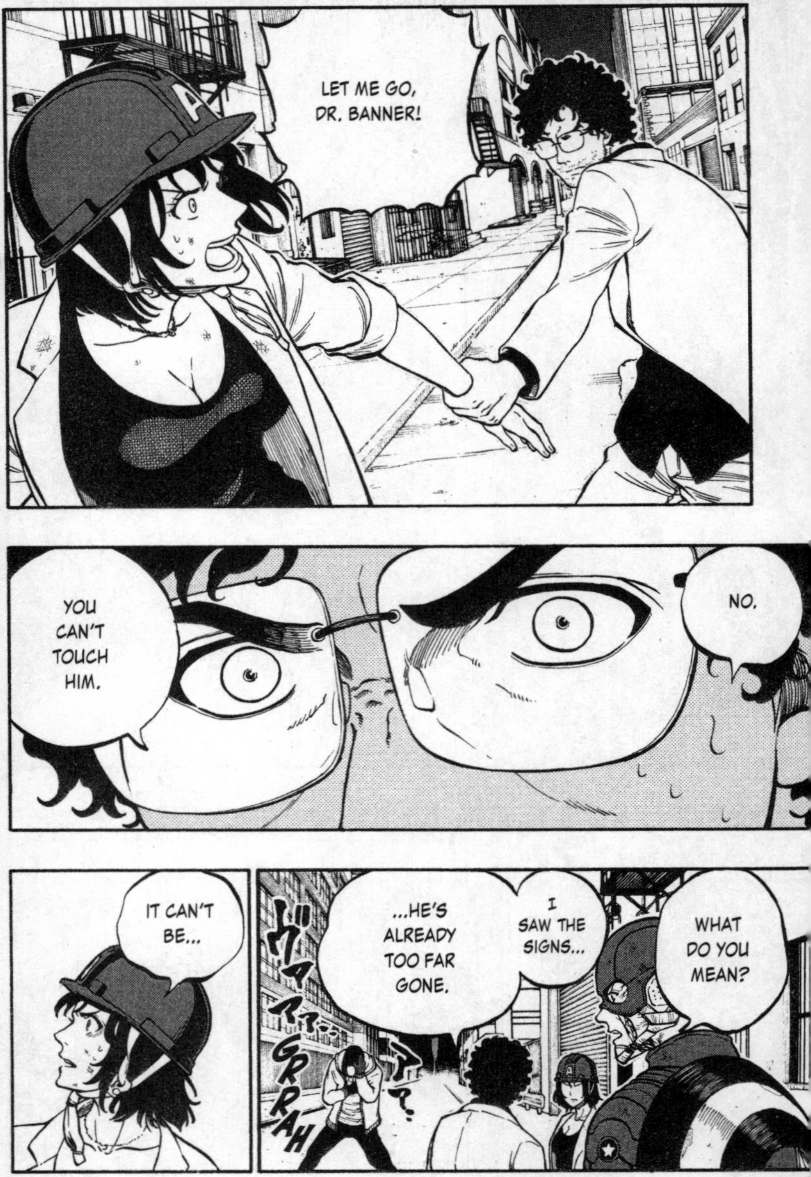
LET ME GO, DR. BANNER!
NO.
YOU CAN'T TOUCH HIM.
WHAT DO YOU MEAN?
I SAW THE SIGNS...
...HE'S ALREADY TOO FAR GONE.
GRRAH
?
IT CAN'T BE...

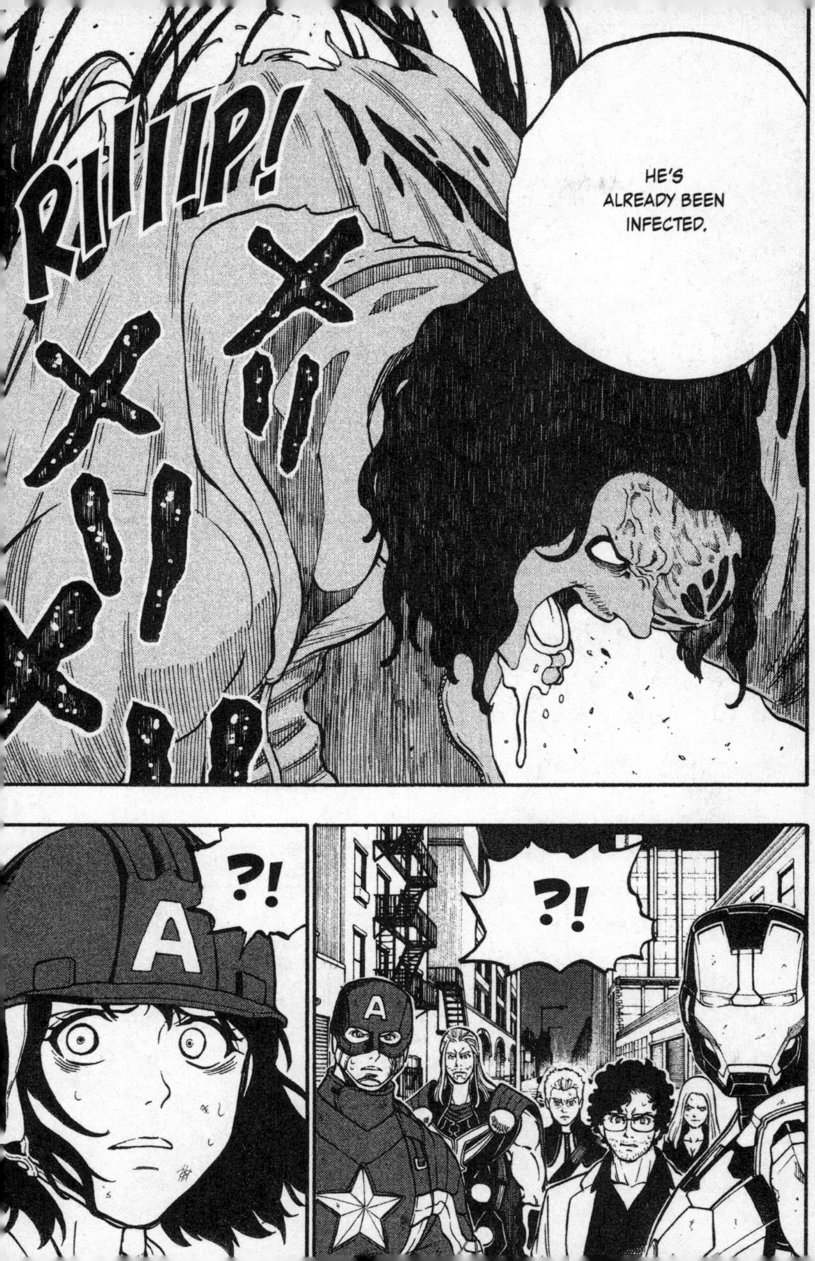
HE'S ALREADY BEEN INFECTED.
RIIIP!
?!
?!

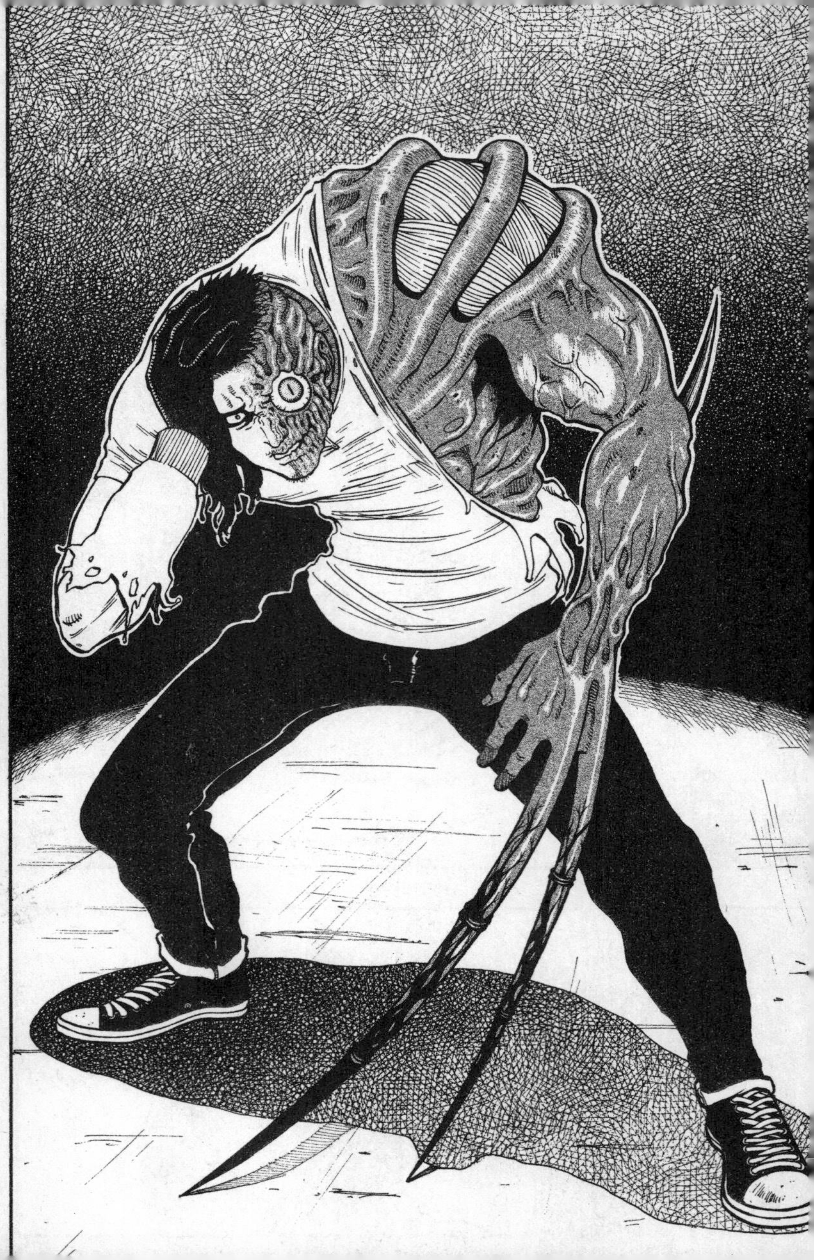

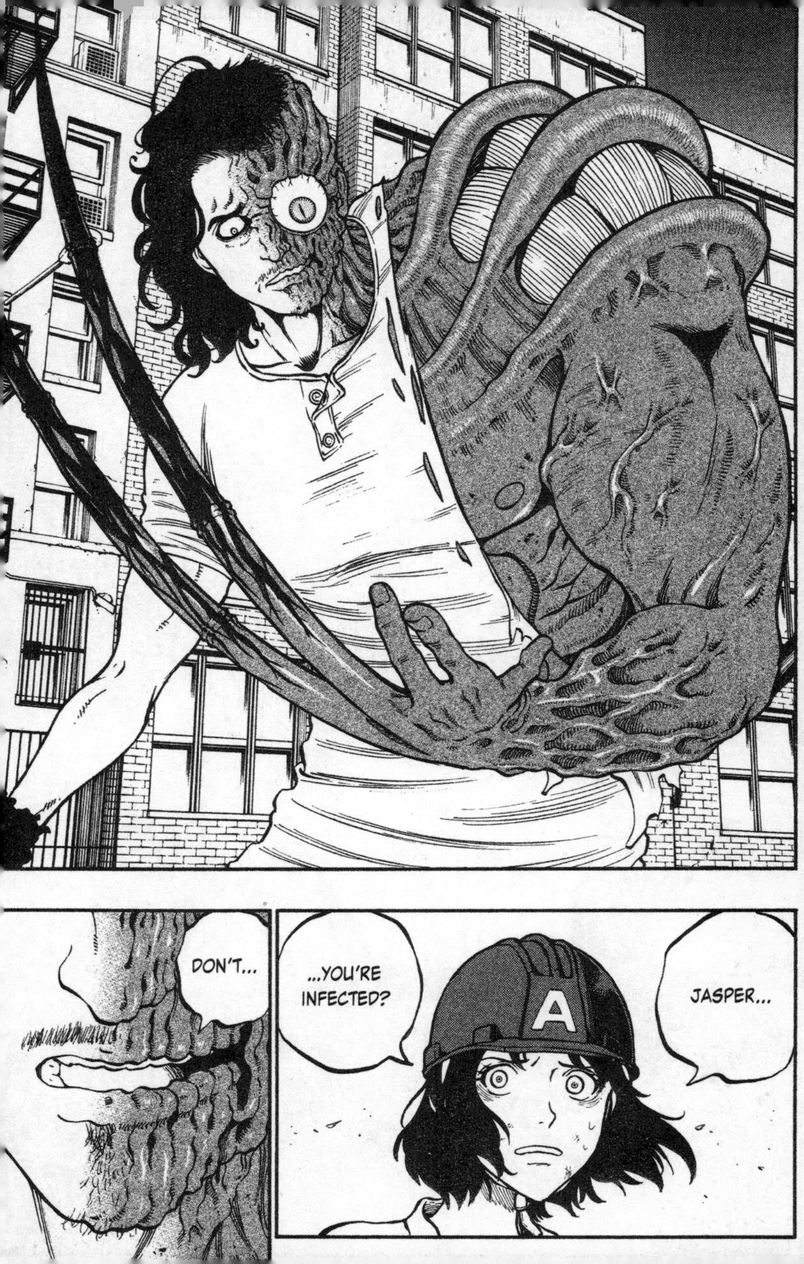
JASPER...
...YOU'RE INFECTED?
DON'T...

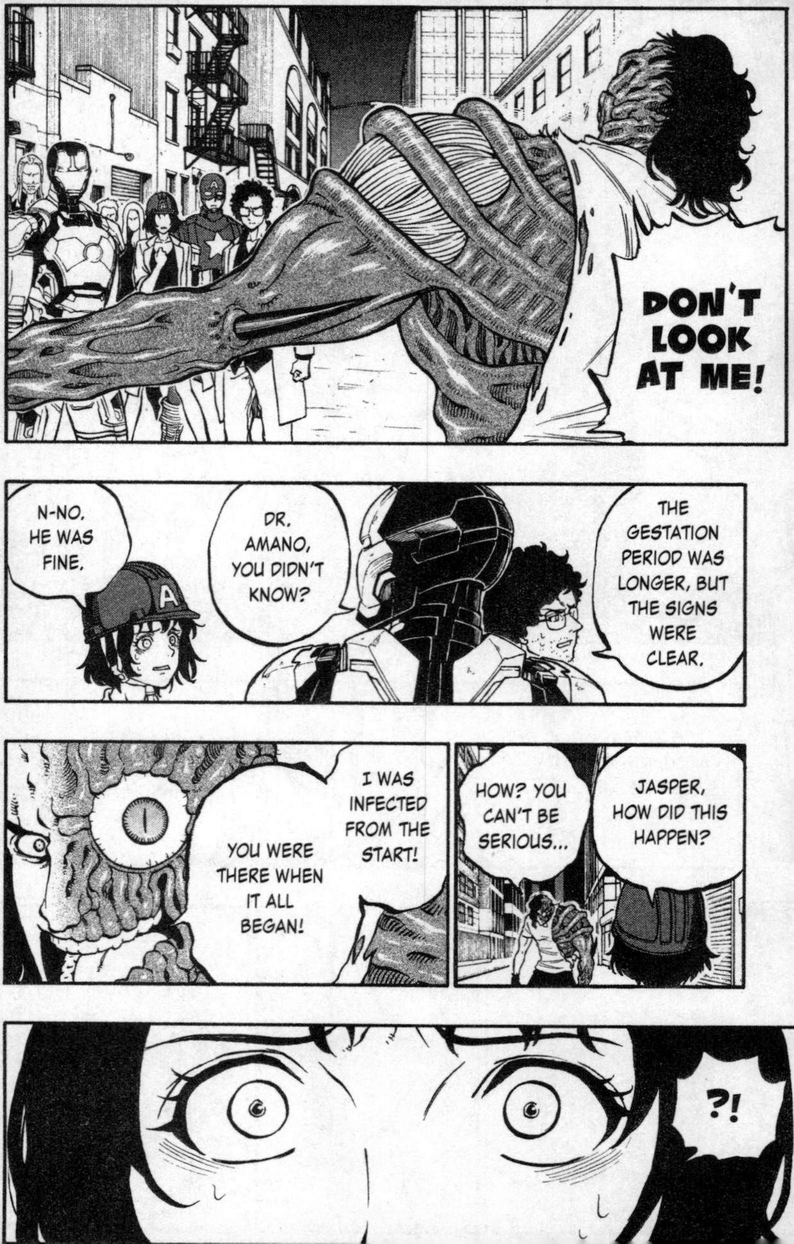
DON'T LOOK AT ME!
THE GESTATION PERIOD WAS LONGER, BUT THE SIGNS WERE CLEAR.
DR. AMANO, YOU DIDN'T KNOW?
N-NO. HE WAS FINE.
JASPER, HOW DID THIS HAPPEN?
HOW? YOU CAN'T BE SERIOUS...
I WAS INFECTED FROM THE START!
YOU WERE THERE WHEN IT ALL BEGAN!
?!

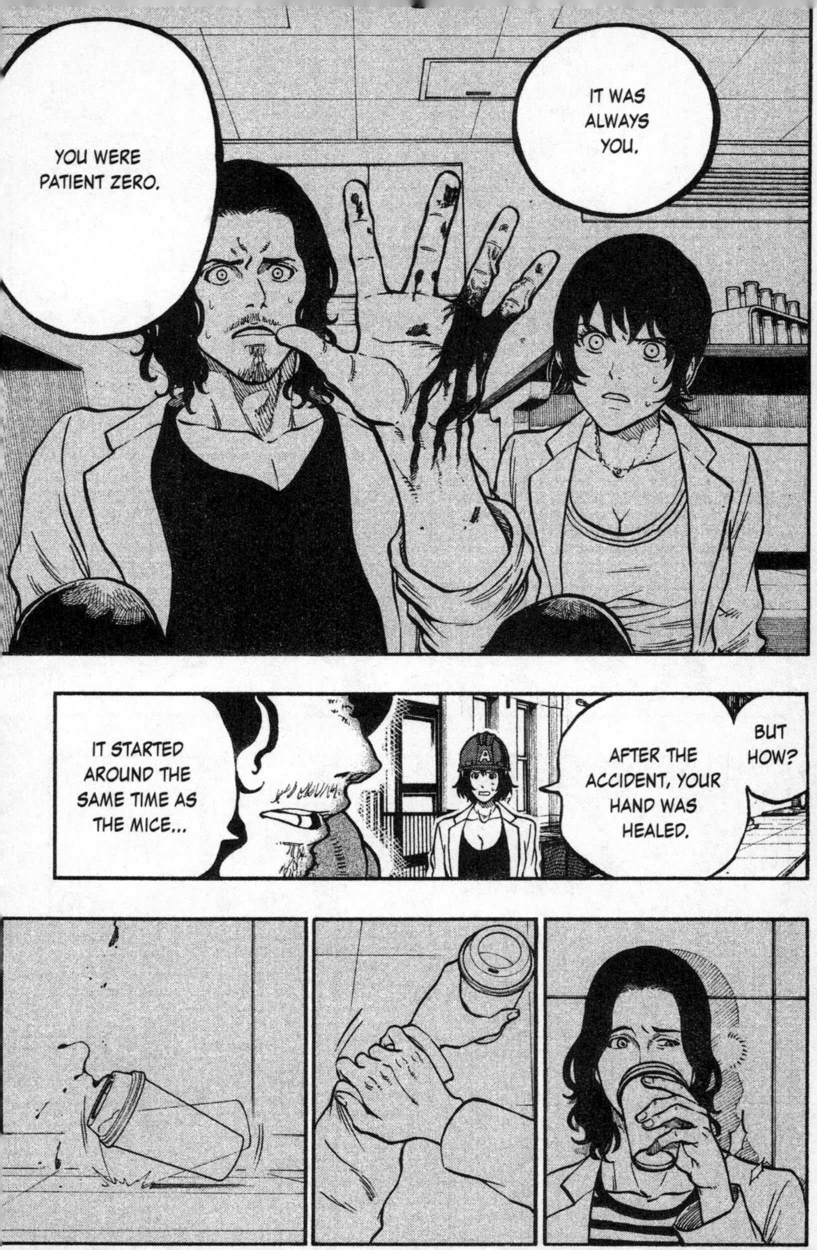
IT WAS ALWAYS YOU.
YOU WERE PATIENT ZERO.
BUT HOW?
AFTER THE ACCIDENT, YOUR HAND WAS HEALED.
IT STARTED AROUND THE SAME TIME AS THE MICE...

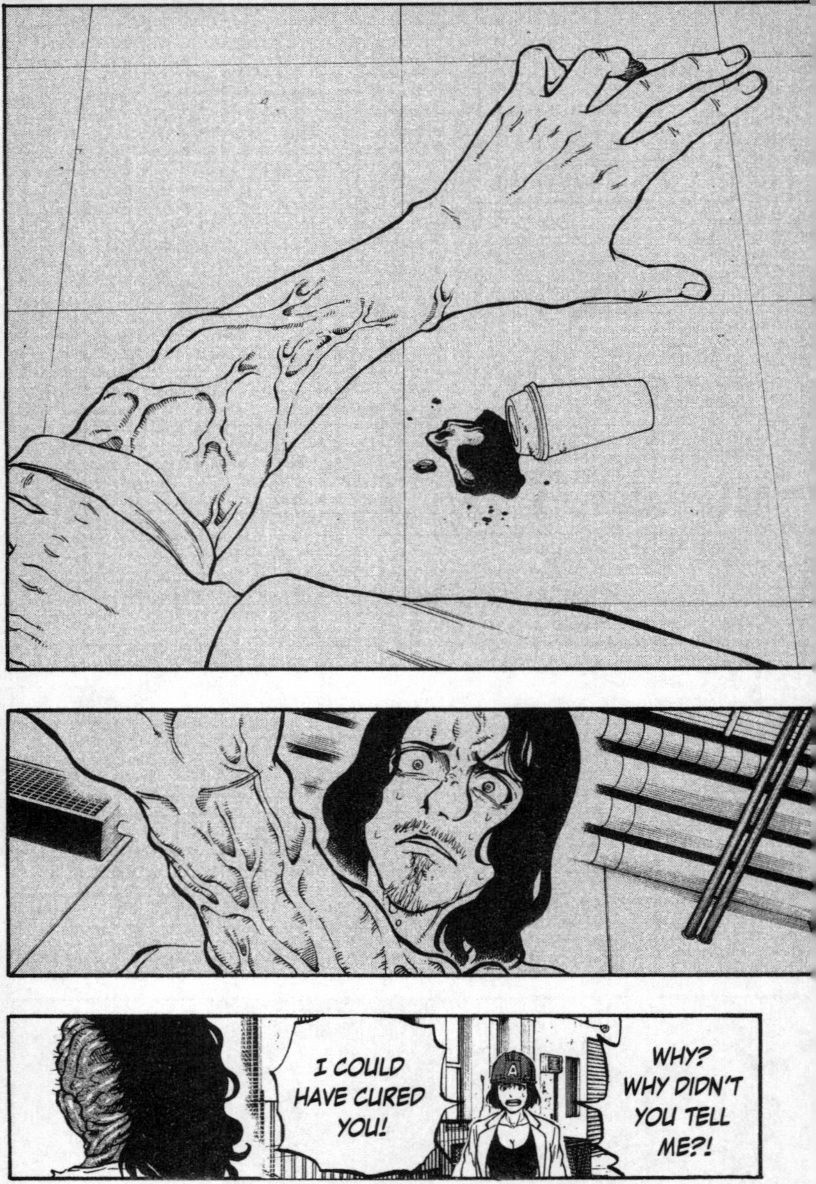
WHY? WHY DIDN'T YOU TELL ME?!
I COULD HAVE CURED YOU!

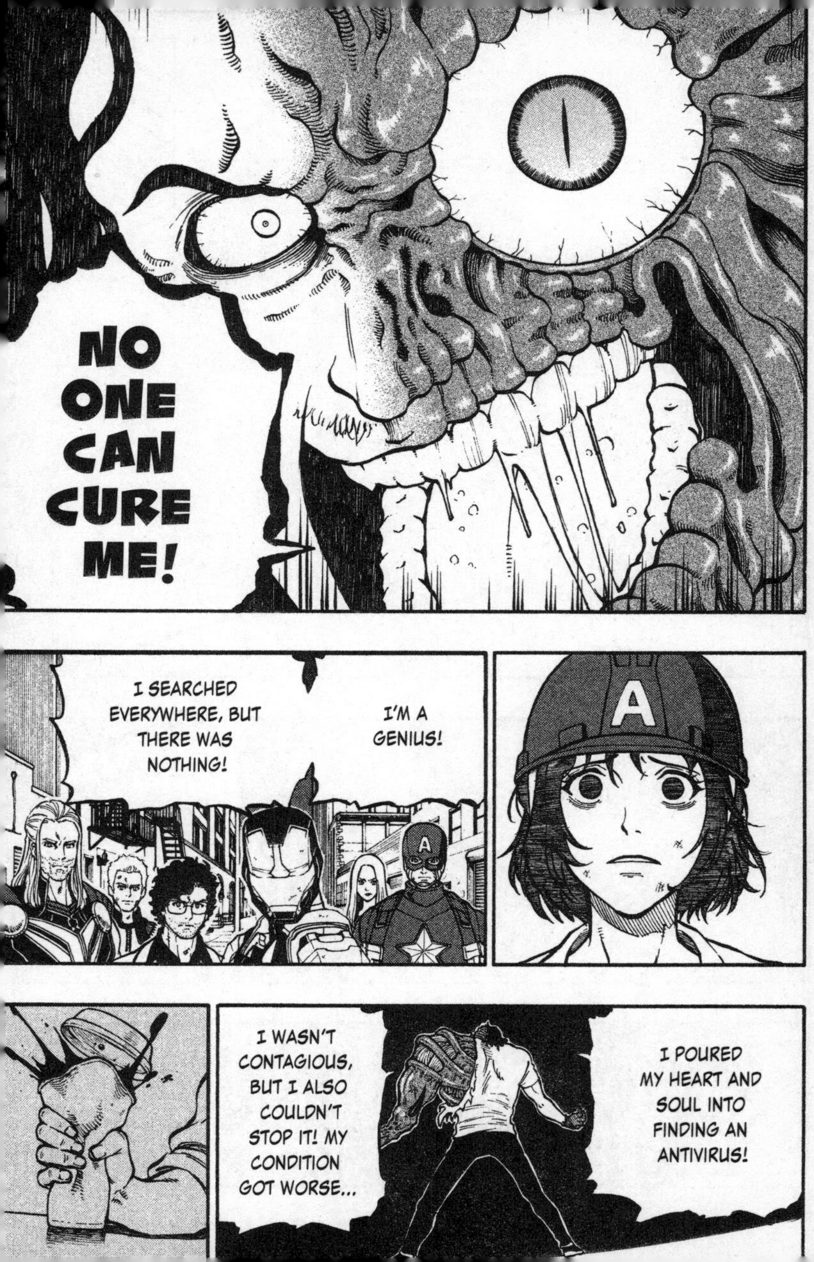
NO ONE CAN CURE ME!
I'M A GENIUS!
I SEARCHED EVERYWHERE, BUT THERE WAS NOTHING!
I POURED MY HEART AND SOUL INTO FINDING AN ANTIVIRUS!
I WASN'T CONTAGIOUS, BUT I ALSO COULDN'T STOP IT! MY CONDITION GOT WORSE...

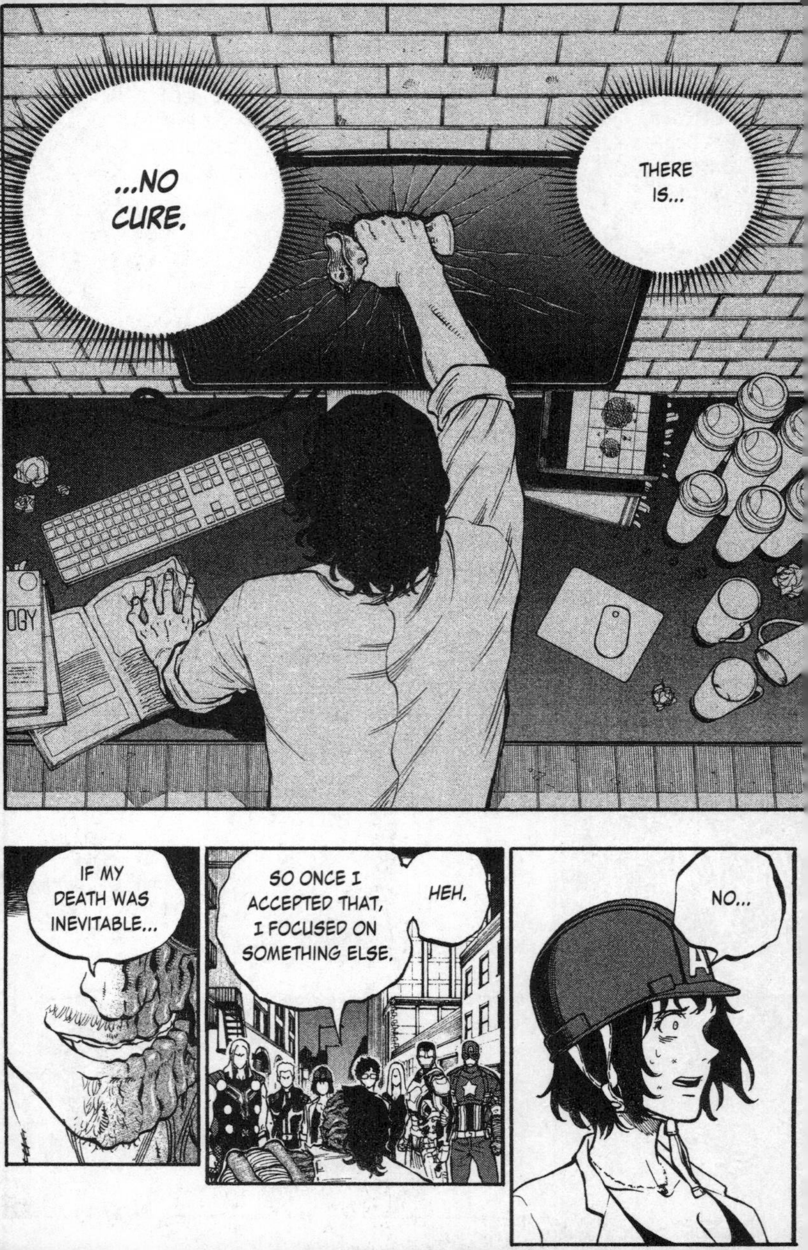
THERE IS...
...NO CURE.
OGY
NO...
HEH.
SO ONCE I ACCEPTED THAT, I FOCUSED ON SOMETHING ELSE.
IF MY DEATH WAS INEVITABLE...

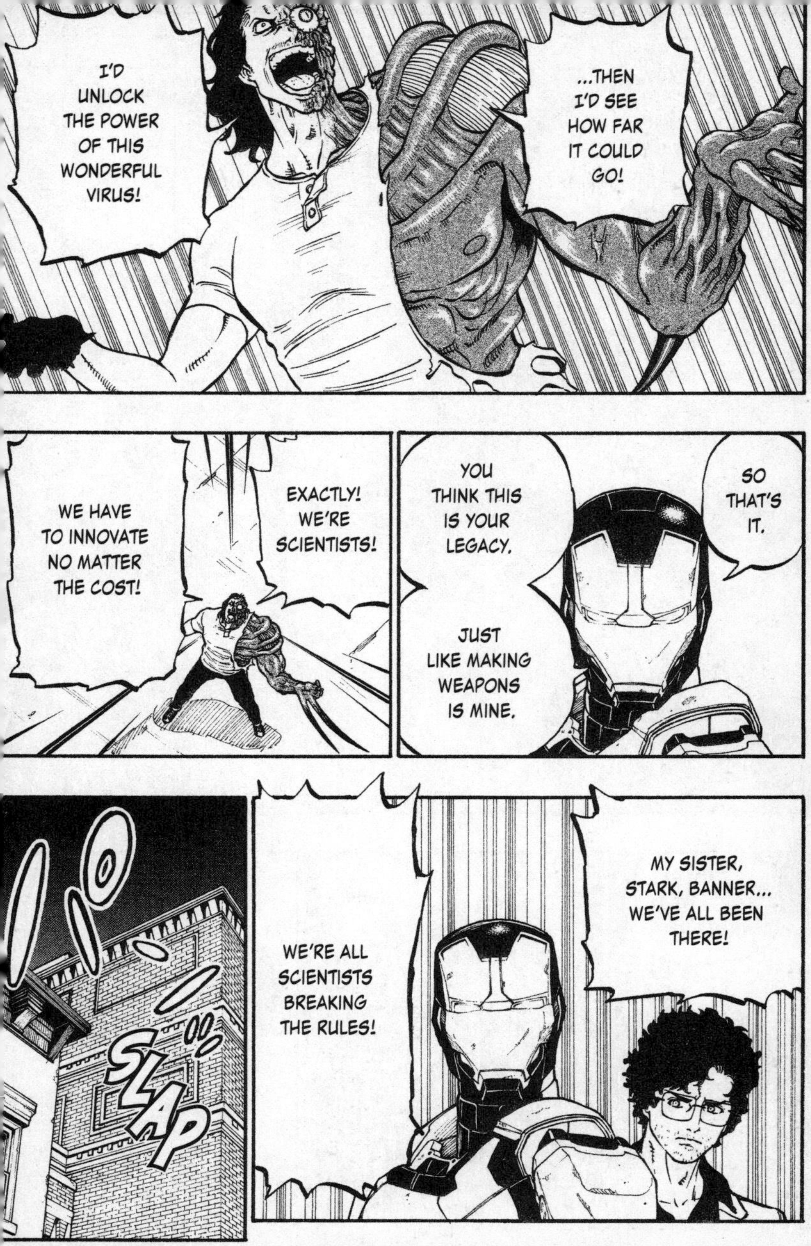
...THEN I'D SEE HOW FAR IT COULD GO!
I'D UNLOCK THE POWER OF THIS WONDERFUL VIRUS!
SO THAT'S IT.
YOU THINK THIS IS YOUR LEGACY.
JUST LIKE MAKING WEAPONS IS MINE.
EXACTLY! WE'RE SCIENTISTS!
WE HAVE TO INNOVATE NO MATTER THE COST!
MY SISTER, STARK, BANNER... WE'VE ALL BEEN THERE!
WE'RE ALL SCIENTISTS BREAKING THE RULES!
SLAP

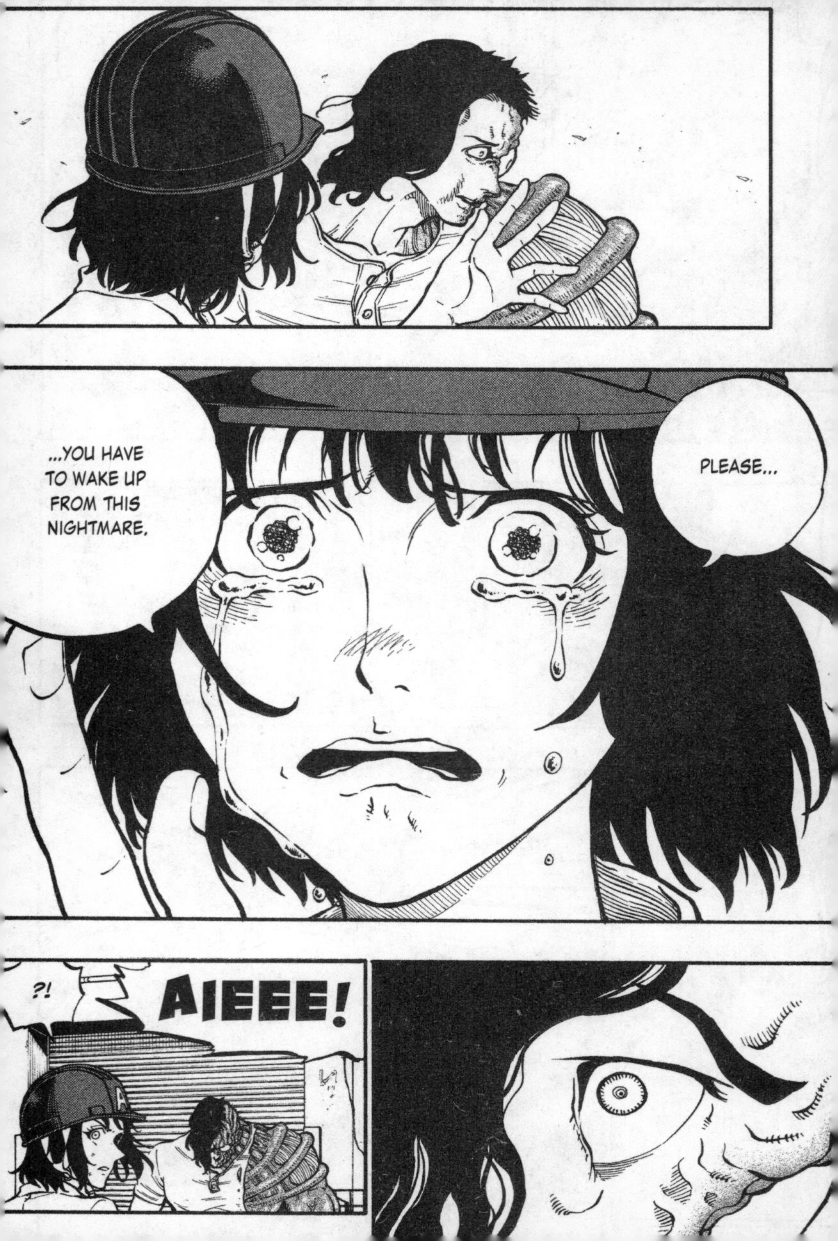
PLEASE...
...YOU HAVE TO WAKE UP FROM THIS NIGHTMARE.
AIEEE!
?!

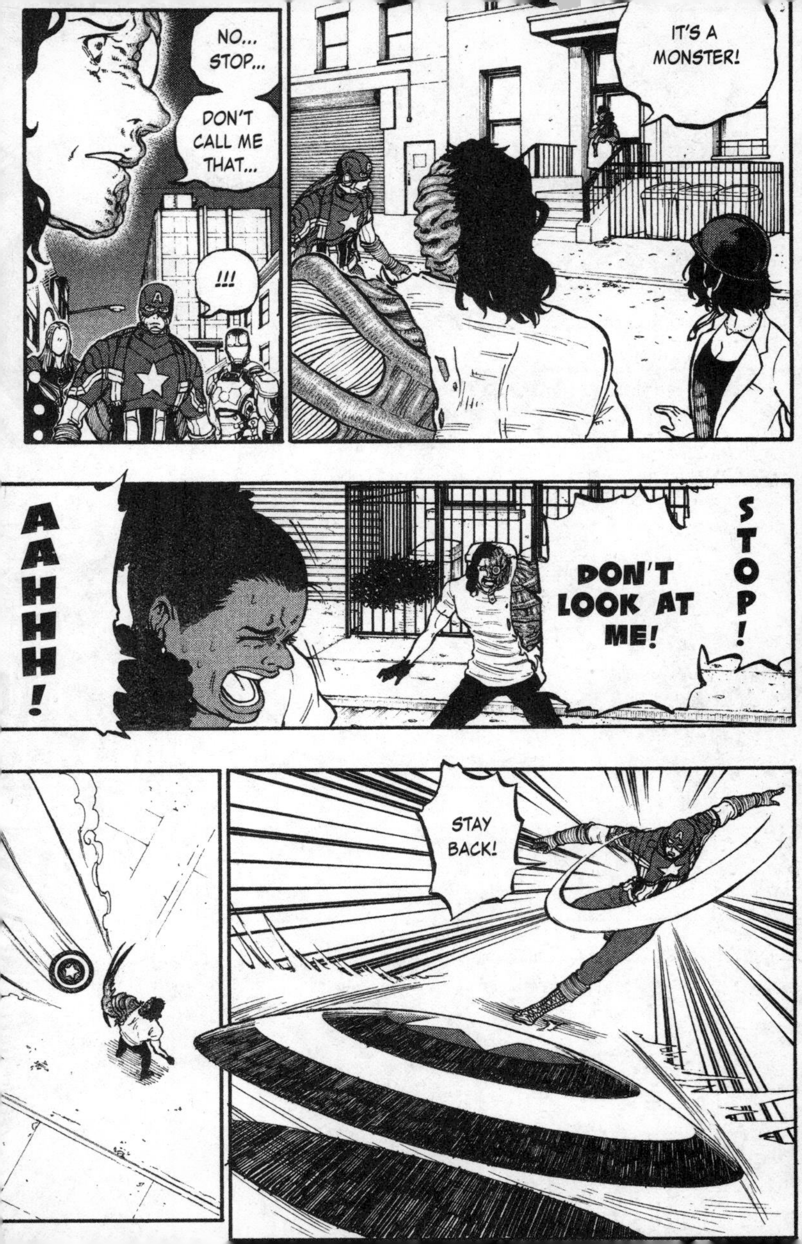
IT'S A MONSTER!
NO... STOP...
DON'T CALL ME THAT...
!!!
STOP!
DON'T LOOK AT ME!
AAHHH!
STAY BACK!

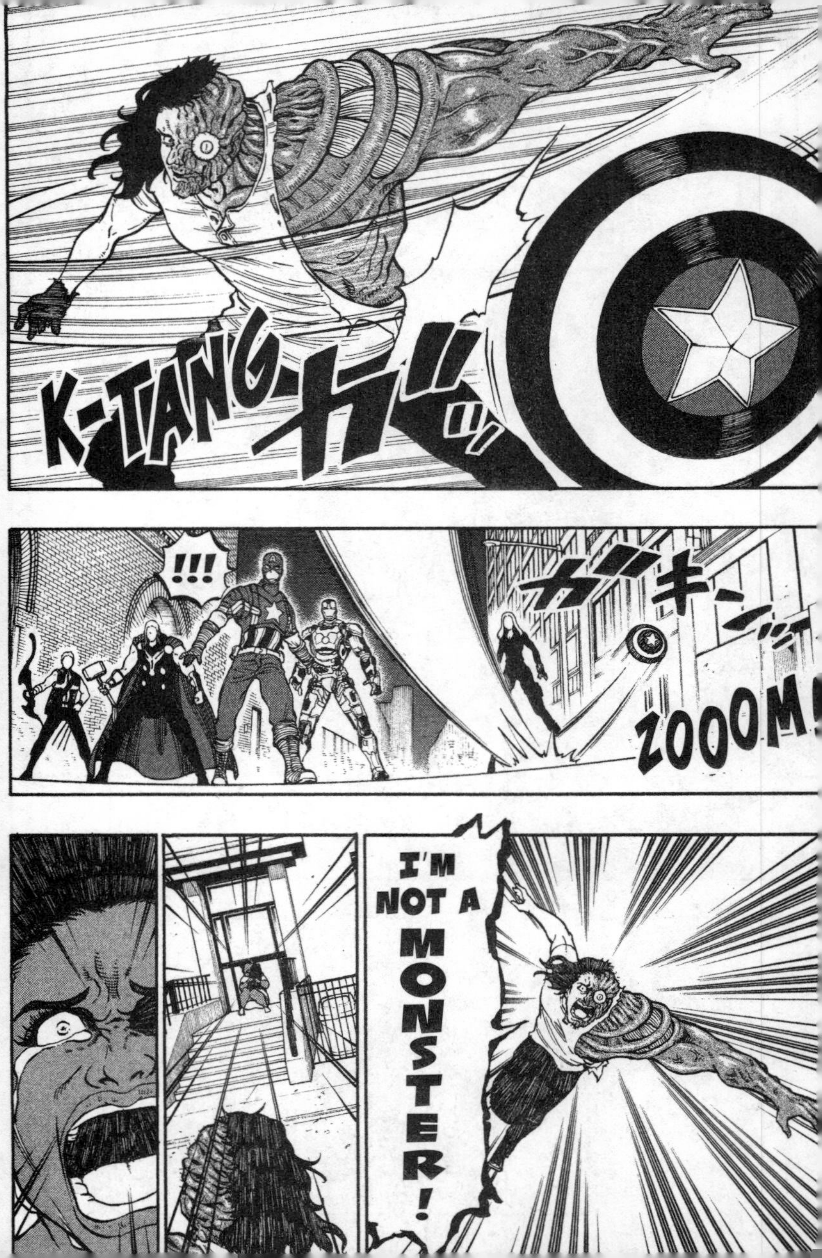
K-TANG
ZOOOM
!!!
I'M NOT A MONSTER!

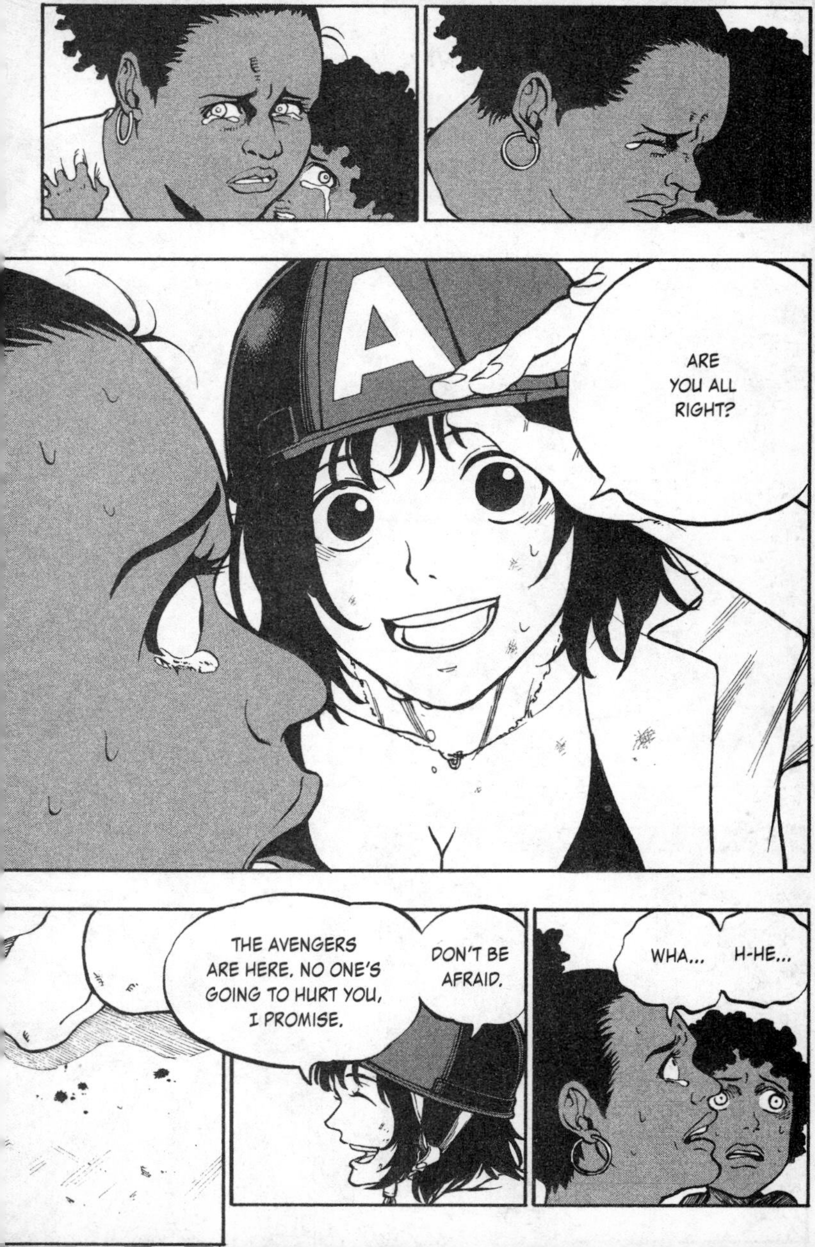
ARE YOU ALL RIGHT?
WHA... H-HE...
DON'T BE AFRAID.
THE AVENGERS ARE HERE. NO ONE'S GOING TO HURT YOU, I PROMISE.

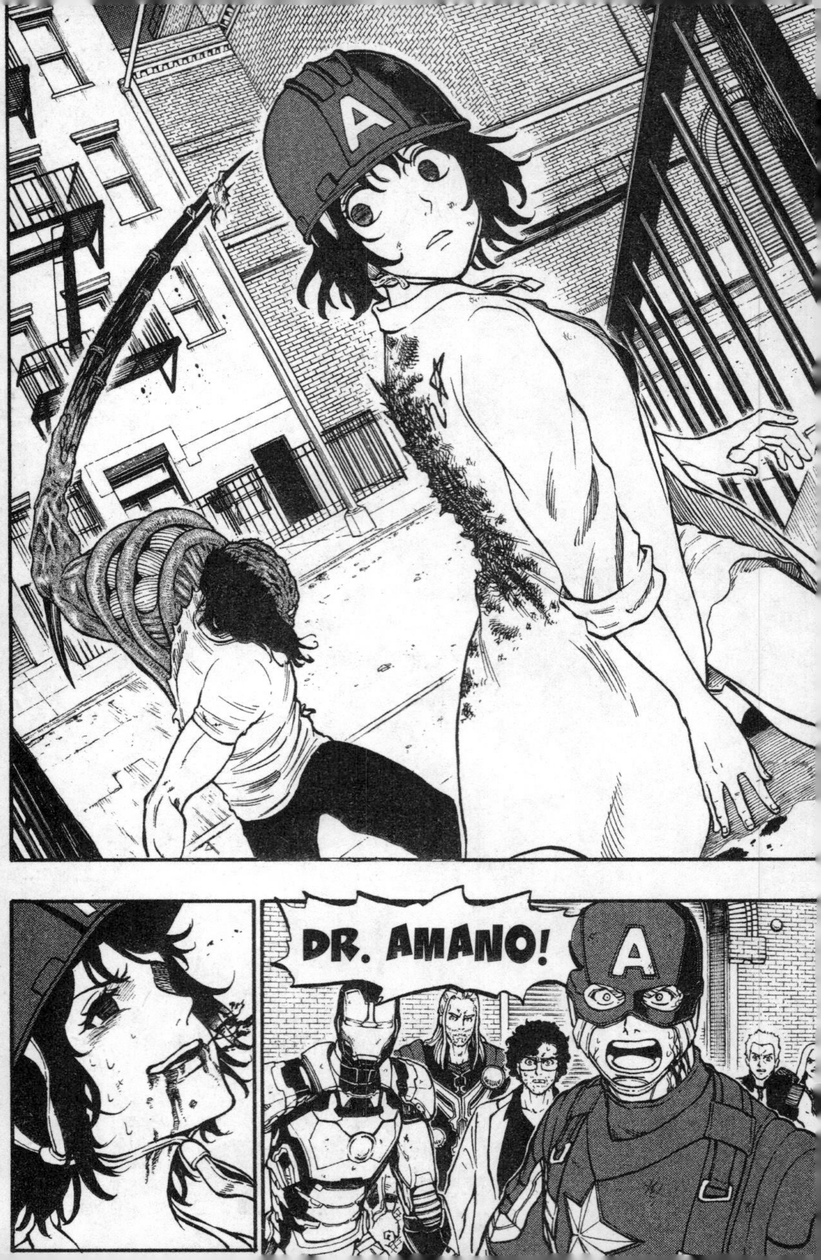
DR. AMANO!

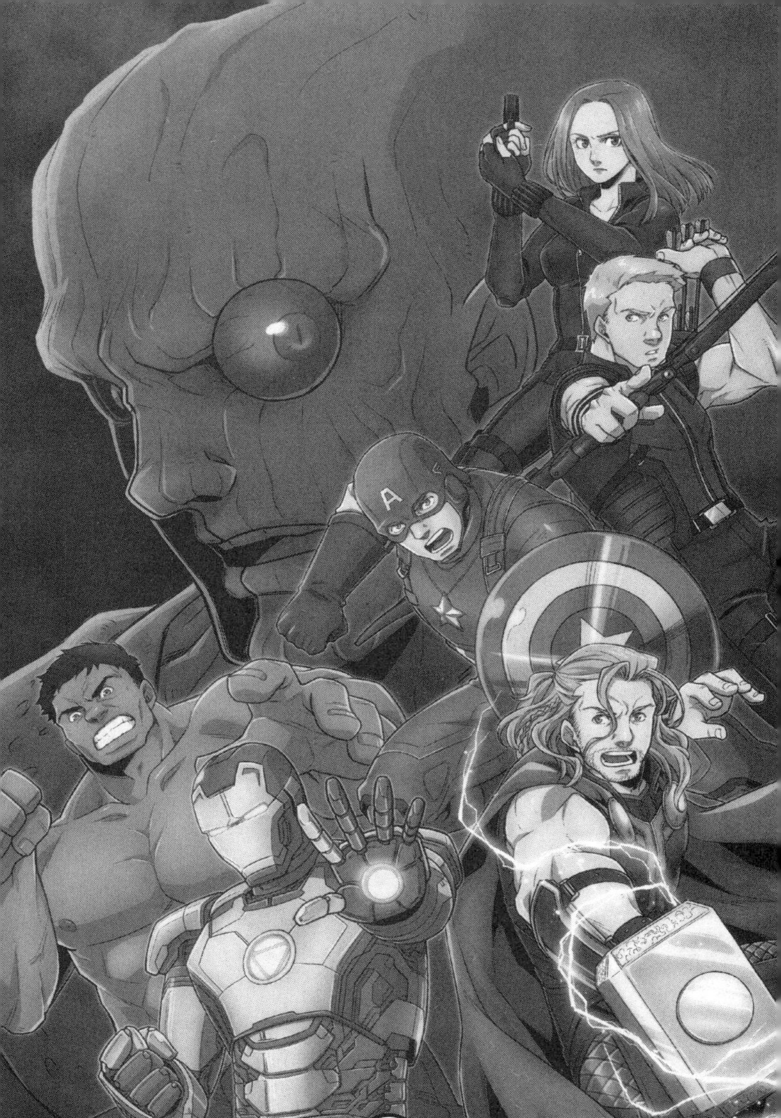

4

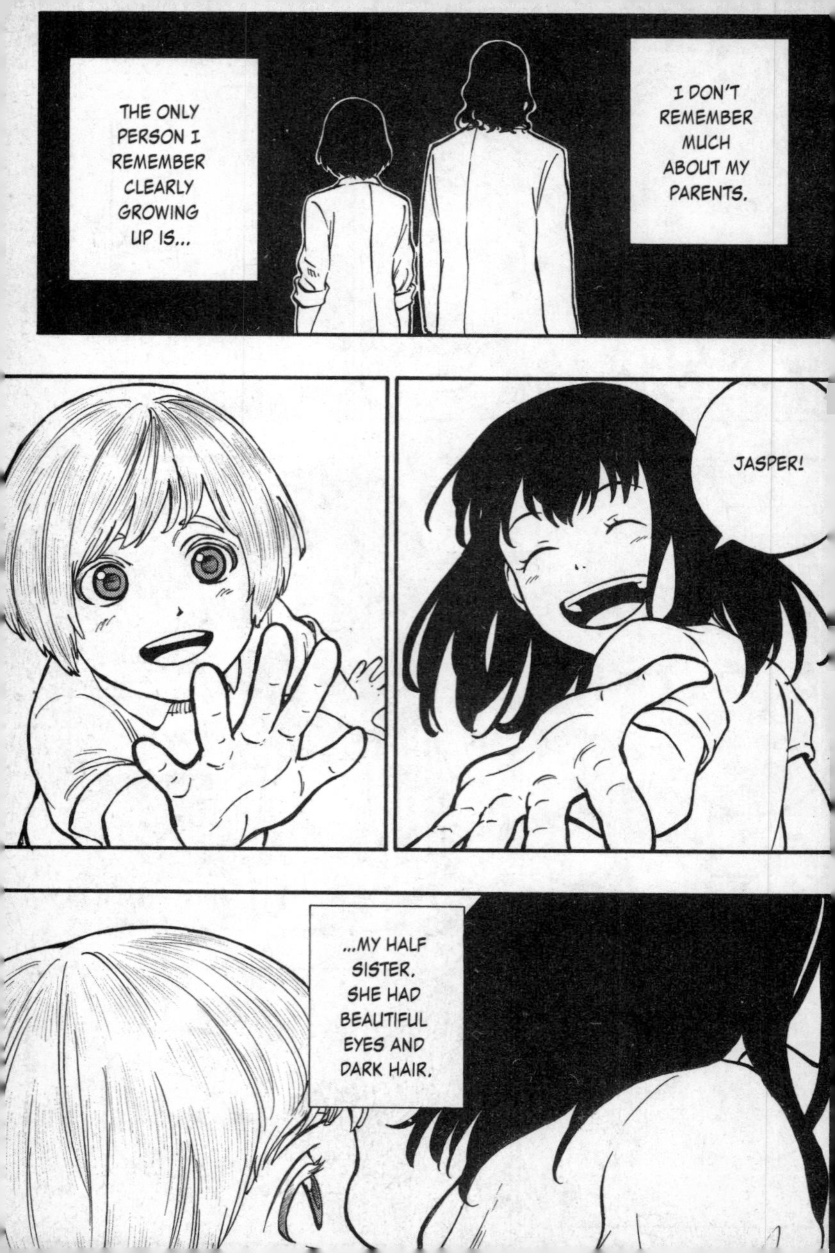
I DON'T REMEMBER MUCH ABOUT MY PARENTS.
THE ONLY PERSON I REMEMBER CLEARLY GROWING UP IS...
JASPER!
...MY HALF SISTER. SHE HAD BEAUTIFUL EYES AND DARK HAIR.

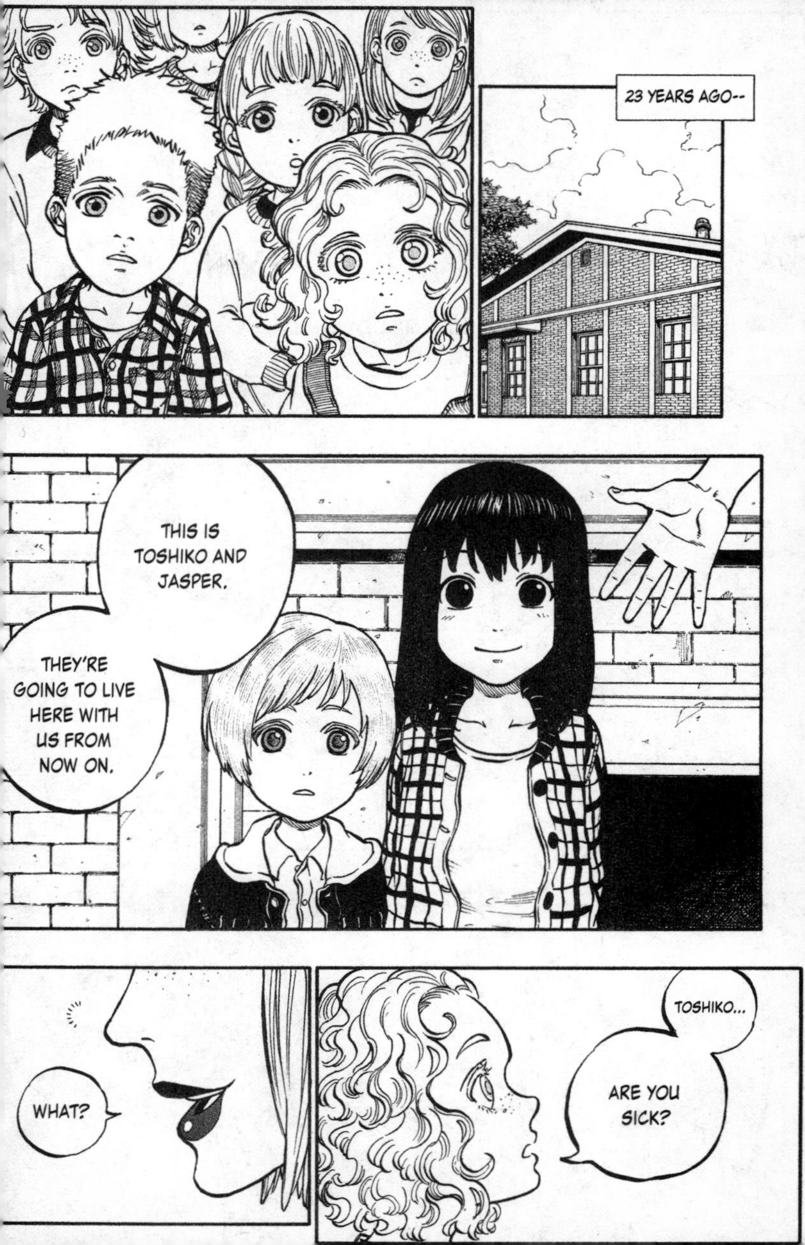
23 YEARS AGO--
THIS IS TOSHIKO AND JASPER.
THEY'RE GOING TO LIVE HERE WITH US FROM NOW ON.
TOSHIKO...
ARE YOU SICK?
WHAT?

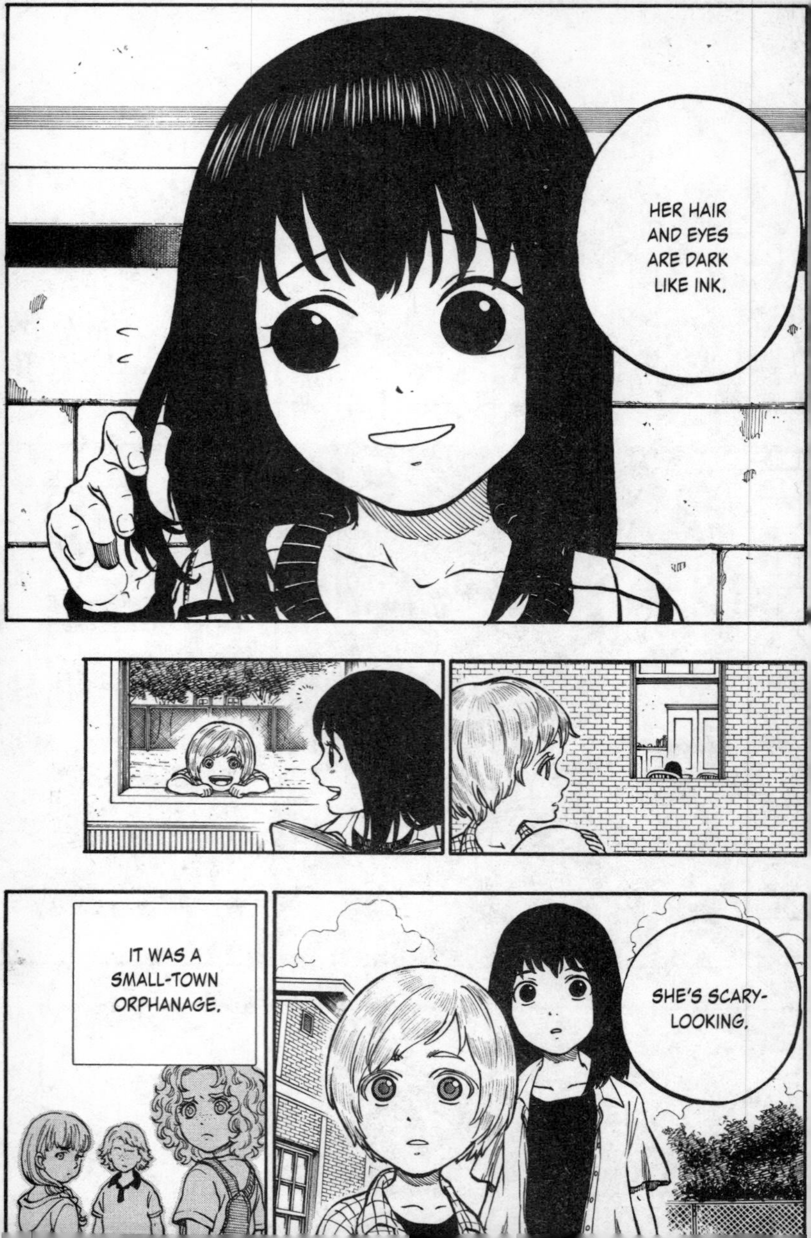
HER HAIR AND EYES ARE DARK LIKE INK.
SHE'S SCARY-LOOKING.
IT WAS A SMALL-TOWN ORPHANAGE.

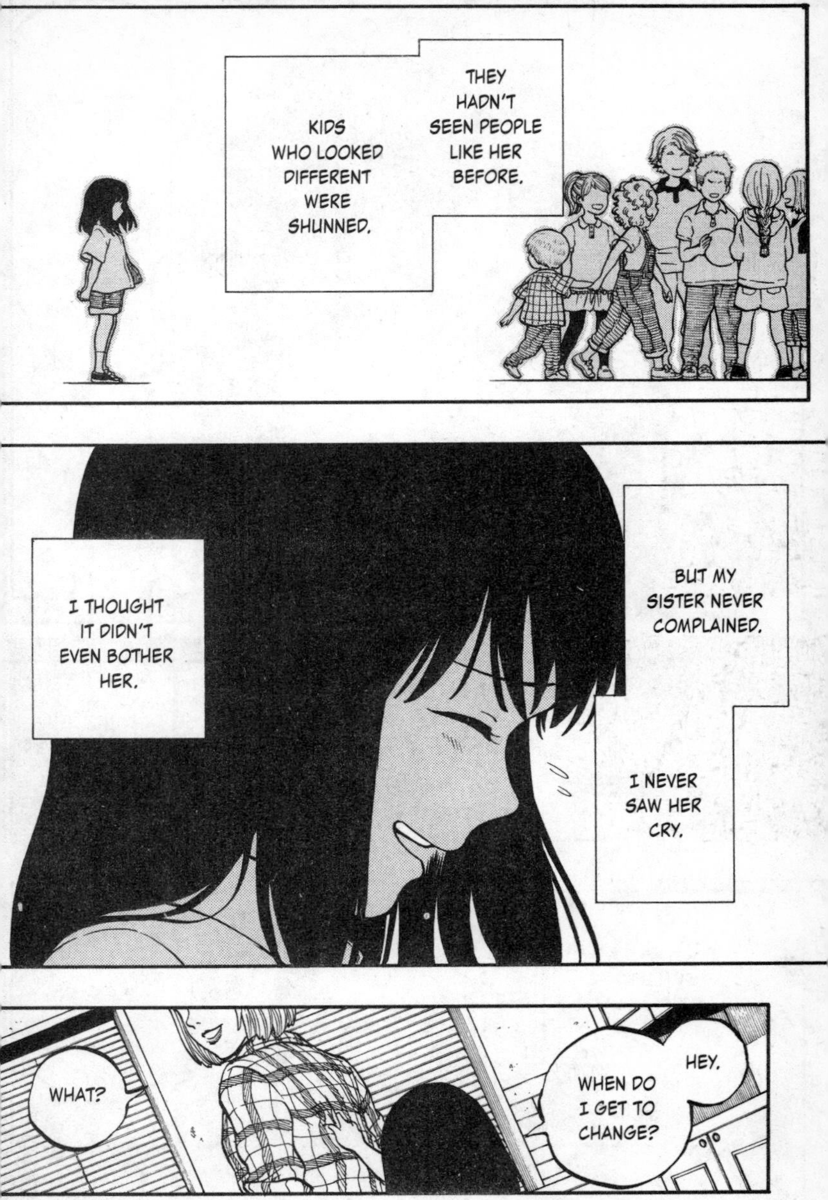
THEY HADN'T SEEN PEOPLE LIKE HER BEFORE.
KIDS WHO LOOKED DIFFERENT WERE SHUNNED.
BUT MY SISTER NEVER COMPLAINED.
I NEVER SAW HER CRY.
I THOUGHT IT DIDN'T EVEN BOTHER HER.
HEY.
WHEN DO I GET TO CHANGE?
WHAT?

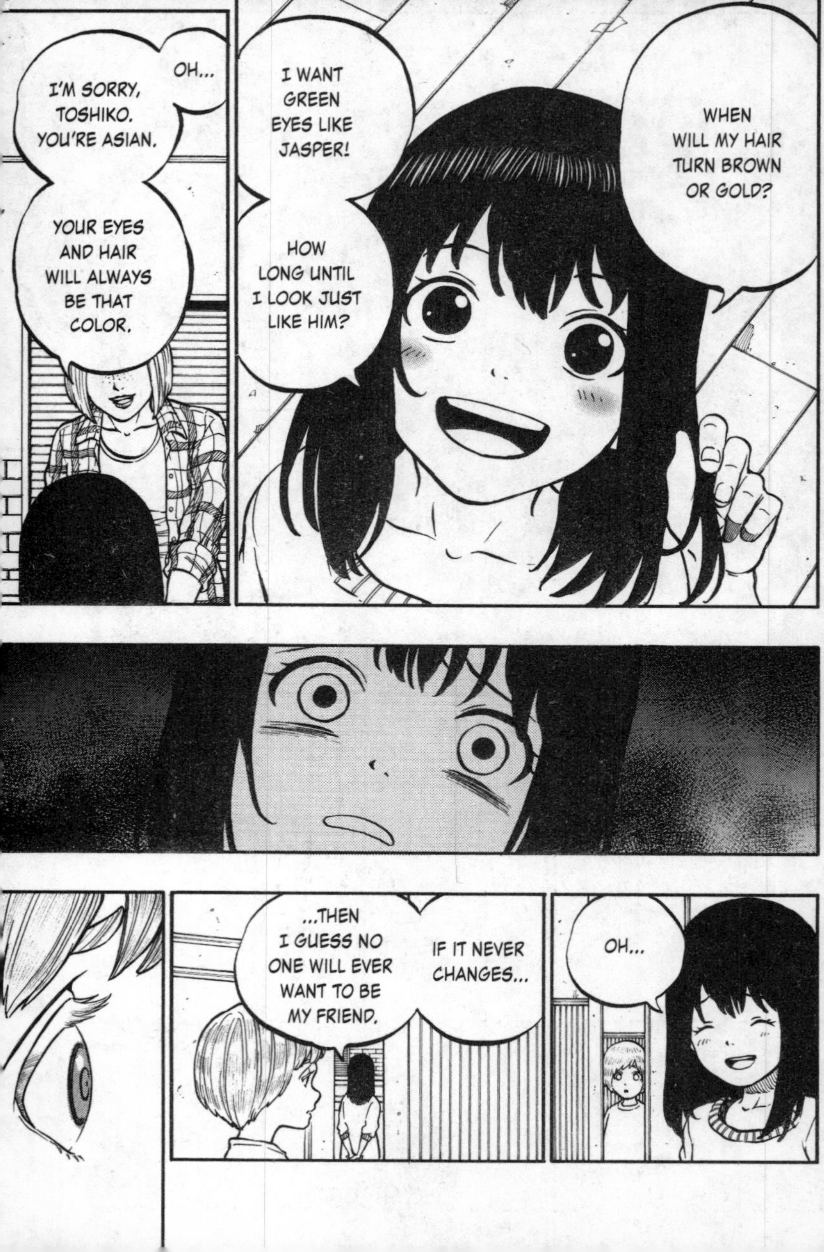
WHEN WILL MY HAIR TURN BROWN OR GOLD?
I WANT GREEN EYES LIKE JASPER!
HOW LONG UNTIL I LOOK JUST LIKE HIM?
OH...
I'M SORRY, TOSHIKO. YOU'RE ASIAN.
YOUR EYES AND HAIR WILL ALWAYS BE THAT COLOR.
OH...
IF IT NEVER CHANGES...
...THEN I GUESS NO ONE WILL EVER WANT TO BE MY FRIEND.

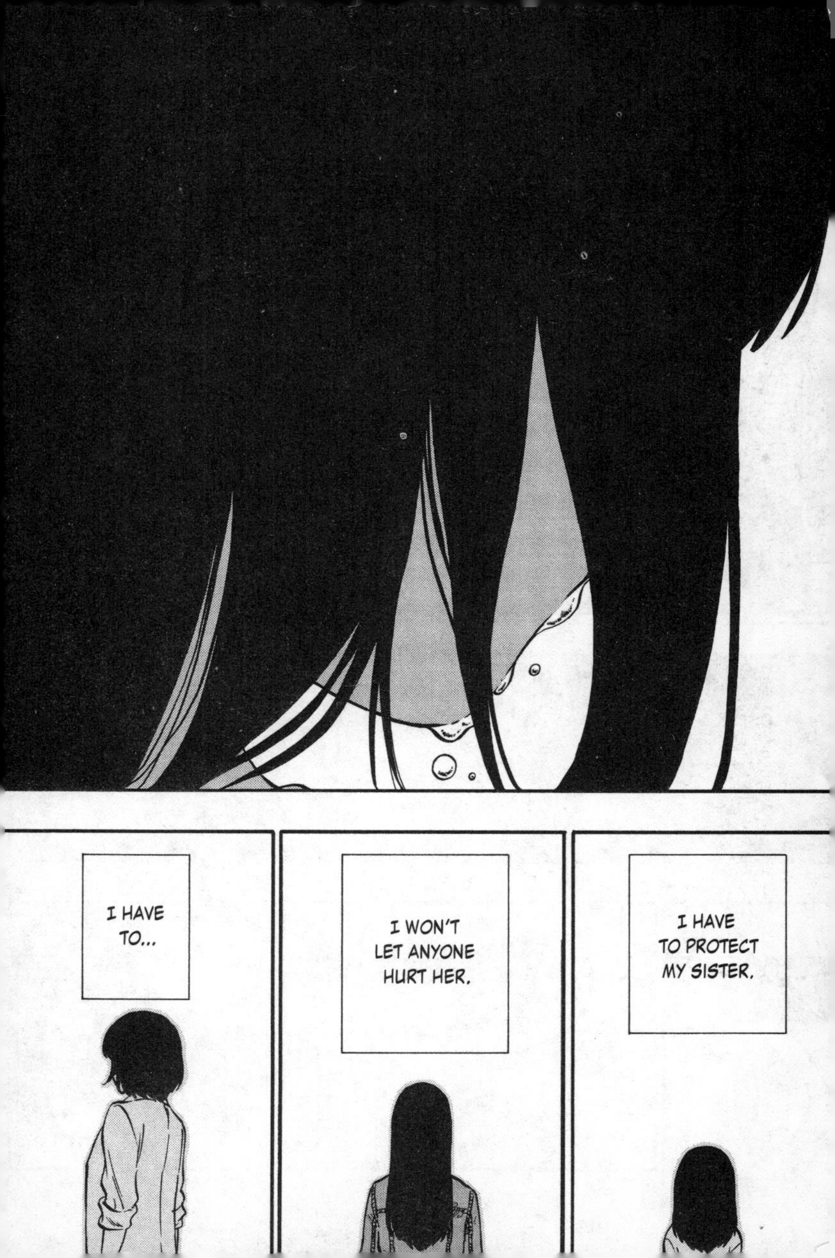
I HAVE TO PROTECT MY SISTER.
I WON'T LET ANYONE HURT HER.
I HAVE TO...

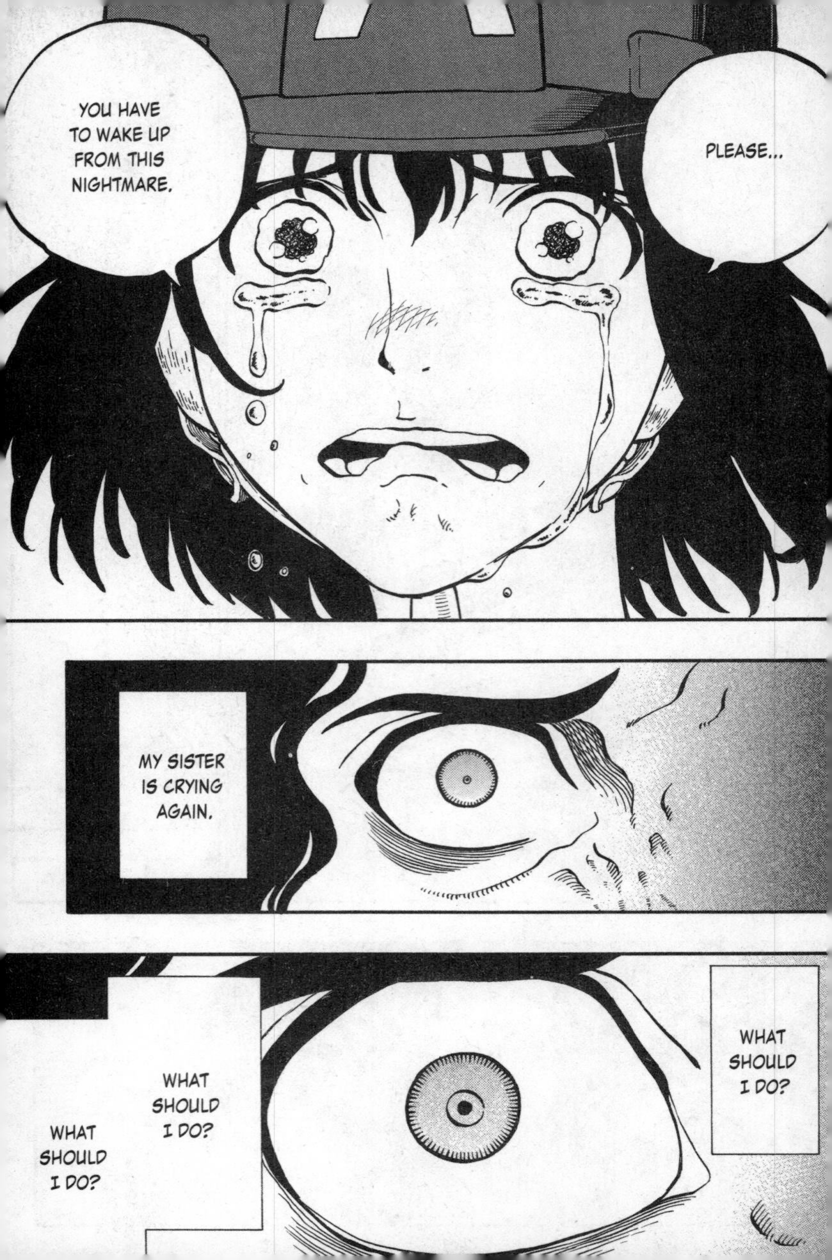
PLEASE...
YOU HAVE TO WAKE UP FROM THIS NIGHTMARE.
MY SISTER IS CRYING AGAIN.
WHAT SHOULD I DO?
WHAT SHOULD I DO?
WHAT SHOULD I DO?

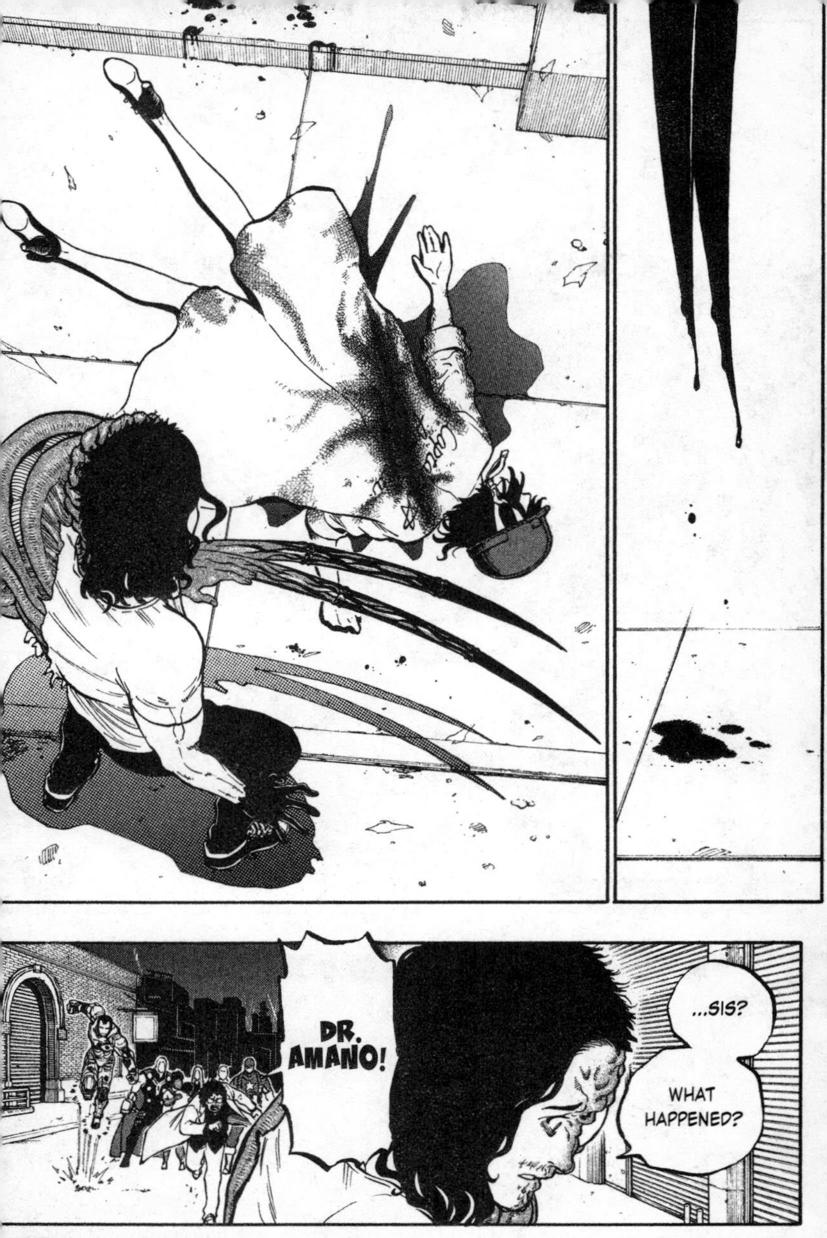
...SIS?
WHAT HAPPENED?
DR. AMANO!

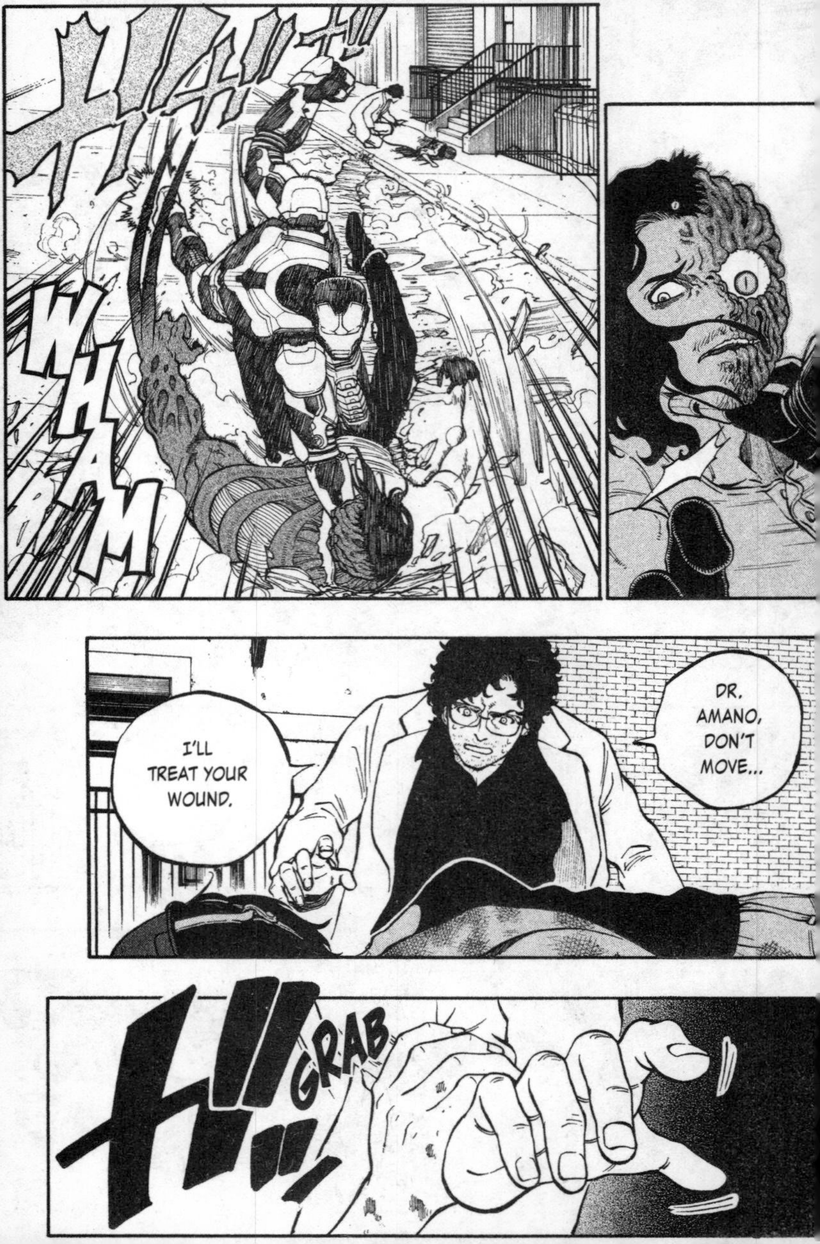
WHAM
DR. AMANO, DON'T MOVE...
I'LL TREAT YOUR WOUND.
GRAB

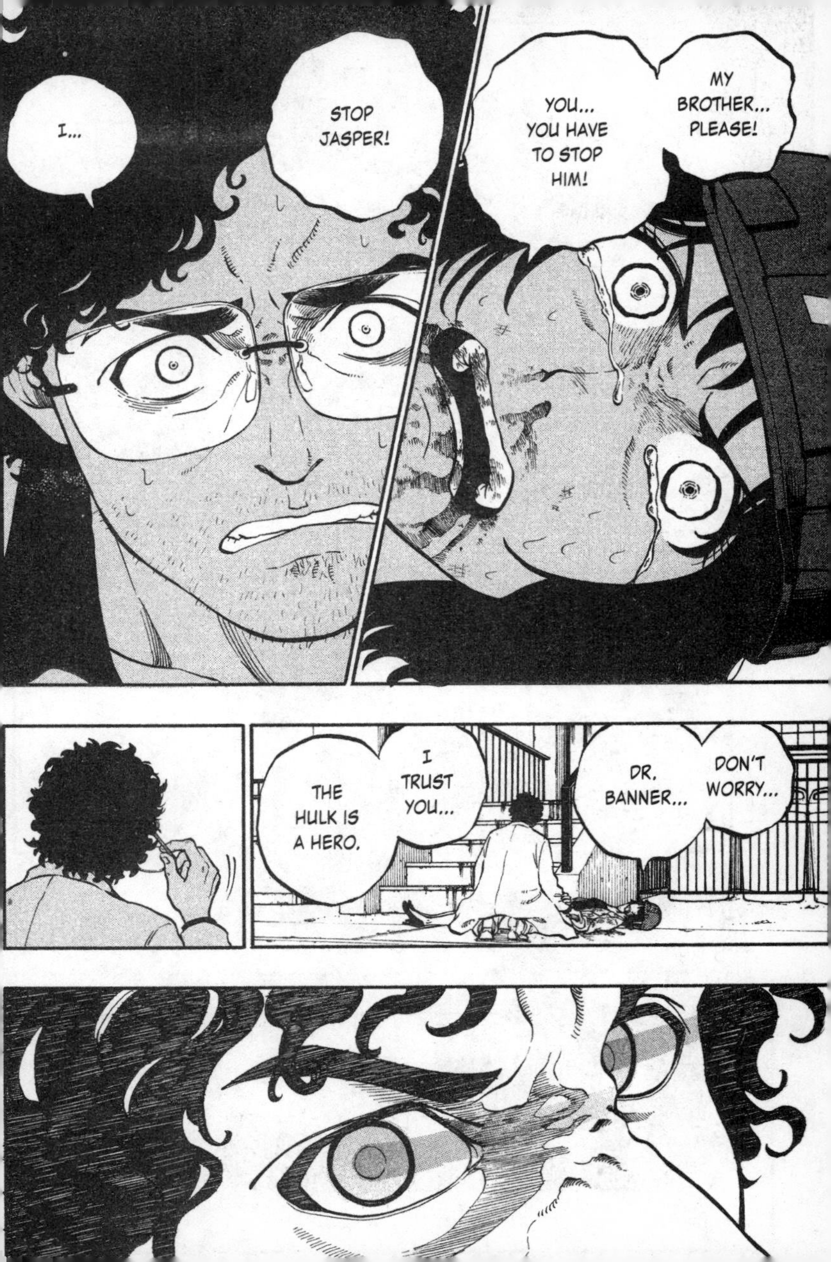
MY BROTHER... PLEASE!
YOU... YOU HAVE TO STOP HIM!
STOP JASPER!
I...
DON'T WORRY...
DR. BANNER...
I TRUST YOU...
THE HULK IS A HERO.

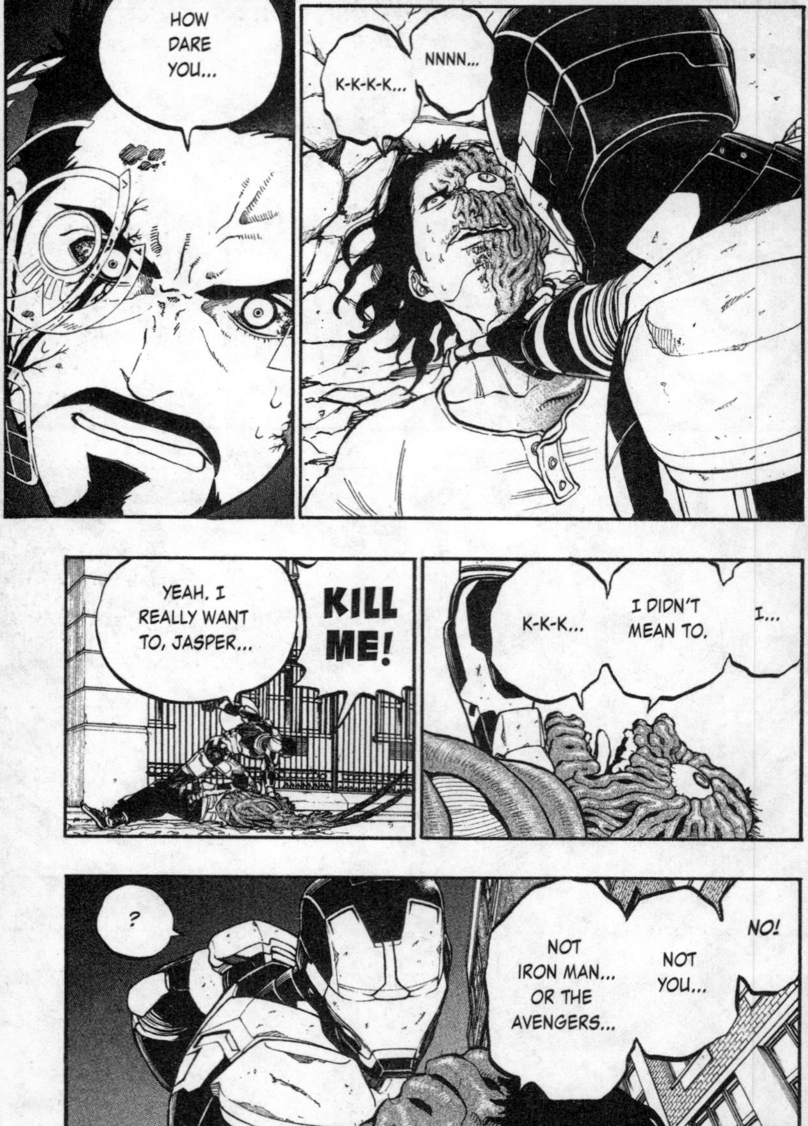
NNNN...
K-K-K-K...
HOW DARE YOU...
K-K-K... I DIDN'T MEAN TO. I...
KILL ME!
YEAH. I REALLY WANT TO, JASPER...
NOT IRON MAN... OR THE AVENGERS... NOT YOU... NO!
?

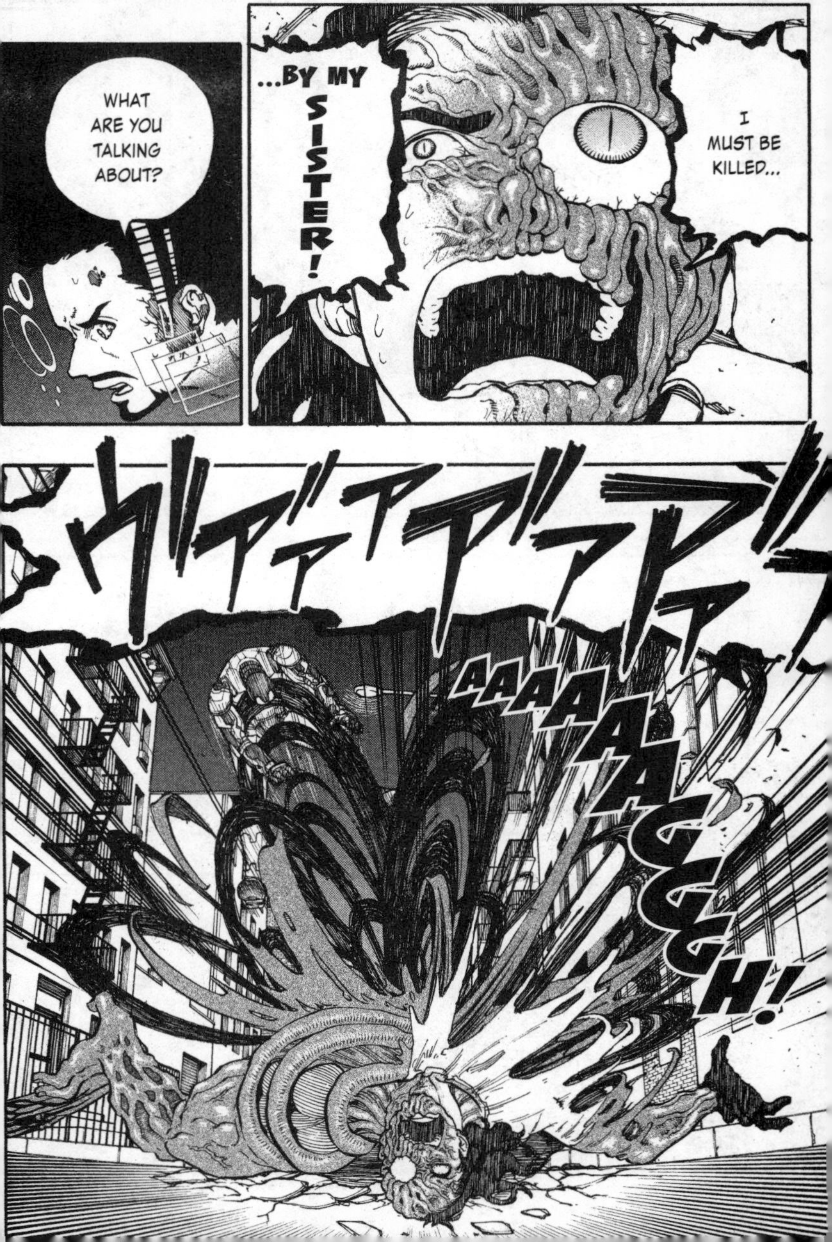

I MUST BE KILLED...
...BY MY SISTER!
WHAT ARE YOU TALKING ABOUT?
AAAAAAAGGGH!

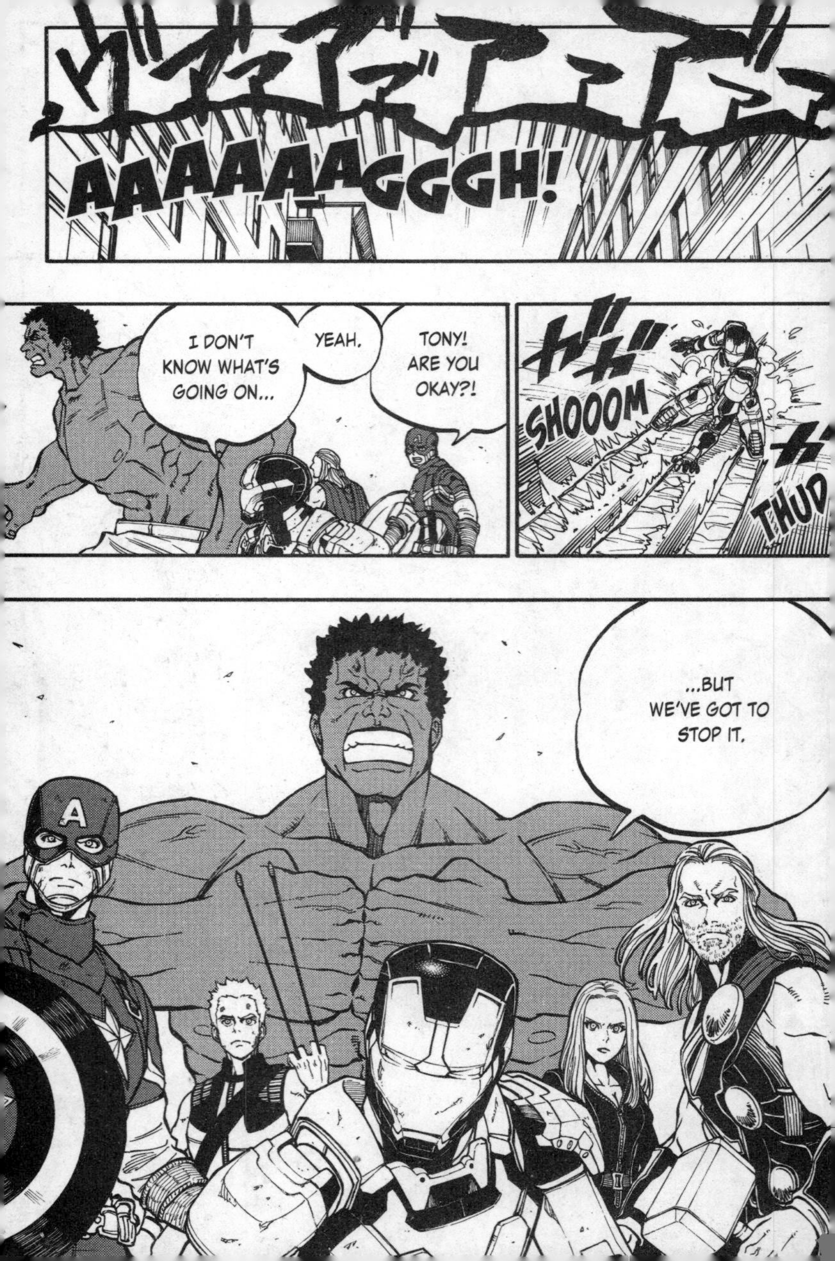
AAAAAAGGGH!
SHOOOM
THUD
TONY! ARE YOU OKAY?!
YEAH.
I DON'T KNOW WHAT'S GOING ON...
...BUT WE'VE GOT TO STOP IT.

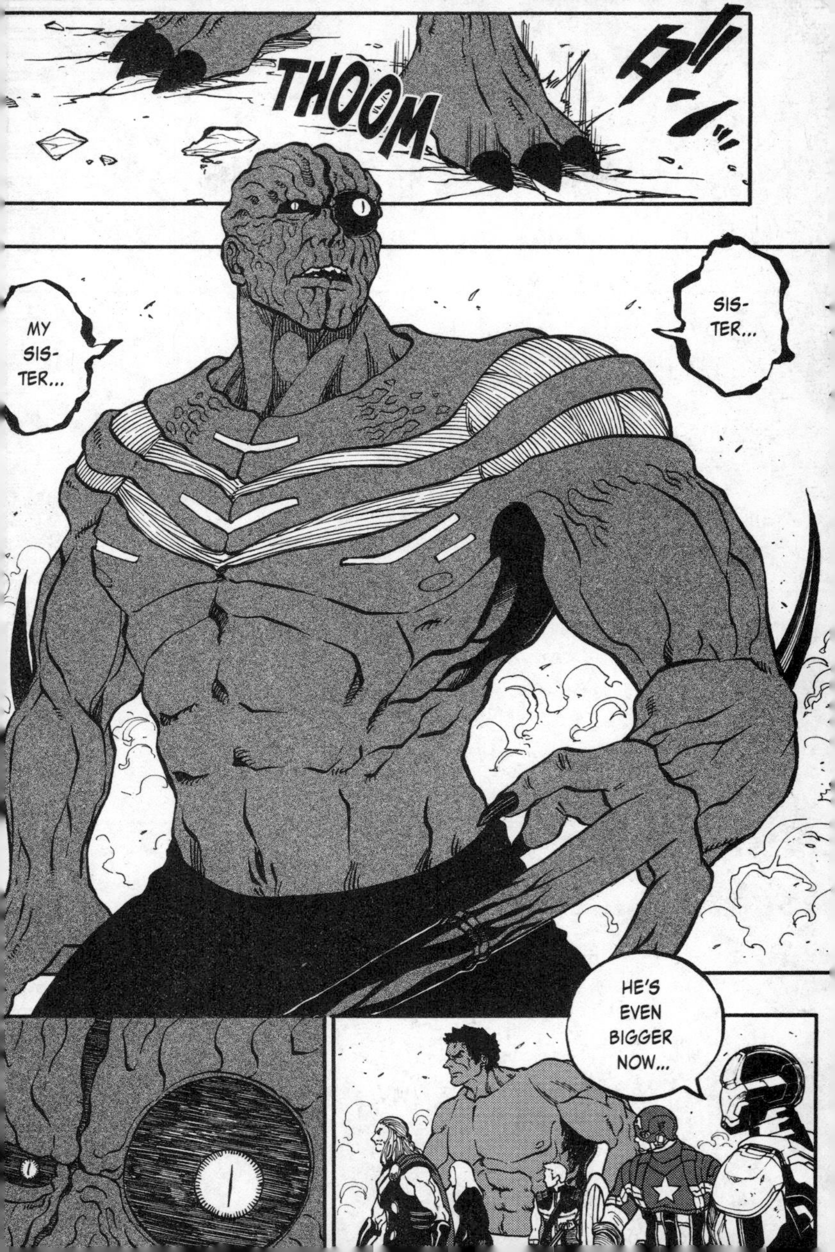
THOOM
SISTER...
MY SISTER...
HE'S EVEN BIGGER NOW...

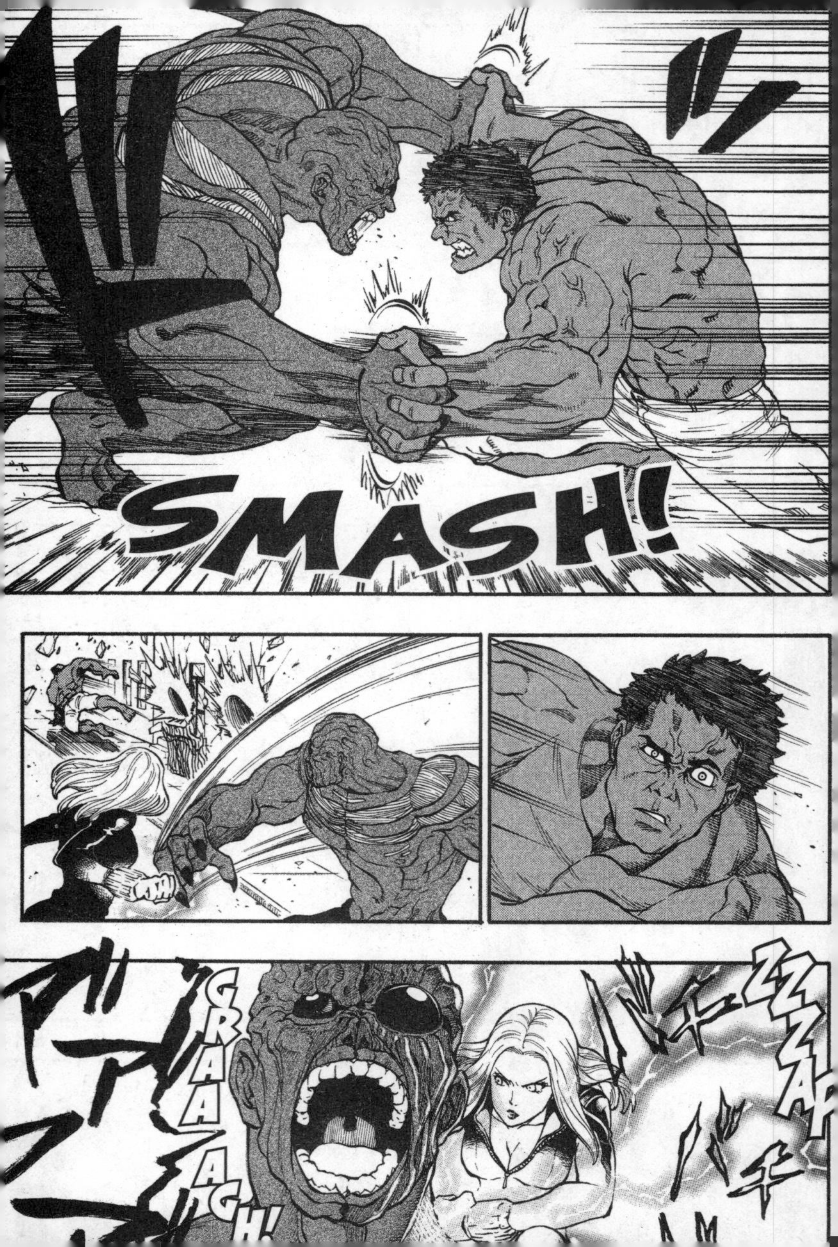
SMASH!
ZZZZAP
GRAAAAGH!

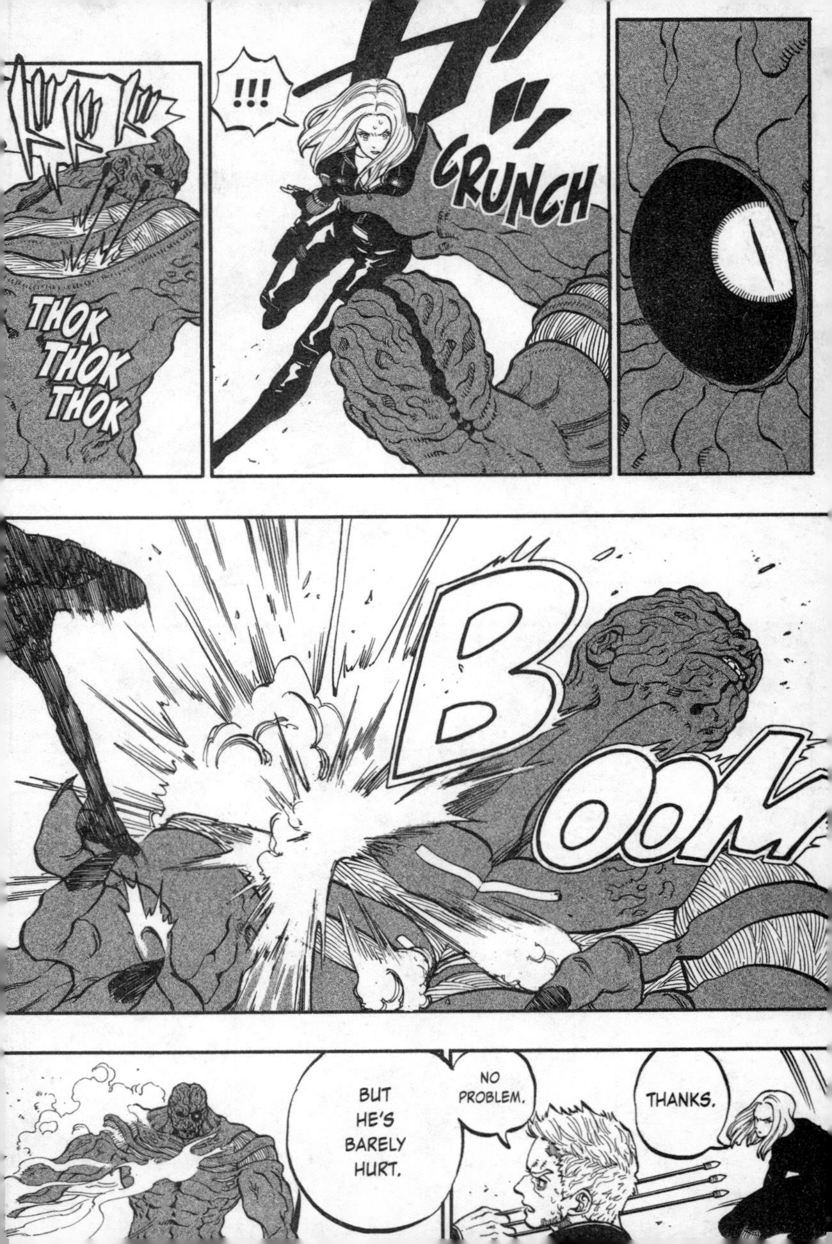
!!!
GRUNCH
THOK THOK THOK
BOOM
THANKS.
NO PROBLEM.
BUT HE'S BARELY HURT.

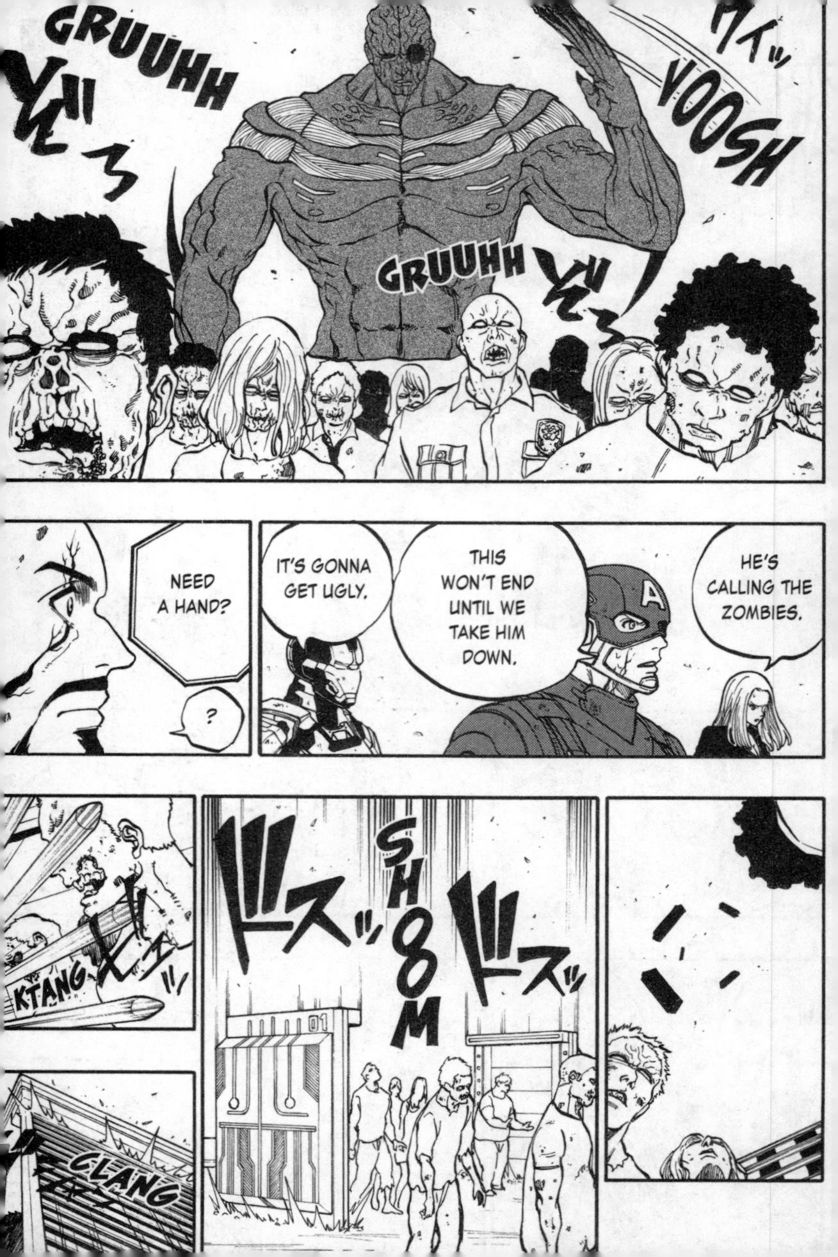
VOOSH
GRUUHH
GRUUHH
HE'S CALLING THE ZOMBIES.
THIS WON'T END UNTIL WE TAKE HIM DOWN.
IT'S GONNA GET UGLY.
NEED A HAND?
?
SHOOM
KTANG
CLANG

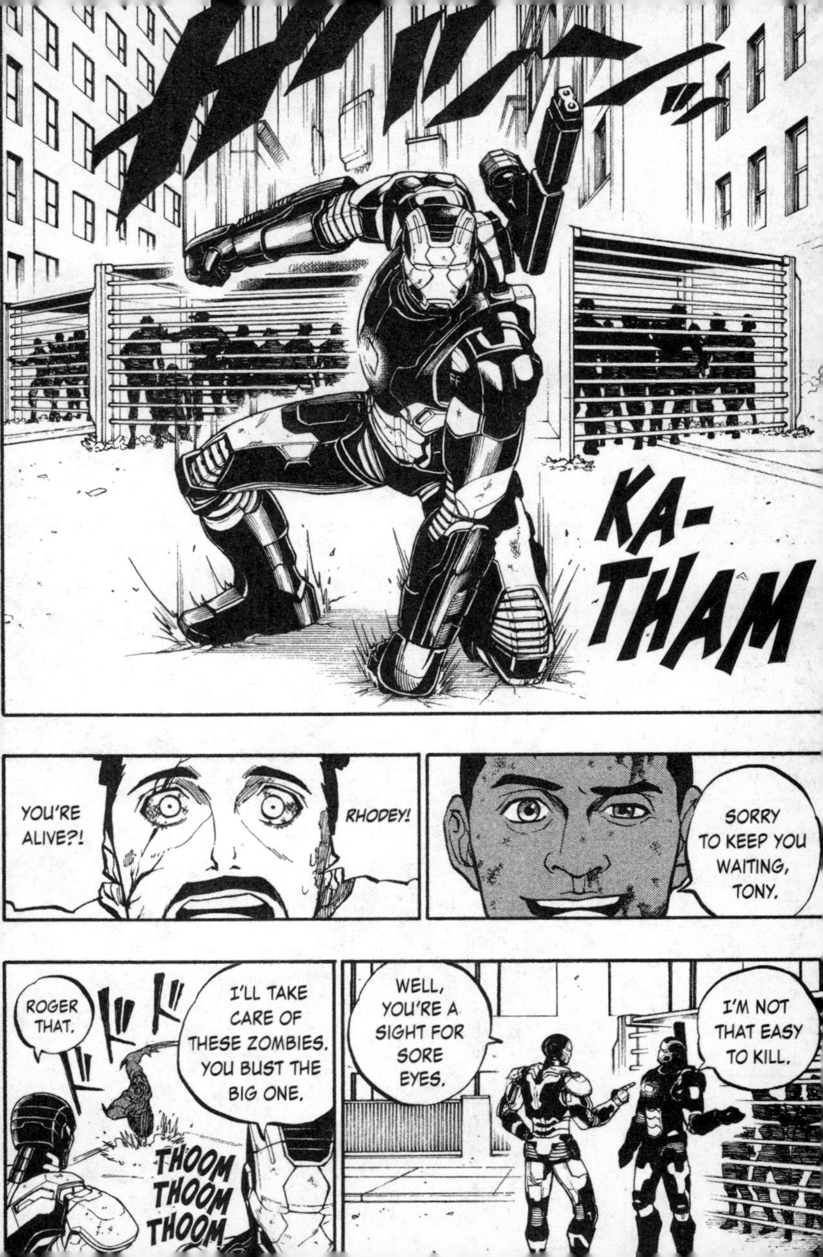
KA-THAM
SORRY TO KEEP YOU WAITING, TONY.
RHODEY!
YOU'RE ALIVE?!
I'M NOT THAT EASY TO KILL.
WELL, YOU'RE A SIGHT FOR SORE EYES.
I'LL TAKE CARE OF THESE ZOMBIES. YOU BUST THE BIG ONE.
ROGER THAT.
THOOM THOOM THOOM

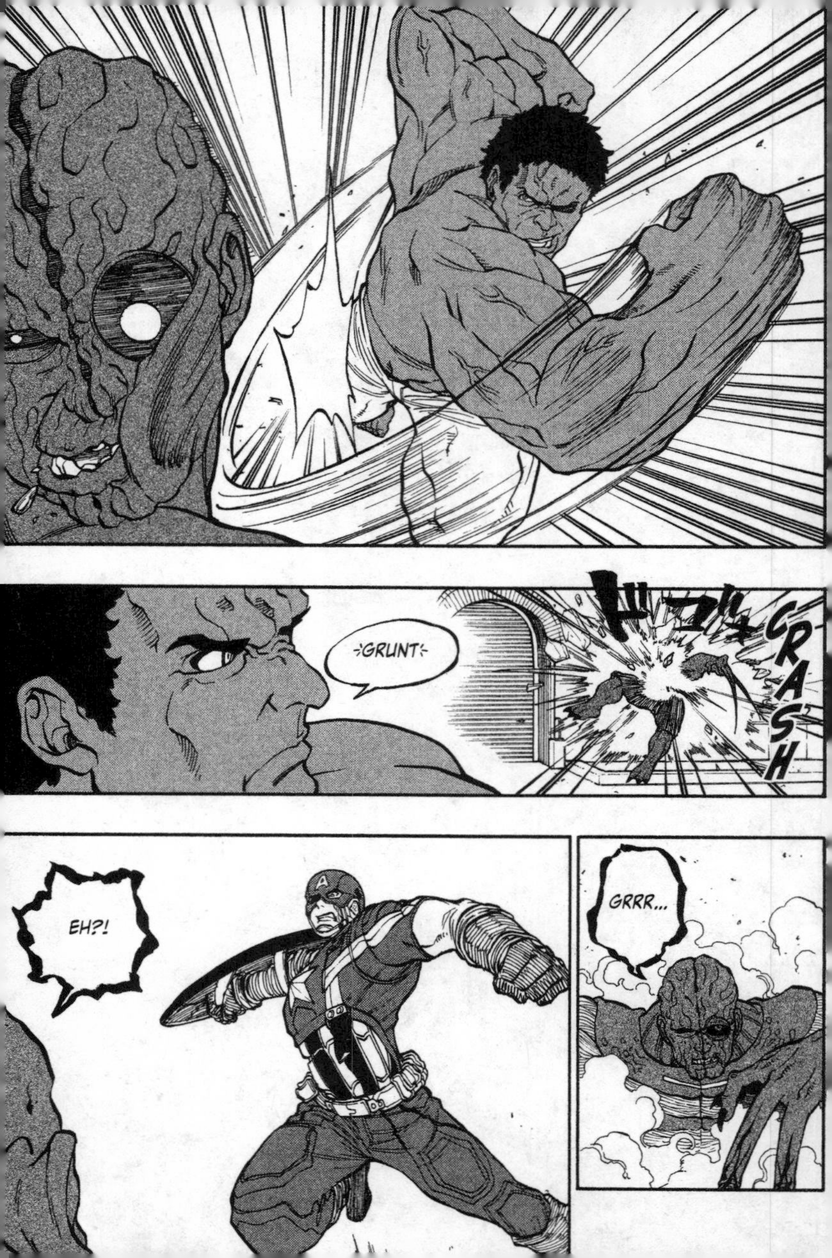
CRASH
GRUNT
GRRR...
EH?!

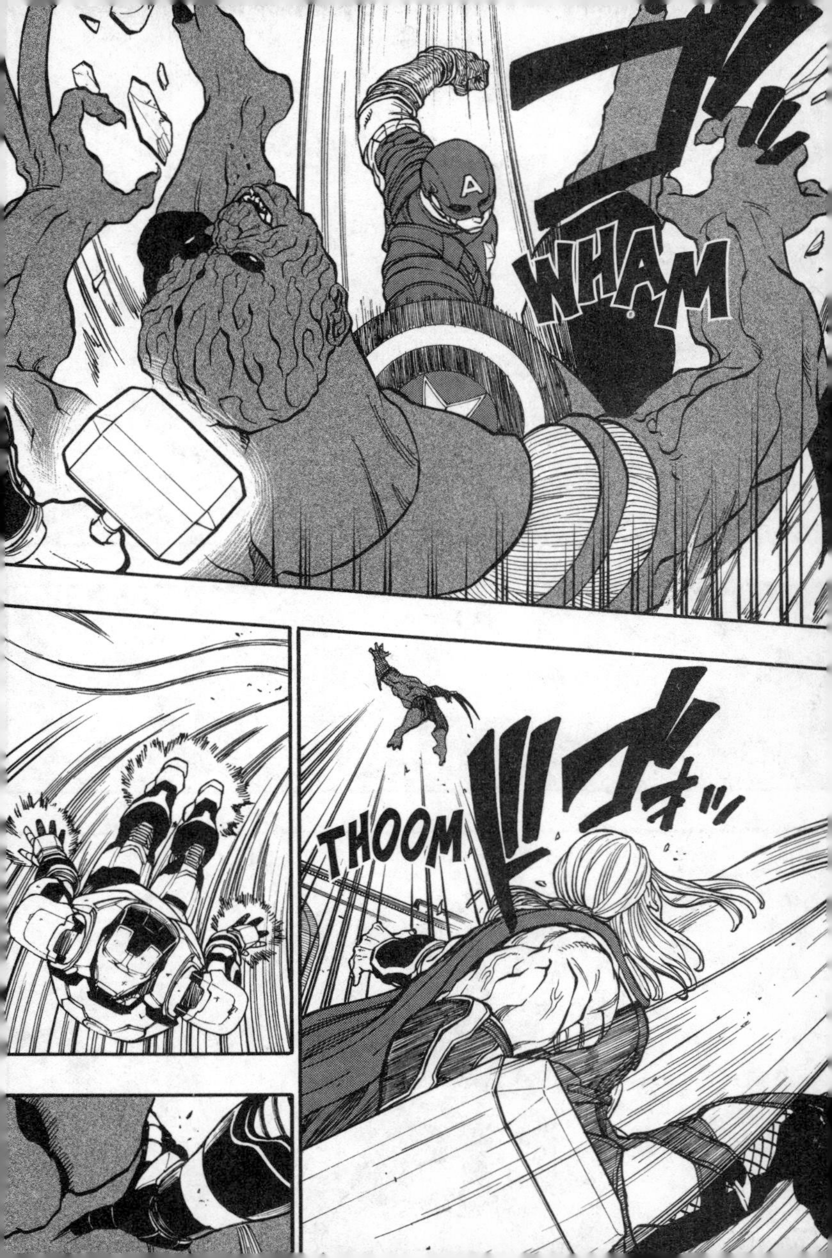
WHAM
THOOM

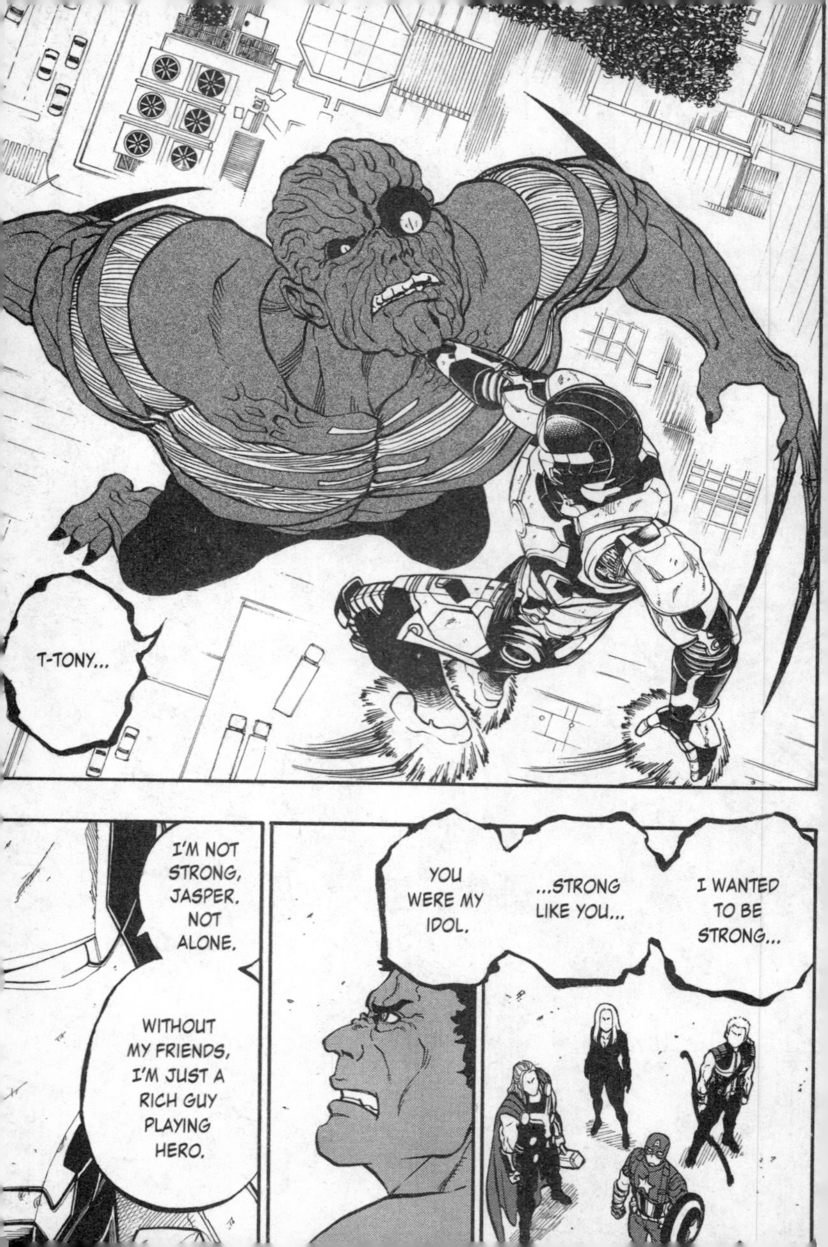
T-TONY...
I WANTED TO BE STRONG...
...STRONG LIKE YOU...
YOU WERE MY IDOL.
I'M NOT STRONG, JASPER. NOT ALONE.
WITHOUT MY FRIENDS, I'M JUST A RICH GUY PLAYING HERO.

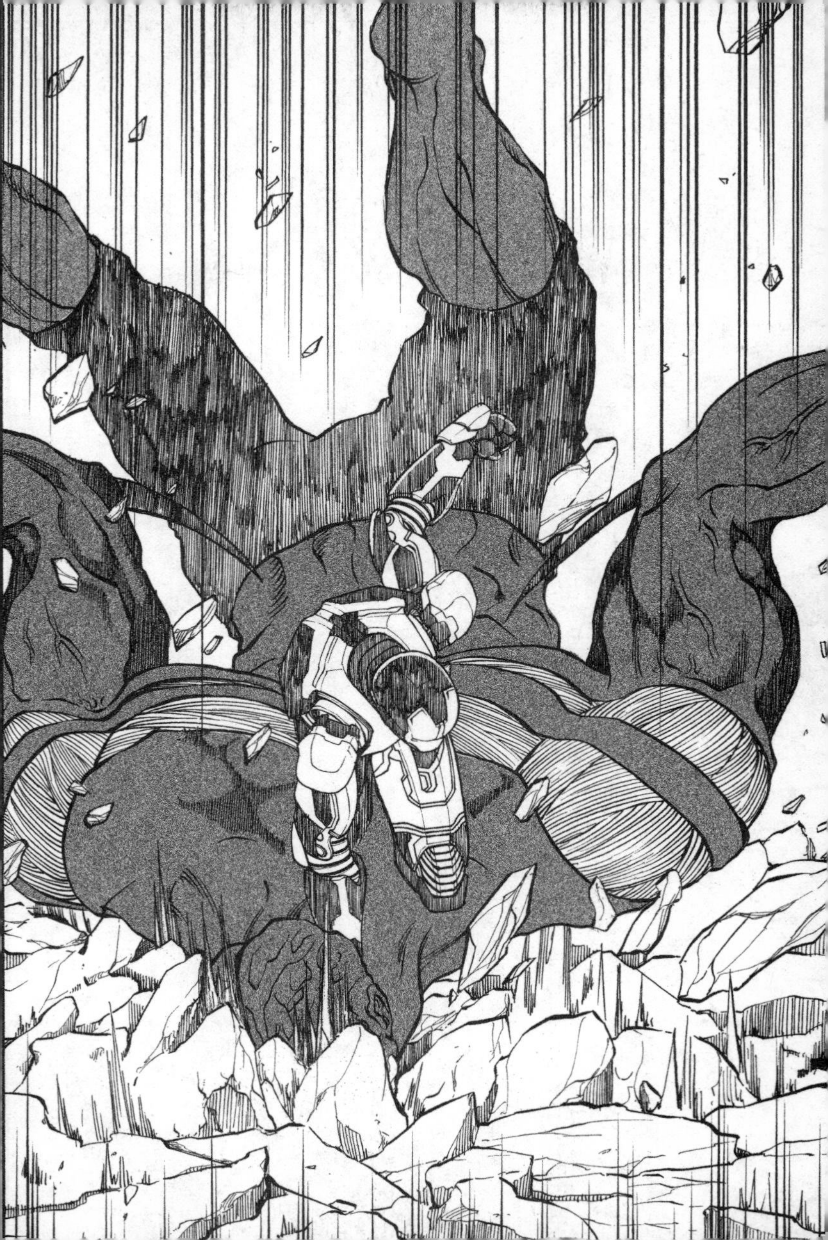

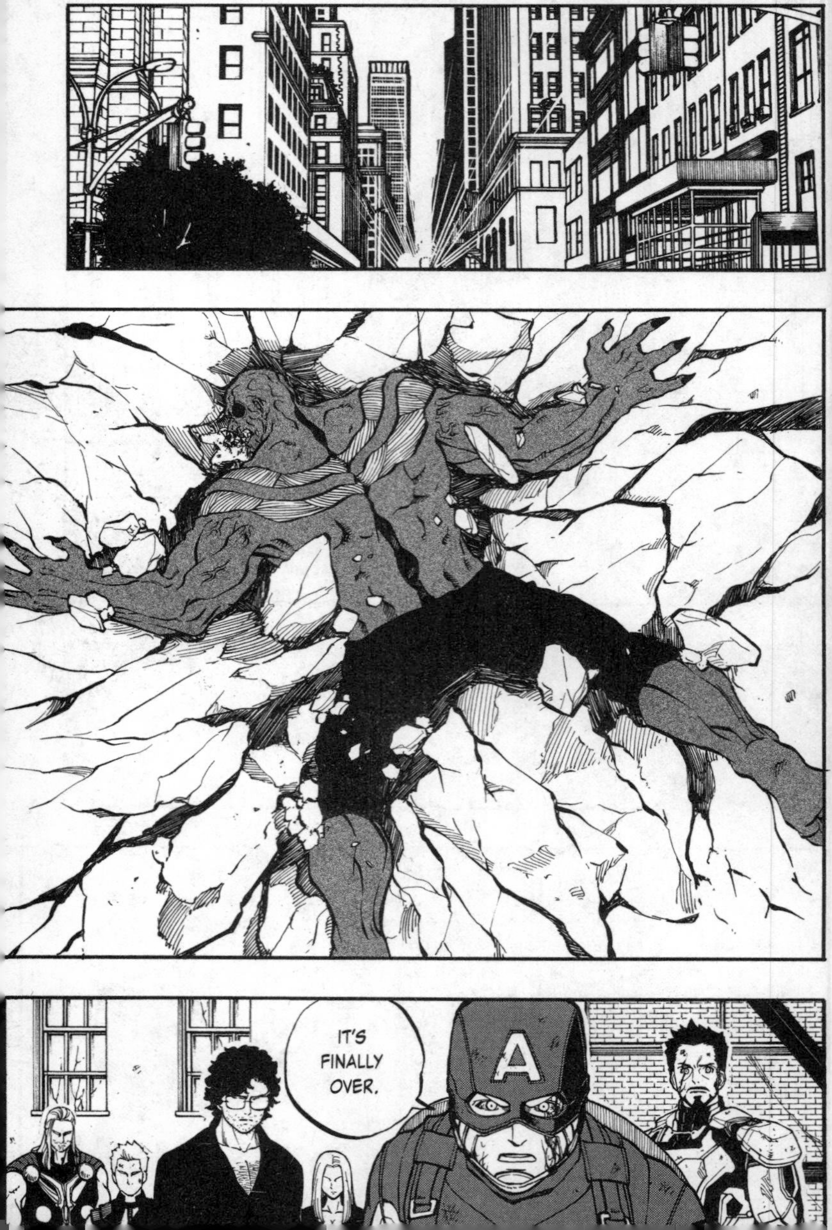
IT'S FINALLY OVER.

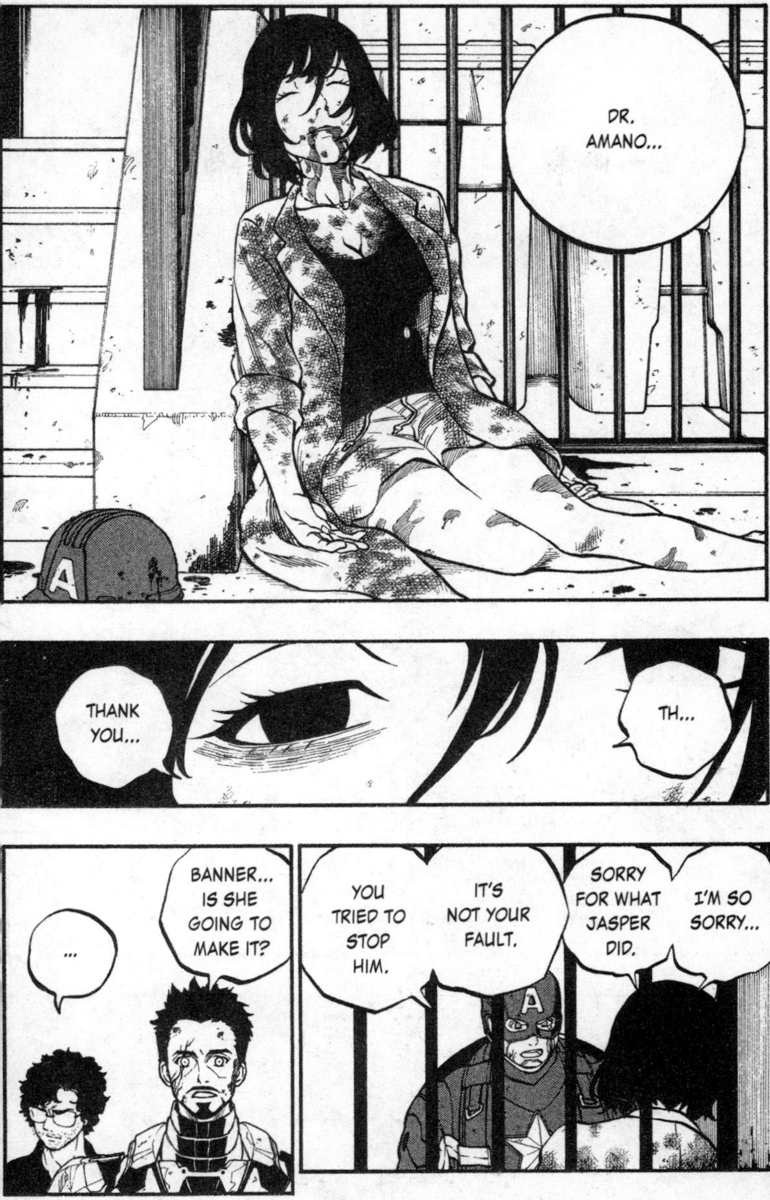

DR. AMANO...
TH...
THANK YOU...
I'M SO SORRY...
SORRY FOR WHAT JASPER DID.
IT'S NOT YOUR FAULT.
YOU TRIED TO STOP HIM.
BANNER... IS SHE GOING TO MAKE IT?
...

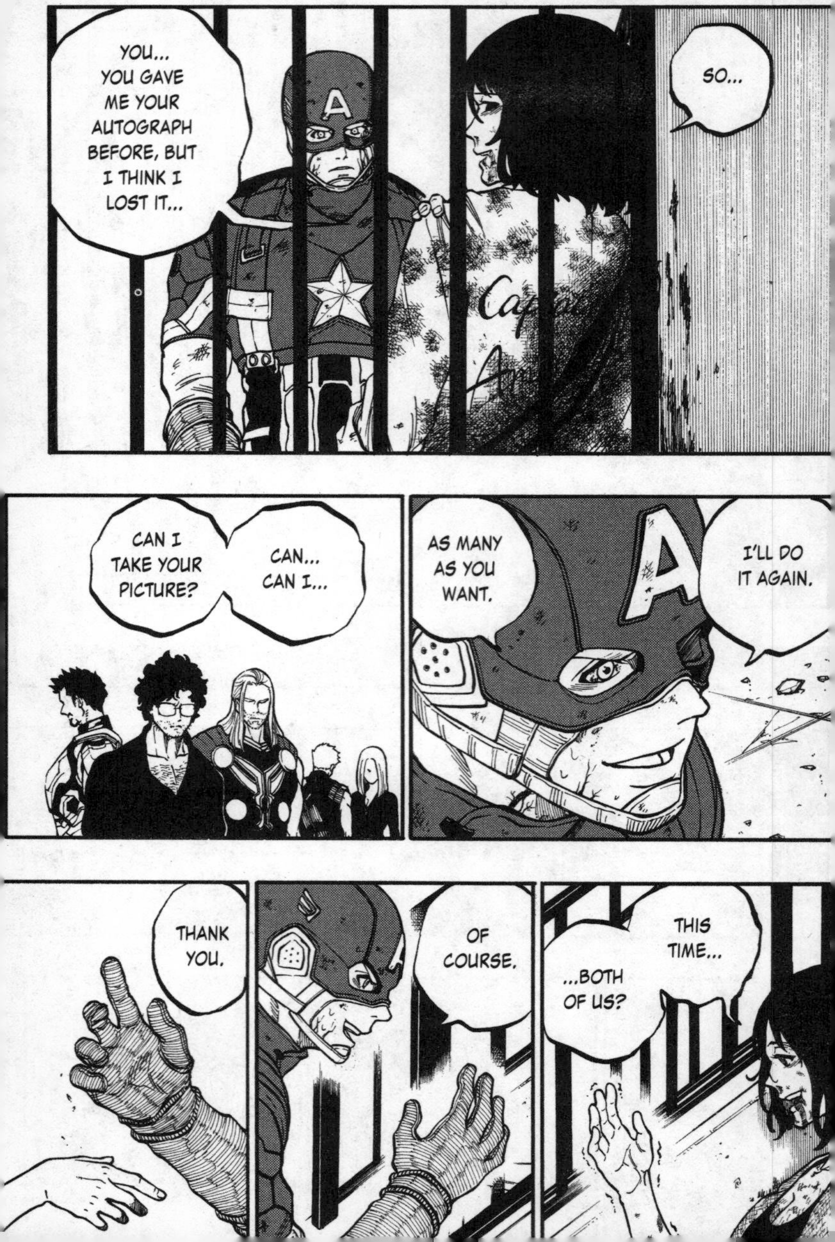
SO...
YOU... YOU GAVE ME YOUR AUTOGRAPH BEFORE, BUT I THINK I LOST IT...
I'LL DO IT AGAIN.
AS MANY AS YOU WANT.
CAN... CAN I...
CAN I TAKE YOUR PICTURE?
THIS TIME...
...BOTH OF US?
OF COURSE.
THANK YOU.

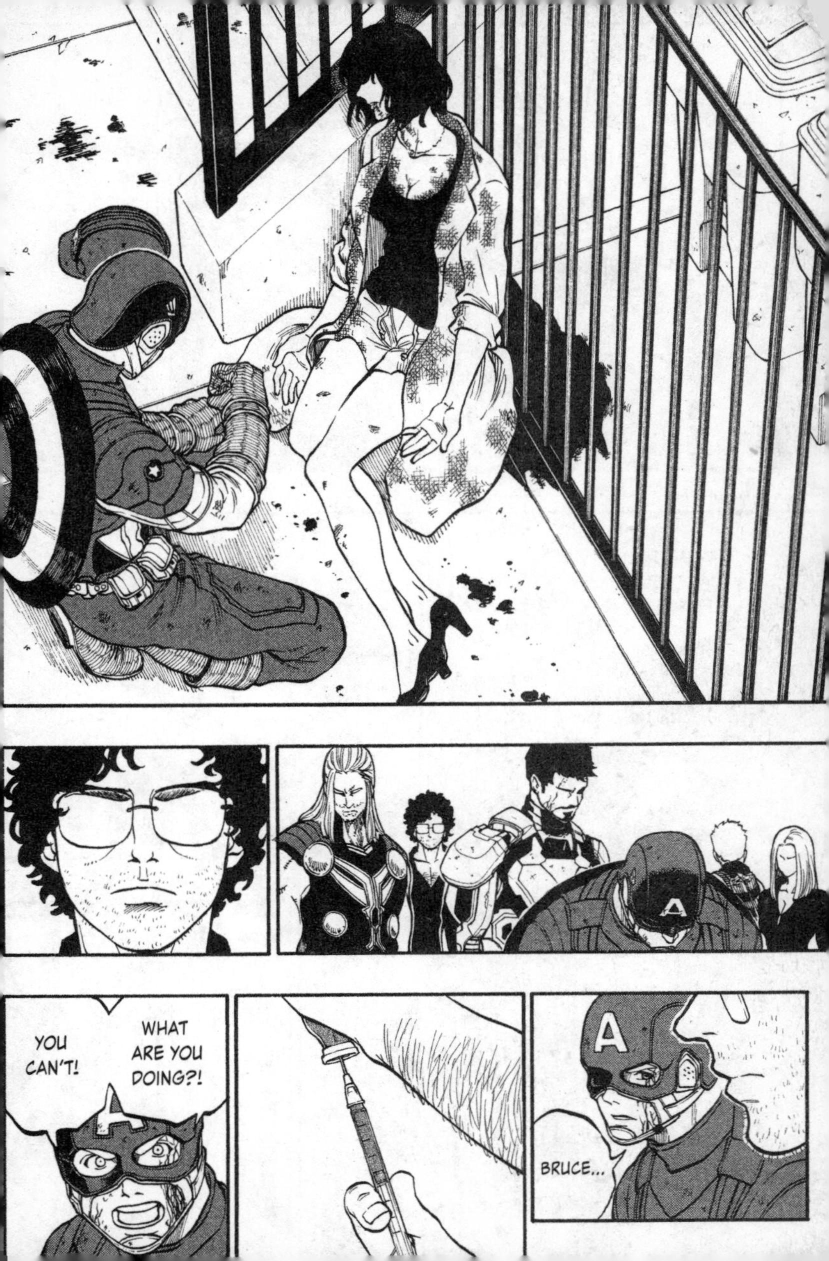
BRUCE...
WHAT ARE YOU DOING?!
YOU CAN'T!

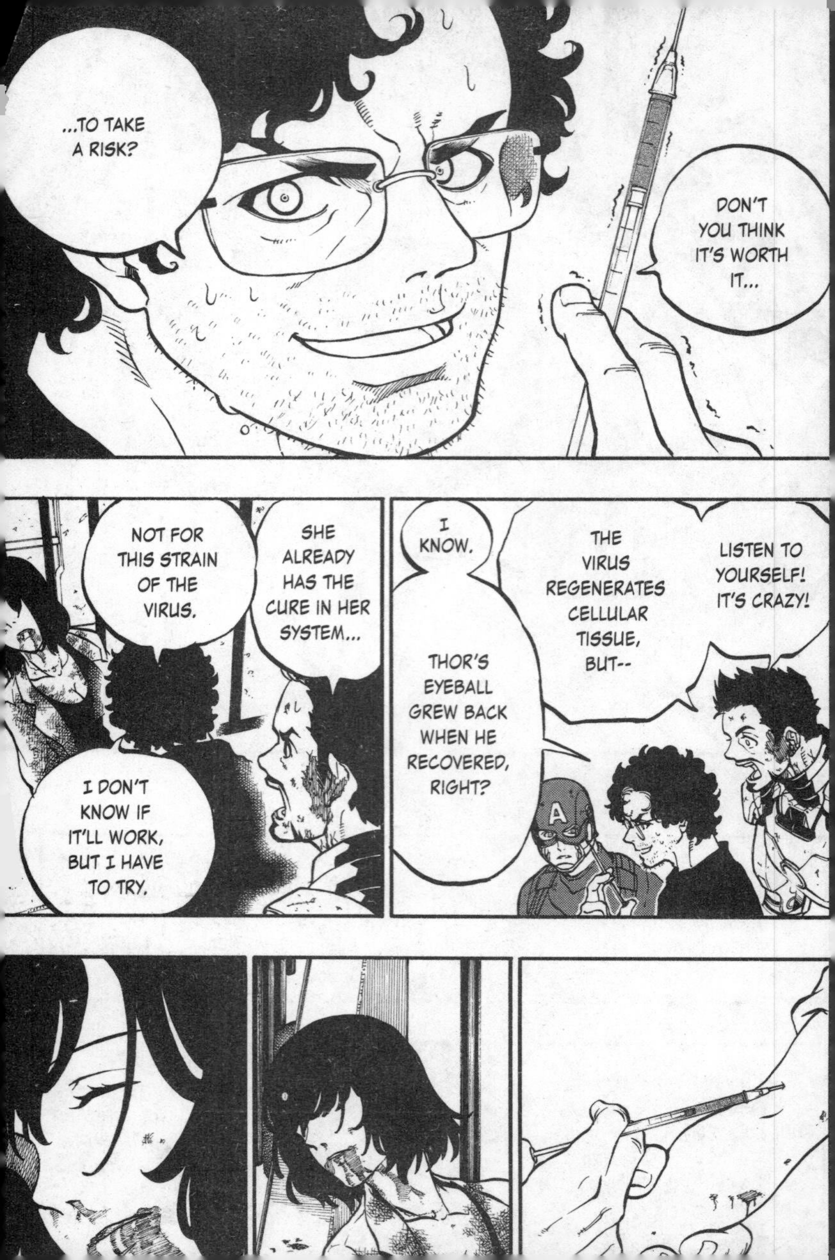
DON'T YOU THINK IT'S WORTH IT...
...TO TAKE A RISK?
LISTEN TO YOURSELF! IT'S CRAZY!
THE VIRUS REGENERATES CELLULAR TISSUE, BUT--
I KNOW.
THOR'S EYEBALL GREW BACK WHEN HE RECOVERED, RIGHT?
SHE ALREADY HAS THE CURE IN HER SYSTEM...
NOT FOR THIS STRAIN OF THE VIRUS.
I DON'T KNOW IF IT'LL WORK, BUT I HAVE TO TRY.

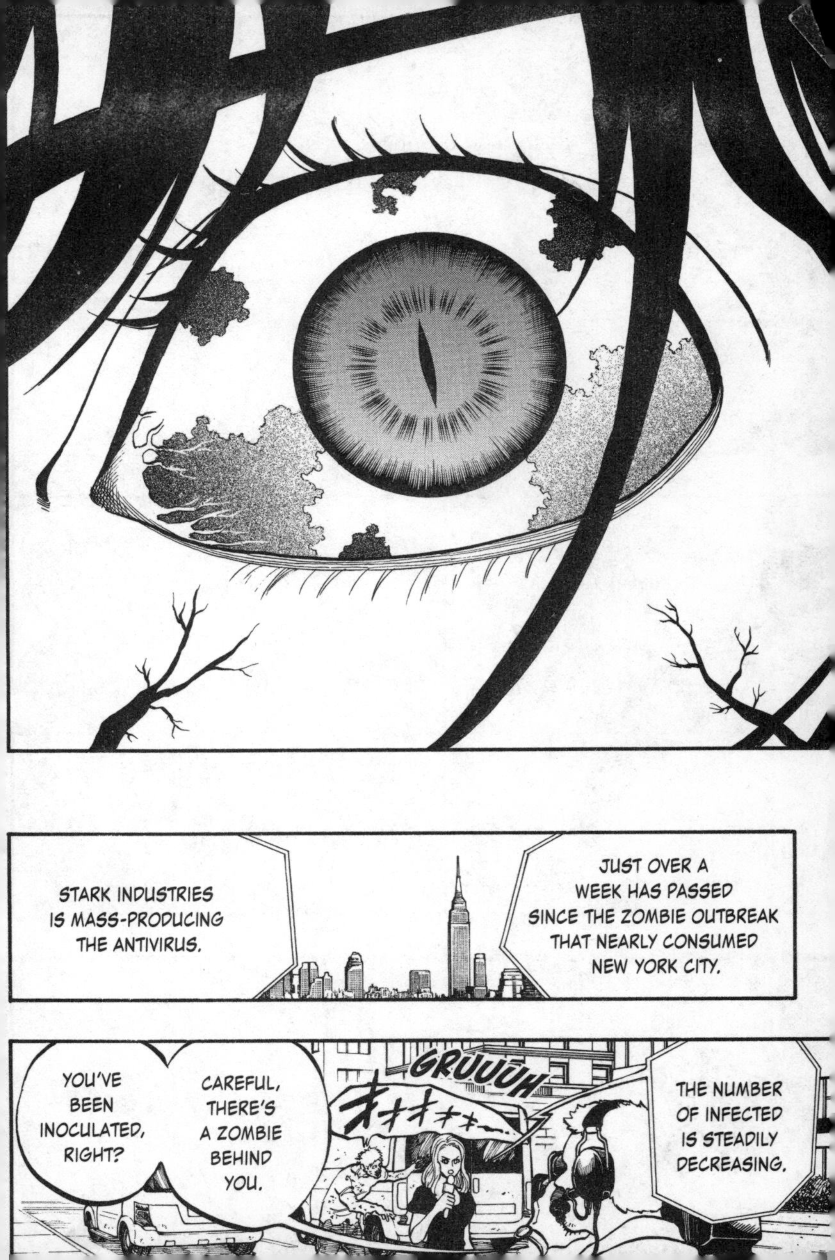
JUST OVER A WEEK HAS PASSED SINCE THE ZOMBIE OUTBREAK THAT NEARLY CONSUMED NEW YORK CITY.
STARK INDUSTRIES IS MASS-PRODUCING THE ANTIVIRUS.
THE NUMBER OF INFECTED IS STEADILY DECREASING.
GRUUUH
CAREFUL, THERE'S A ZOMBIE BEHIND YOU.
YOU'VE BEEN INOCULATED, RIGHT?

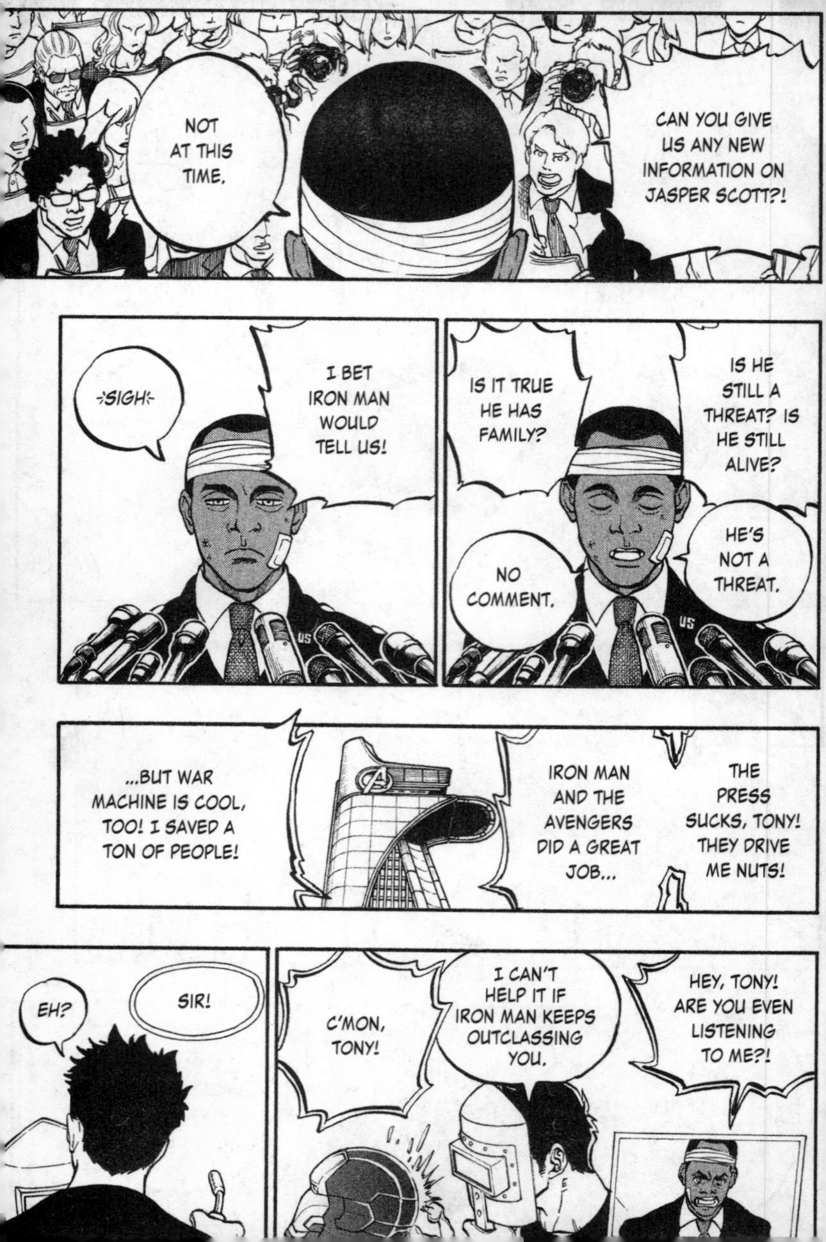
CAN YOU GIVE US ANY NEW INFORMATION ON JASPER SCOTT?!
NOT AT THIS TIME.
IS HE STILL A THREAT? IS HE STILL ALIVE?
IS IT TRUE HE HAS FAMILY?
HE'S NOT A THREAT.
NO COMMENT.
I BET IRON MAN WOULD TELL US!
-SIGH-
THE PRESS SUCKS, TONY! THEY DRIVE ME NUTS!
IRON MAN AND THE AVENGERS DID A GREAT JOB...
...BUT WAR MACHINE IS COOL, TOO! I SAVED A TON OF PEOPLE!
HEY, TONY! ARE YOU EVEN LISTENING TO ME?!
I CAN'T HELP IT IF IRON MAN KEEPS OUTCLASSING YOU.
C'MON, TONY!
SIR!
EH?

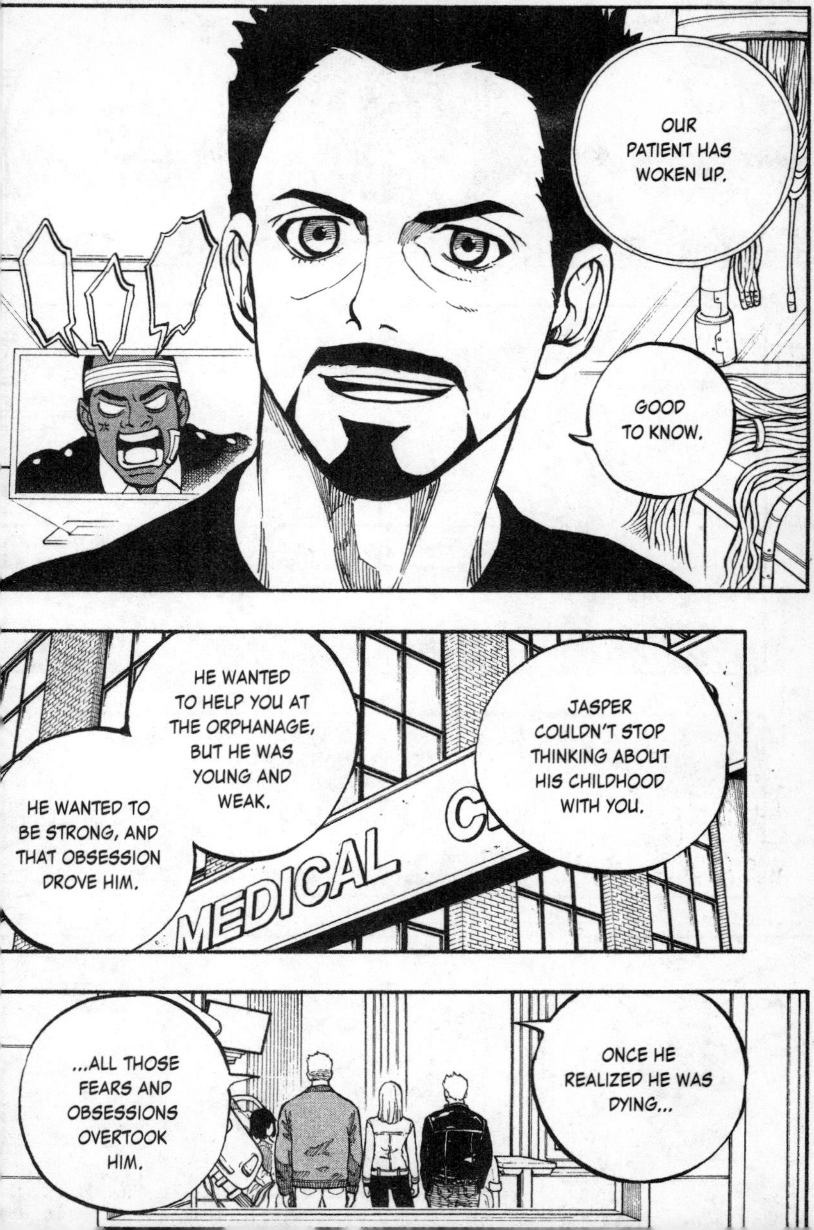
OUR PATIENT HAS WOKEN UP.
GOOD TO KNOW.
JASPER COULDN'T STOP THINKING ABOUT HIS CHILDHOOD WITH YOU.
HE WANTED TO HELP YOU AT THE ORPHANAGE, BUT HE WAS YOUNG AND WEAK.
HE WANTED TO BE STRONG, AND THAT OBSESSION DROVE HIM.
MEDICAL
ONCE HE REALIZED HE WAS DYING...
...ALL THOSE FEARS AND OBSESSIONS OVERTOOK HIM.

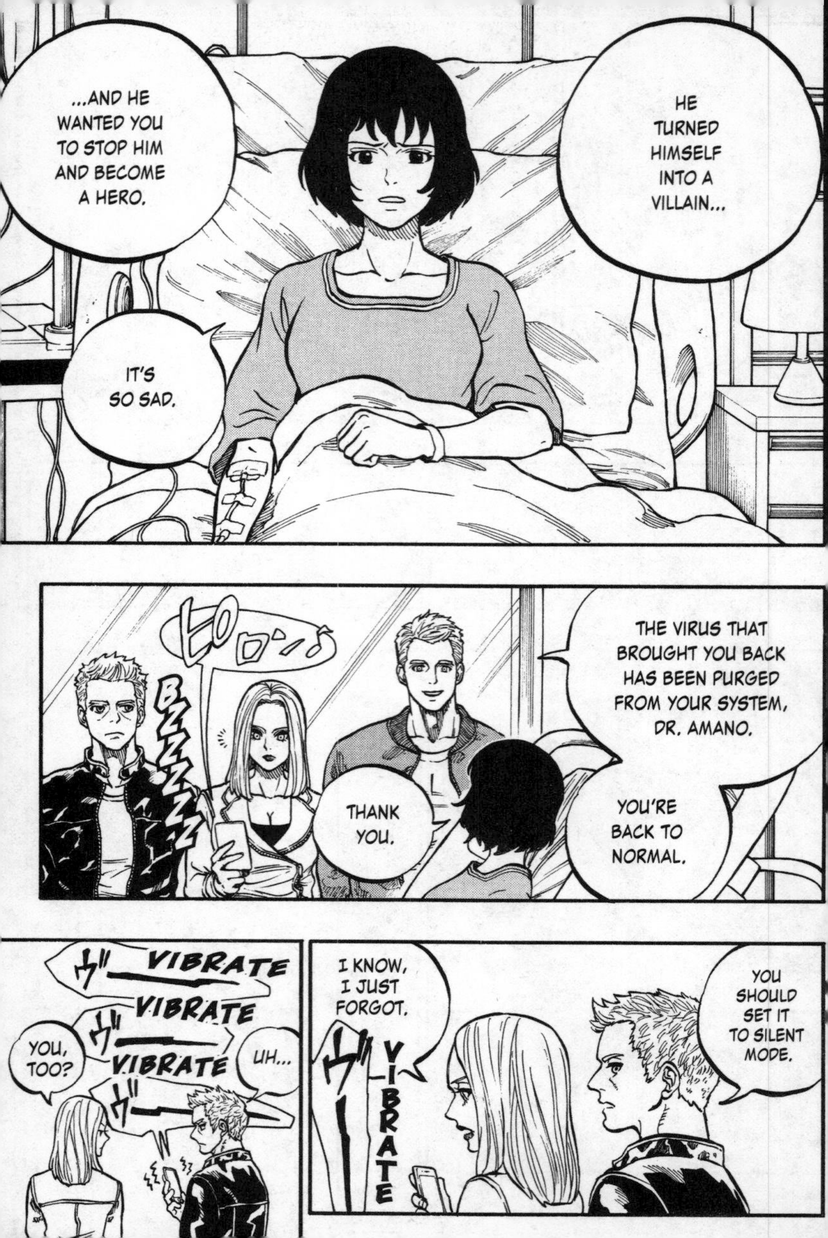
HE TURNED HIMSELF INTO A VILLAIN...
...AND HE WANTED YOU TO STOP HIM AND BECOME A HERO.
IT'S SO SAD.
THE VIRUS THAT BROUGHT YOU BACK HAS BEEN PURGED FROM YOUR SYSTEM, DR. AMANO.
YOU'RE BACK TO NORMAL.
THANK YOU.
ピロン♪
BZZZZZZ
YOU SHOULD SET IT TO SILENT MODE.
I KNOW, I JUST FORGOT.
ヴー VIBRATE
UH...
ヴー VIBRATE
ヴー VIBRATE
ヴー VIBRATE
YOU, TOO?

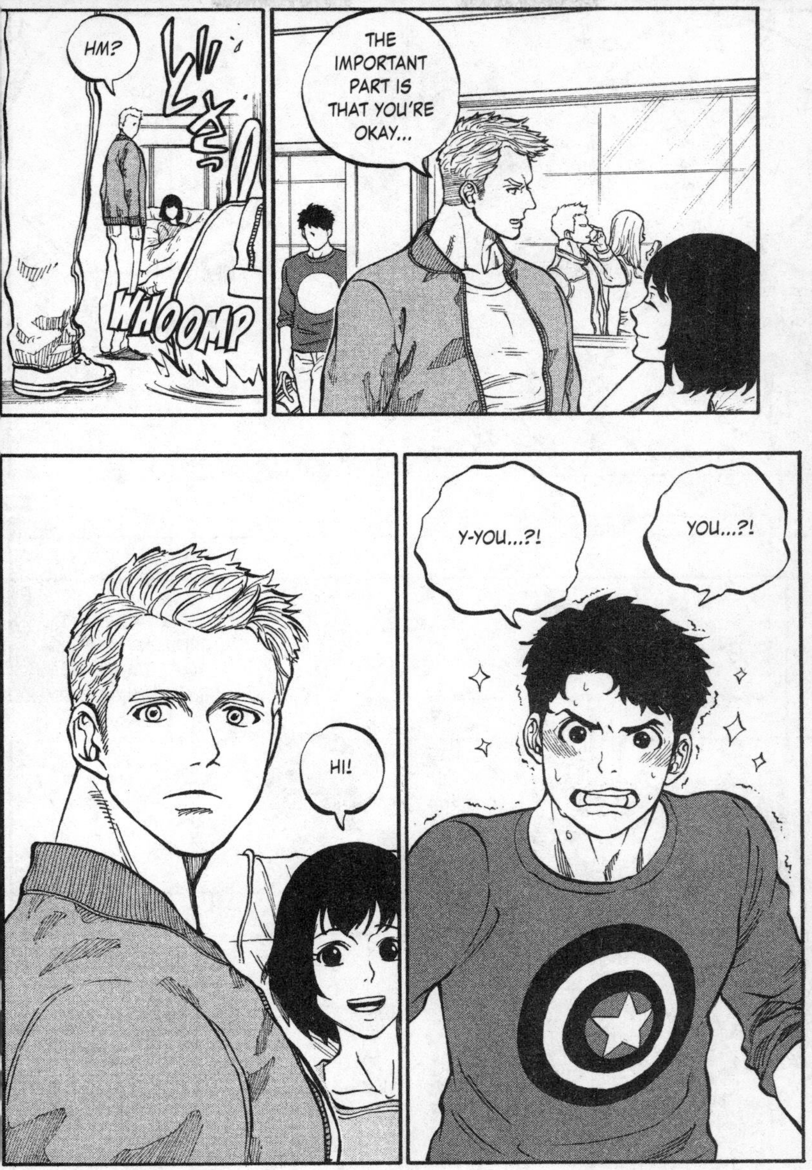
THE IMPORTANT PART IS THAT YOU'RE OKAY...
HM?
WHOOMP
YOU...?!
Y-YOU...?!
HI!

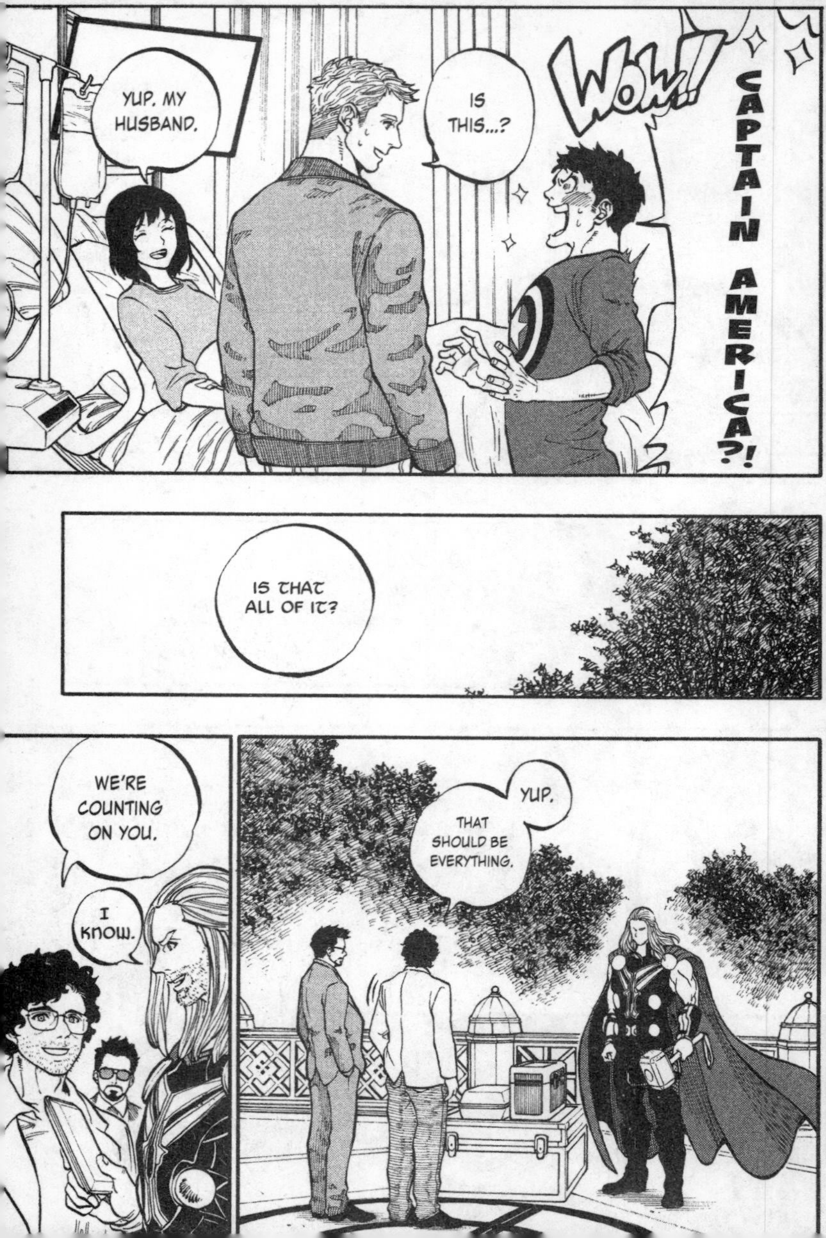
CAPTAIN AMERICA?!
WOW!!
IS THIS...?
YUP. MY HUSBAND.
IS THAT ALL OF IT?
YUP.
THAT SHOULD BE EVERYTHING.
WE'RE COUNTING ON YOU.
I KNOW.

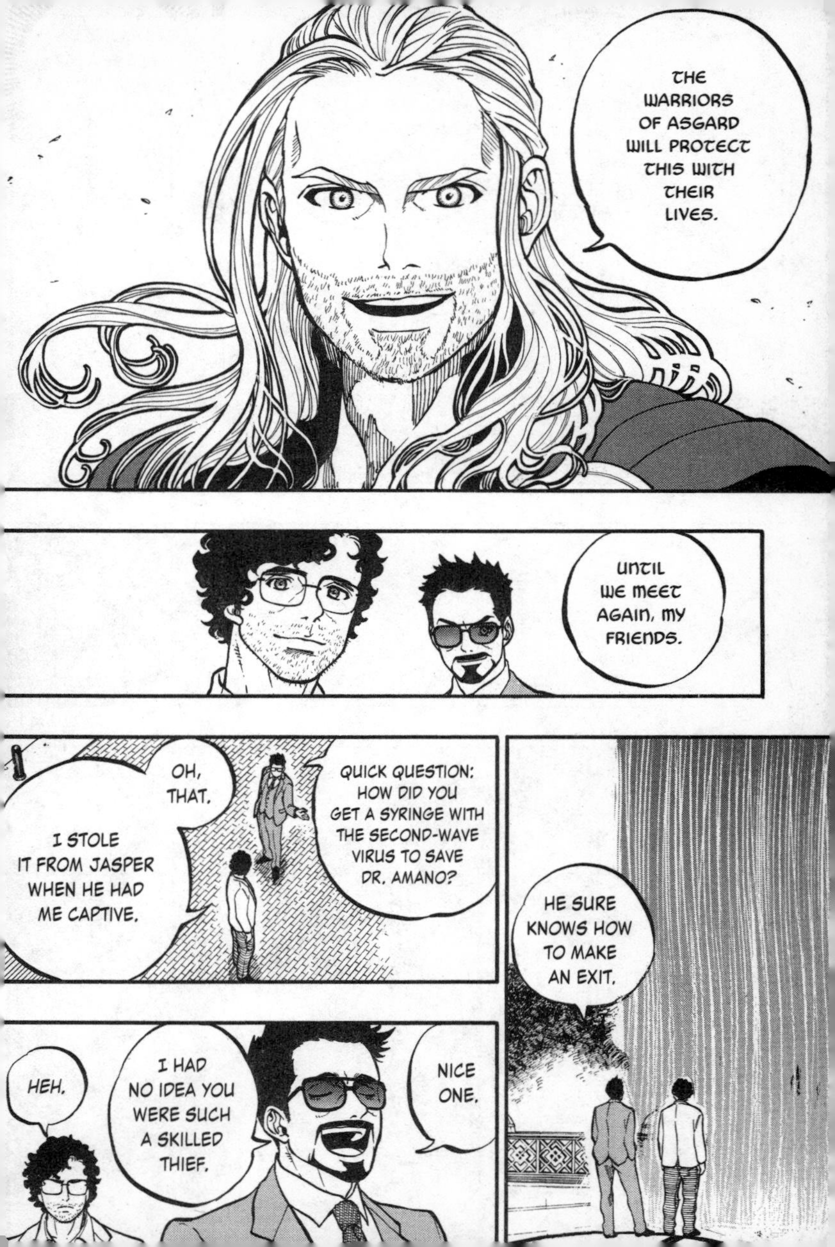
THE WARRIORS OF ASGARD WILL PROTECT THIS WITH THEIR LIVES.
UNTIL WE MEET AGAIN, MY FRIENDS.
HE SURE KNOWS HOW TO MAKE AN EXIT.
QUICK QUESTION: HOW DID YOU GET A SYRINGE WITH THE SECOND-WAVE VIRUS TO SAVE DR. AMANO?
OH, THAT.
I STOLE IT FROM JASPER WHEN HE HAD ME CAPTIVE.
NICE ONE.
I HAD NO IDEA YOU WERE SUCH A SKILLED THIEF.
HEH.

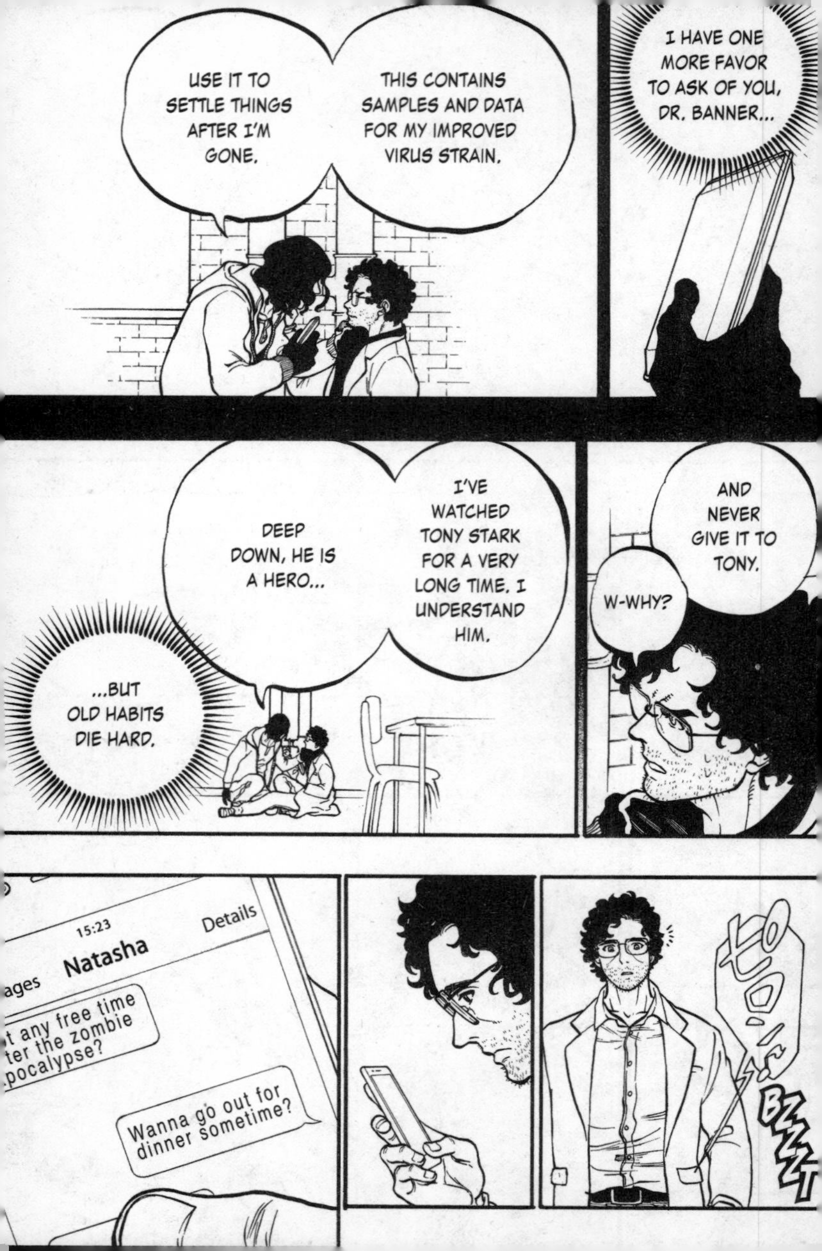
I HAVE ONE MORE FAVOR TO ASK OF YOU, DR. BANNER...
THIS CONTAINS SAMPLES AND DATA FOR MY IMPROVED VIRUS STRAIN.
USE IT TO SETTLE THINGS AFTER I'M GONE.
AND NEVER GIVE IT TO TONY.
W-WHY?
I'VE WATCHED TONY STARK FOR A VERY LONG TIME. I UNDERSTAND HIM.
DEEP DOWN, HE IS A HERO...
...BUT OLD HABITS DIE HARD.
BZZZT
15:23
Details
Natasha
ages
t any free time ter the zombie pocalypse?
Wanna go out for dinner sometime?

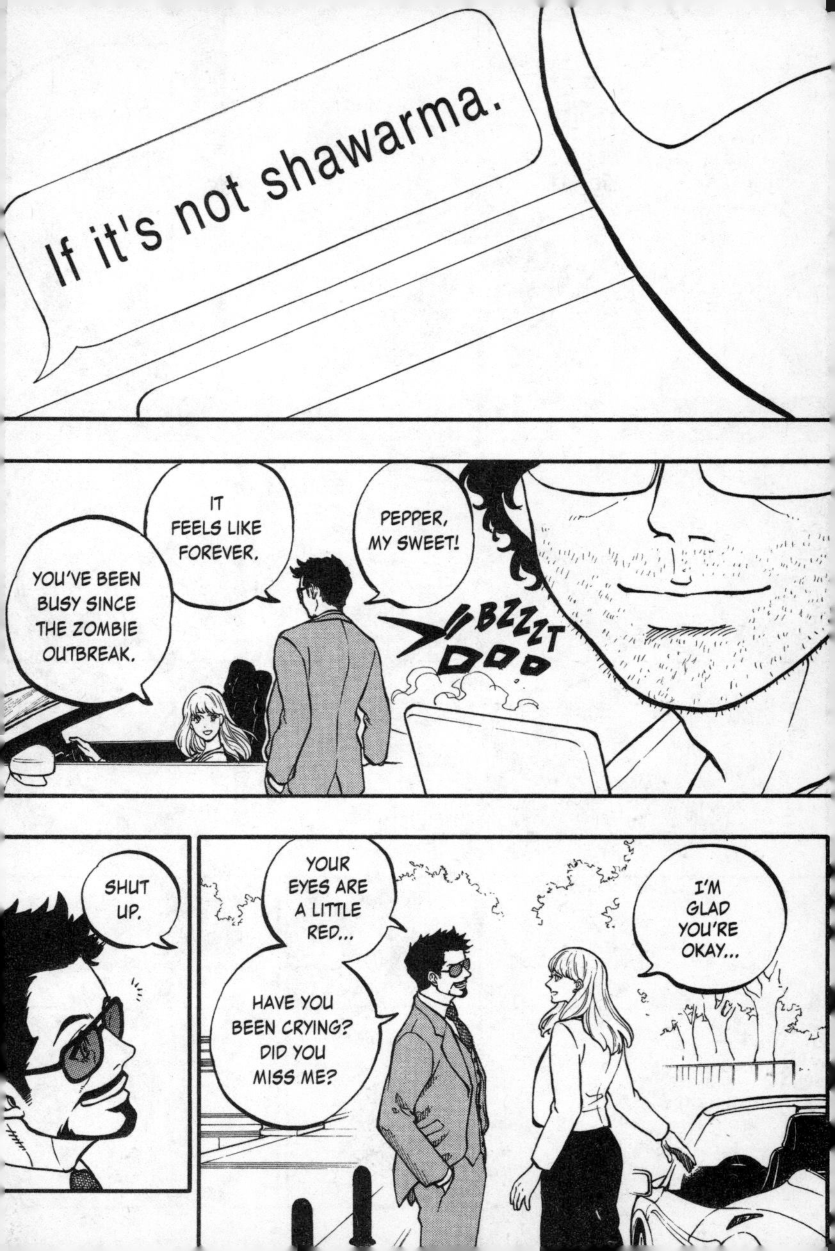
If it's not shawarma.
PEPPER, MY SWEET!
BZZZZT DOO
IT FEELS LIKE FOREVER.
YOU'VE BEEN BUSY SINCE THE ZOMBIE OUTBREAK.
I'M GLAD YOU'RE OKAY...
YOUR EYES ARE A LITTLE RED...
HAVE YOU BEEN CRYING? DID YOU MISS ME?
SHUT UP.

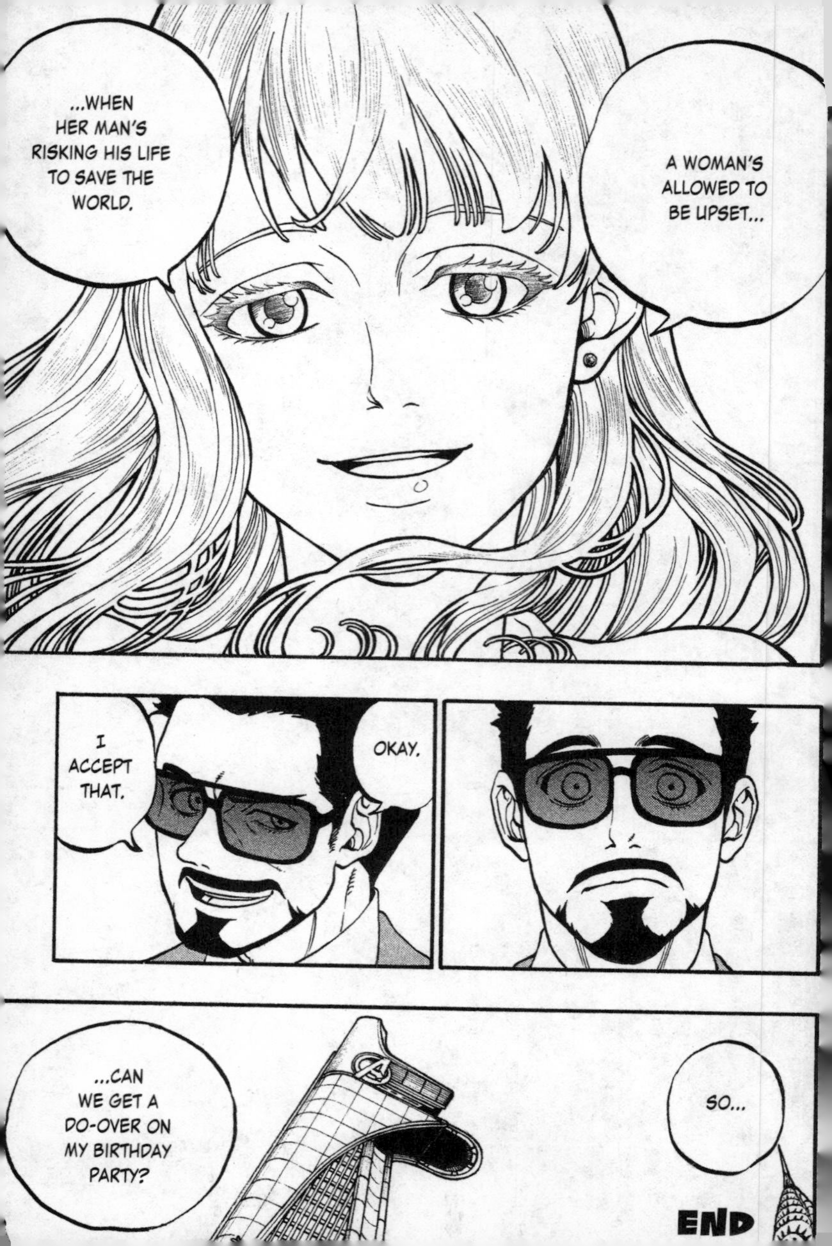
A WOMAN'S ALLOWED TO BE UPSET...
...WHEN HER MAN'S RISKING HIS LIFE TO SAVE THE WORLD.
OKAY.
I ACCEPT THAT.
SO...
...CAN WE GET A DO-OVER ON MY BIRTHDAY PARTY?
END

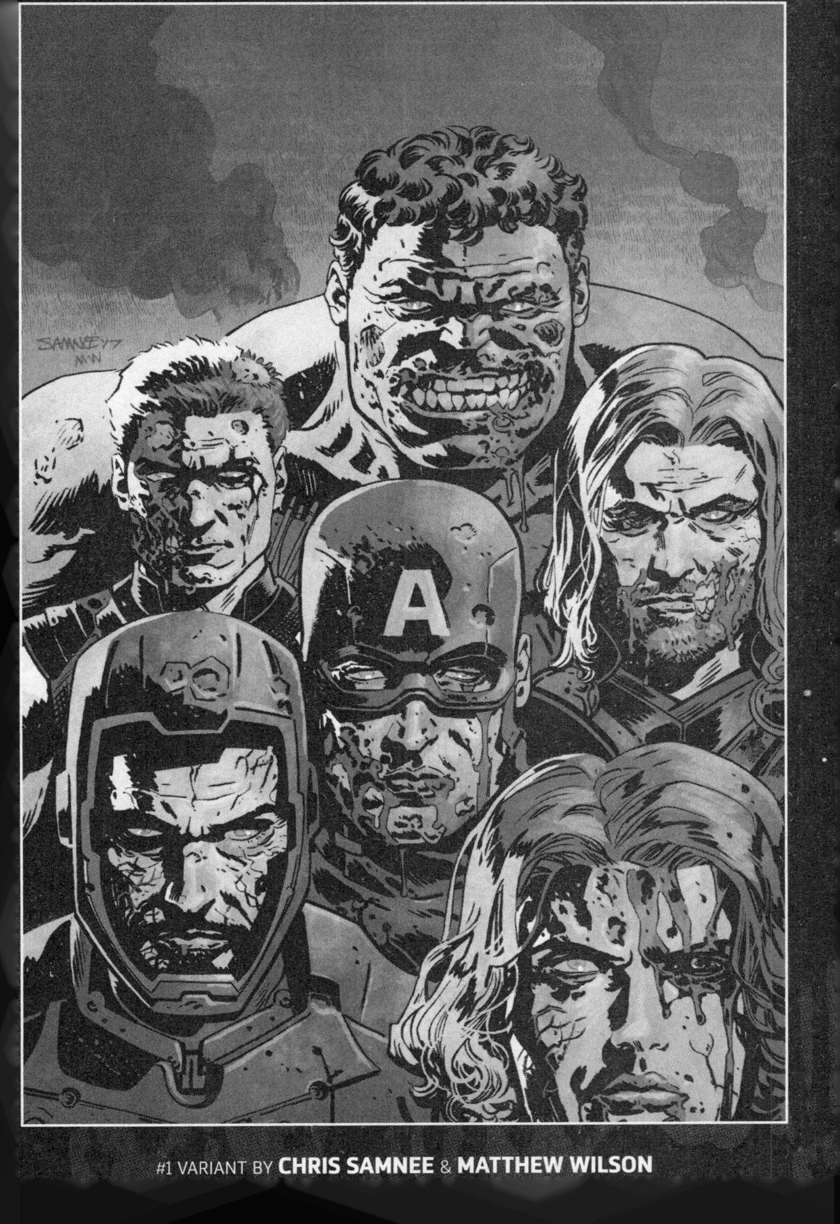
SAMNEE '17
MW

#1 VARIANT BY **CHRIS SAMNEE** & **MATTHEW WILSON**

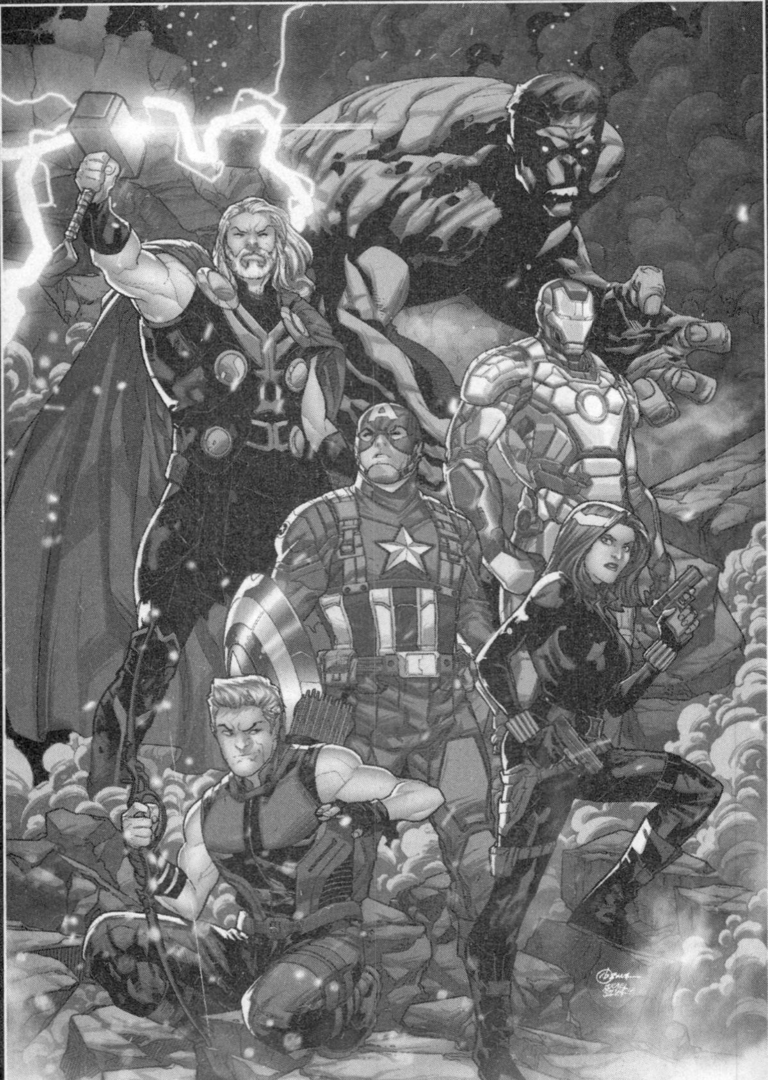

#2 VARIANT BY **R.B. SILVA** & **ISRAEL SILVA**

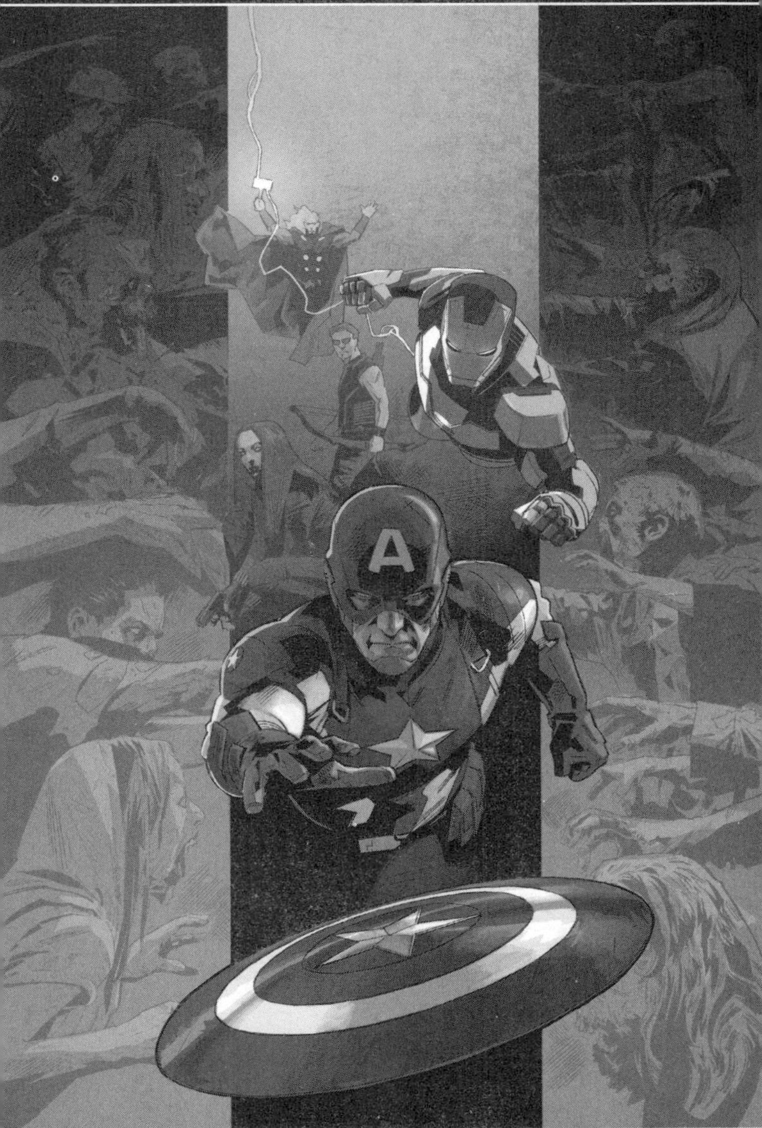

#3 VARIANT BY **MATTEO BUFFAGNI**

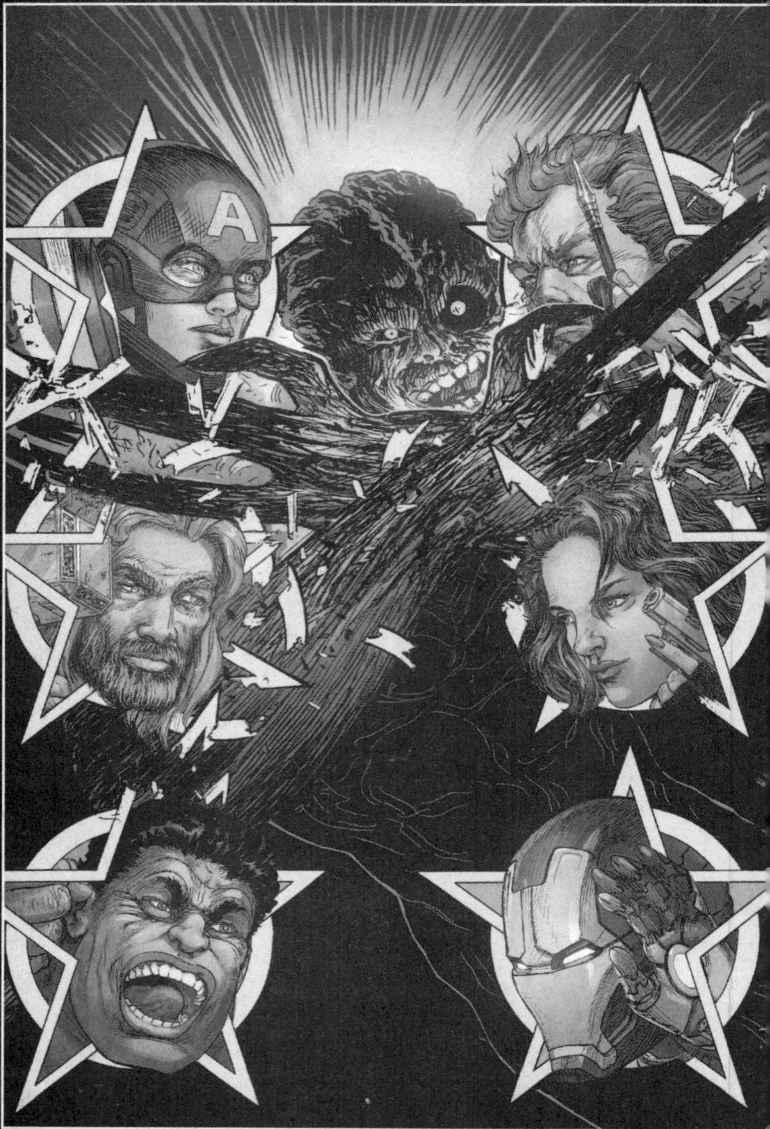

#4 VARIANT BY **MICHAEL KALUTA** & **JIM CHARALAMPIDIS**

STOP

FACE FRONT, TRUE BELIEVER!

This book is printed in traditional Japanese style, which means this is the back of the book! To read this manga, flip the book over and read from right to left, and within each panel from top to bottom (just like you would with an American comic).

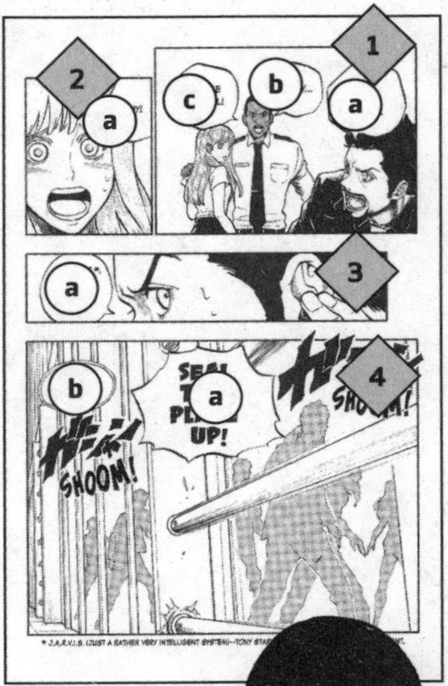
1
a
b
c
2
a
3
a
4
SHOOM!
a
UP!
b
SHOOM!

◄ START READING IN THE UPPER RIGHT-HAND CORNER.

PANEL ORDER

WORD BALLOON ORDER

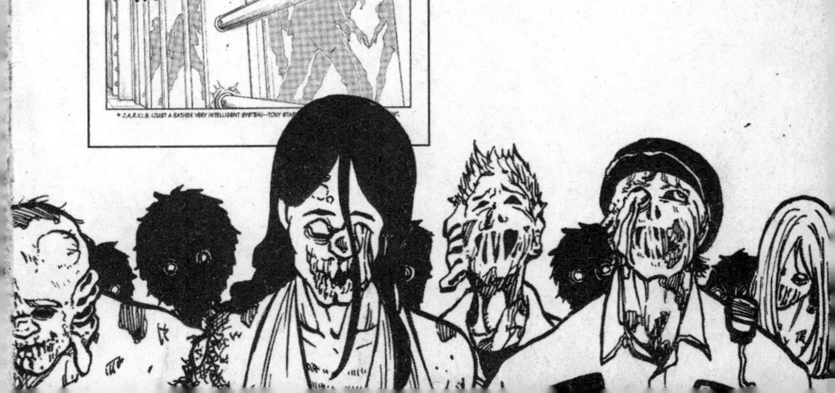